The J.M. Pyne Stories
& other selected writings by Lucian Cary

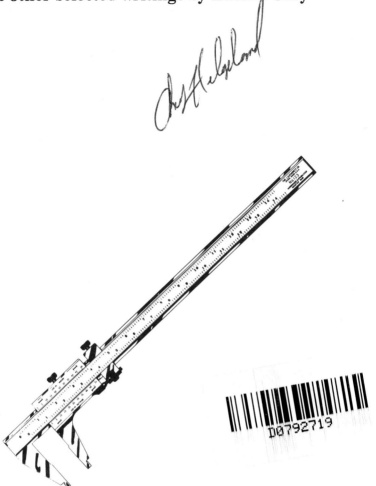

D0792719

The J.M. Pyne Stories
& other selected writings by Lucian Cary

compiled, edited, and published by

Guy Lautard
2570 Rosebery Avenue
West Vancouver, B.C.
CANADA V7V 2Z9

Published by Guy Lautard; Printed in Canada

1st Printing

Canadian Cataloging in Publication Data:
   Cary, Lucian, 1886-1971.
   The J.M. Pyne stories and other selected writings

   Previously published in: The Saturday evening post.
   ISBN 0-9690980-8-1

   I. Lautard, Guy, 1946-   II. Title.
   PS3505.A793A6 1991   813'.54   C91-091707-8

ACKNOWLEDGEMENTS

As the publisher of this book, I would like to thank:
Lucian Cary's grandchildren - Eve, Sheila, Sylvia, Brian and Roger - for their permission to compile and publish this book.
Mr. Adrian Lopez, President, Magazine Associates Inc. for permission to reprint herein "H.M. Pope - Last of the Great Gunsmiths" from TRUE Magazine, April & May, 1945.
The L.S. Starrett Company for the photo of a Starrett 12" Master Vernier Caliper, which is used in the cover design, and...
Last but not least, my good friend Bryan Boutry, for the drawing of the Schuetzen rifle which appears on the cover and elsewhere in this book.

                                                        Guy Lautard

CREDITS

The several short stories, and the article **Almost A Gun Crank,** are reprinted in this book with the permission of the decendants of Lucian Cary.

The article **H.M. Pope - Last of the Great Gunsmiths,** is reprinted from *True Magazine,* April and May 1945, with the permission of the copyright holder, Magazine Associates Inc., New York, NY.

The Lucian Cary stories found in this book originally apeared in *The Saturday Evening Post* in the issues cited below:

A NOTE ABOUT THE AUTHOR

Lucian Cary was born January 1, 1886 in Hamlin, Kansas. He was a writer, an editor, and a noted authority on guns and shooting. He spent some of his boyhood years in Milwaukee, and tells, in one of his articles, of a summer spent on his grandfather's farm in southern Ohio when he was 12. He had asked his father for a BB gun to take with him for the summer, but when they tried one out at a local gun store, neither he nor his father could hit anything with it. His father therefore decided to let Lucian take instead a fine little Marlin .22 equipped with good target peep sights. Lucian Cary's interest in shooting and good guns stayed with him for the next 70 years or so.

Lucian Cary started his professional career in 1910 as a reporter for the *Chicago Tribune*. Over the years, many of his short stories appeared in *The Saturday Evening Post, Colliers*, and other magazines; in addition he wrote several novels, and did some writing for the movie industry. "Saturday's Millions," one of his *Saturday Evening Post* stories about a football star, was made into a movie. Lucian Cary was also the gun editor of *TRUE* magazine for about 20 years.

Lucian Cary died on September 7, 1971. In one of his last articles, which appeared in *TRUE* magazine for November 1970, he reminisced about his favorite guns, and concluded by saying that if he had it all to do over again, he would be more of a gun crank.

INTRODUCTION

I first encountered Lucian Cary's writings in the book **Lucian Cary on Guns**, back in the early 1960's, in my early high school years. I had that book out of the library quite a few times. My next encounter with Mr. Cary's work was in the 1964 **Gun Digest**, where "Forty-Rod Gun" was reprinted from *The Saturday Evening Post* of April 18th, 1936. To my delight - and I am sure to the delight of countless others - over the next 20 years or so, several (but not all) of the "J.M. Pyne" stories were reprinted in **Gun Digest**.

As a boy with a serious interest in shooting, I thoroughly enjoyed Lucian Cary's stories. Later, having become somewhat of a machinist, I enjoyed them even more. I would also like to think that some of Lucian Cary's style and technique as a story teller has rubbed off on me - see, for example, my story "The Bullseye Mixture", in **The Machinist's Second Bedside Reader.**[1]

In 1986, I wrote and published **The Machinist's Bedside Reader.**[2] In it, with the permission of Lucian Cary's granddaughter Eve Cary, I included "The Secret of the Old Master" - one of the J.M. Pyne stories. **The Machinist's Bedside Reader** has enjoyed a wide popularity of its own, and generated numerous letters from readers, some commenting on fond recollections of Lucian Cary's writings in *The Saturday Evening Post*.

This lead me to the idea of bringing out a book of some of the collected short stories of Lucian Cary, which I felt would appeal to a dual audience: machinists and shooters/gunsmiths.

Not all of Lucian Cary's short stories were centered around the character of J.M. Pyne. Some were about football players, failed marriages and so on. But Lucian Cary was himself a shooter, and he was a personal friend of the legendary master gunsmith and barrel maker H.M. Pope. The J.M. Pyne stories were a direct reflection of that friendship - as you will find, some of J.M. Pyne's activities and statements bear a very close resemblance to those of H.M. Pope (see next paragraph). Some of Cary's other stories stemmed from his own activities as a shooter.

I have also included 2 items by Lucian Cary which are not short stories *per se*, but which show where some of Cary's story material came from. If you read these 2 items first, as they are placed in the book, I think you will enjoy the fictional pieces even more. For example, when J.M. Pyne moves to Gaylord's Corner, in the New England hills, to make rifle barrels, and does a little "hunting" with a .25 caliber rifle of his own making, you will know that the story grew (in part) from the fact that Pope's first rifle barrel was a .25 caliber he made for himself (when no such rifles were being made in the United States), plus Cary's ability as a story teller.

Although these stories were originally written and published over a period of about a dozen years as a series of separate short stories, I believe Mr. Cary would be pleased to see his J.M. Pyne stories brought out in book form for the enjoyment of a whole new generation of readers, today.

The Lucian Cary stories in this book appeared in *The Saturday Evening Post* in an era entirely different from our own. Many of them were written in the years of the Great Depression, before WWII. Prices, as well as tastes and taboos, were different then. Our society was much less urbanized then, and I suspect that a far greater percentage of the population could relate to stories about a master gunsmith and shooters than would be the case today. None the less, there are countless gun enthusiasts and many talented gunsmiths today in Canada and the US, as well as elsewhere in the world, who share the same wholesome and genuine interest in good guns and good shooting which Cary, Pope and others had in that day. There are also vast areas of Canada and the US, as well as elsewhere in the world, where the competent use of firearms is as necessary today as it was then and before.

I have found Lucian Cary's fiction stories entertaining, instructive and uplifting. I have read and re-read them all, with fresh enjoyment each time. I hope that this book will enable others to get from his stories what I have gotten: many pleasant hours of enjoyable reading.

Guy Lautard
West Vancouver, Canada
June, 1991

1/ published by Guy Lautard, 1988
2/ published by Guy Lautard, 1986

iv

TABLE of CONTENTS

ALMOST A GUN CRANK

My enthusiasm for rifle and pistol shooting is like the madness of golfers, or dry-fly fishermen, or collectors of antiques, except that it is a reasonable enthusiasm.

I have been called a gun crank. That is an exaggeration. I would say merely that I am more interested in fine shooting rifles than the average man. I do not go in for collecting guns. I never buy a gun unless I really need it. As a matter of fact, I really only need about a dozen, or possibly fourteen, more guns than I have now.

But even if I were a gun crank I should think it nothing for my family and my friends to be funny about. A gun crank will sometimes talk about guns when other people would rather talk about something else, or anything else. A gun crank sometimes does foolish things, such as buying two guns in the same week, or going some place where there is a fine Ballard for sale cheap and meeting an old-timer who was actually present at that famous match in the 1880's when muzzle-loading rifles outshot breechloaders, and forgetting all about the dinner party and never having a fair chance to explain until he is in so deep that a man too innocent to know the difference between a bullet mold and a false muzzle couldn't square himself.

A Cure for Tired Nerves
But compared with people who play bridge, hold post-mortems on bridge hands, and have theories about bridge, I find gun cranks to be remarkably sane, sound, responsible men. I do not know anything about bridge. I could not tell you the difference between a big slam and a little slam, and I would just as soon that you didn't tell me. But I have seen a good deal of bridge players, and I can only imagine that the game is not a

1

pleasurable one, but rather a painful ordeal, which produces deep feelings of exasperation and frustration.

I have often wondered why nerve specialists do not prescribe rifle or pistol shooting for people who have cracked up at the bridge table. Nothing is more soothing to the nerves than shooting -- which explains why gun cranks are so good-natured except when they have been forced to neglect their shooting.

I live as much of the year as I can on a farm, several miles from a railway station and several hours from New York. The farm, though narrow, is about a mile long. At the time we bought the place, my wife thought it would give her room for the kind of flower garden she wanted and could not have on the two acres she had been cultivating near a suburban town. I thought a farm would give me the peace and quiet I needed for my work.

It is often said that there is nothing for a writer to do in the country except write, and for some reason this is considered an ideal state of affairs. No one expects a brick-layer to be laying one brick on another throughout his waking hours, but if a man's trade is to put down one word after another, it is taken for granted that he should do nothing else. I had heard, at the time we bought the farm, of writers who got so bored writing in the country that they were driven to hoeing the garden or mowing the lawn. But I felt that this would never happen to me. And, as a matter of fact, it never has. I foresaw that I could put any spare time I might have into making some important experiments with rifles.

The farm had a good-sized shed, built into a side-hill, which had apparently never been used for anything much. I thought this would be a fine place to set up my typewriter. My wife agreed with me. She pointed out that it was a good way from the house and the distractions of an active family. I pointed out that it had windows along one whole side. She said it was really splendid. I could put the right end of my desk against the wall beneath the middle window and my typewriter table at the left end of the desk and at right angles to it, the way I always liked it. When I sat at my typewriter the light would come over my shoulder as it should. So I put a good floor in the shed and built a chimney to take care of a chunk stove, and ordered a rifle I had seen advertised secondhand.

There was a long and solid work bench in the shed. I at first thought that this could be cut down to a height which would make it the kind of big table I have always wanted - one offering endless room on which to spread out letters you intend to answer, clippings you intend to file, notes for stories you intend to write, and books you intend to read. But on looking it over, I decided that the bench was too good for this purpose. I put it lengthwise against the wall under the windows. It reached across three windows, so it was well lighted. I got a machinist's vise for it. I'm not a good mechanic, but there are jobs which require a vise - for example, it is much simpler to clean a rifle properly without injuring the bore if it is held firmly in a vise.

I am interested in the scientific aspects of rifle shooting - that is, in finding out what a rifle will do and, if possible, why. This requires either a muzzle-and-elbow rest or a machine rest. The idea is not to test your skill in rifle shooting but, having eliminated so far as possible the human error, to test the rifle and the ammunition. I did not know then where I could buy a machine rest and I did not have the skill to make one. But with the aid of the work bench that I had so fortunately salvaged and the machinist's vise, I built a solid table, or bench rest, for muzzle-and-elbow-rest shooting.

Perfect Conditions for Not Writing

The rifle I had sent for arrived about the time I finished the rest bench. It was a .22, but it was no child's toy. It weighed between twelve and thirteen pounds, and was fitted with double set triggers. The object of such triggers is to secure the lightest possible trigger pull that will be safe. You pull the rear trigger and the gun does not fire - all you have done is to "set" the front trigger. A mere touch on the front trigger will then fire the gun.

I put up a target seventy-five yards away in the garden and prepared to test the rifle. I found that it was necessary to put one end of my bench rest under one of the two remaining windows. This left no room for my writing desk, so I got the hired man to help me move that out to the barn.

The rifle had been advertised to shoot one-inch groups at 100 yards. I was unable to get groups of much less than two inches at seventy-five yards. For one thing, I discovered that my eyesight was not what it had been. I had never worn glasses or felt the need of them. But I couldn't see a three or four inch bull's-eye sharply at seventy-five yards. I realized that I needed either eyeglasses or a telescope sight, so I went to New York and got both. I also got a spotting telescope with a three-inch objective that was powerful enough to show bullet holes in the black of a distant target - this made it unnecessary to run down to the target to see what I had got. While I was about it I picked up some necessary tools and gadgets and sample lots of all the varieties of .22 long-rifle ammunition on the market and some books on rifle shooting and put in an order for a couple of new rifles.

I found that with the telescope sight and certain varieties of ammunition, I could occasionally get groups as small as seven-eighths of an inch at seventy-five yards. I learned a good deal about rifle shooting that summer and made a number of improvements in my study. Indeed it was one of the happiest summers I ever spent in my life.

By the time cold weather came I had a cabinet in one corner big enough to hold fifteen or twenty guns; racks over the work bench to hold a variety of small tools; a big case of shelves to hold targets and the books on rifle shooting and a file of *The American Rifleman* magazine which I was fortunate enough to pick up secondhand, plus a chest of drawers for this and that.

These simple arrangements would have been inadequate if I had been a real gun crank. The shed was only fifteen feet wide and thirty feet long. There was no room for a lathe or a drill press or a milling machine. In fact, I couldn't, at first, find room for the chunk stove.

I was willing to put up with a cold room, but I discovered that when my trigger finger got chilled I could no longer feel a delicate set trigger, and in consequence, I frequently let off a shot when I didn't intend to. A cold finger is really worse than a calloused finger, although a calloused finger is something to look out for. My trigger finger is the one I use in writing on the typewriter. When the tip of this finger gets calloused from writing too many short stories, I sandpaper it until it is a little too sensitive for pounding a typewriter. It is then just right for touching a set trigger with certainty.

The Gun is Mightier than the Pen
It has often been observed that coincidence is more common in real life than in fiction. A writer of fiction seldom dares to use coincidence as freely as life does. He feels that his readers expect him to make things happen without recourse to coincidence.

The day I made room for the chunk stove was one of those days when life is just one coincidence after another. I put the

4

typewriter and the typewriter table out in the barn and set up the chunk stove and got a fire going. While I was feeding wood into the stove I noticed that there was a considerable space between the stove and the one window which was not occupied by the work bench and the shooting bench. A machine rest is quite small; it need not be more than six inches wide and twenty-four inches long. I got a rule and did some measuring, and found there was room for such a rest between the stove and the window.

A machine rest is a mechanical device for aiming a rifle at the same place every time. In the commonest form, the muzzle of the rifle is held by a clamp that slides freely along a flat surface to a stop. The rear end of the barrel, just forward of the action, is supported in a V groove, and this groove is usually so arranged that it can be moved both vertically and horizontally by fine threaded screws. The gun is free to recoil when fired. After firing a shot, you push the gun forward until the muzzle clamp strikes the stop, and fire again. Such a rest offers less chance of human error than a muzzle-and-elbow rest, and I thought I ought to have one.

It is essential that the base of a machine rest does not move. The floor of my shed was not absolutely solid. But all I had to do to secure a solid foundation for a machine rest was to cut a hole in the floor, dig down to hardpan, and build a small concrete pier.

I laid out a parallelogram of the right size on the floor and got a brace and bit. I bored a couple of holes through the floor, to let in a keyhole saw, and went to work. There was so little space under the floor that I could not get a full stroke with the saw, so it was a slow job. But rifle shooting teaches patience, and I was patiently sawing away when who should appear in the doorway but my literary agent. I had not seen him for months. I had a slightly guilty feeling at seeing him, because I had neglected to answer his last few letters about a serial I was writing, but he greeted me with his usual smile and asked me what I was doing.

His actual words were, "What the hell are you doing?"

I replied that I was sawing a hole in the floor, and since this did not convince him that I was not slightly cuckoo, I explained in some detail why I was sawing a hole in the floor. He was not really interested. He looked about the room instead of listening.

"Where," he asked, "is your typewriter?"

5

I have already explained how it happened that I put my typewriter in the barn. But owing to the unfortunate coincidence by which he arrived a few minutes after I put the typewriter in the barn instead of a few minutes before, he was forever afterward able to maintain that the typewriter had been in the barn all summer. And this was not all. While we were discussing the serial I had been writing all summer and he was asking such questions as what this serial was about, my wife came out to ask what I wanted done with the two long boxes the hired man had just brought out from the express office in the village.

I had supposed that the hired man and I understood each other, but it seems we didn't. And by another coincidence, the two new rifles had arrived at the moment when my agent was beginning to suspect that my shooting had interfered with my writing.

The long and the short of it was that my wife and my agent agreed that I was in danger of becoming a crank about guns, and the best thing for him to do was to drive me and my typewriter to New York. We could discuss what the serial I had been writing would be about on the way to town, and he thought that if I stayed in a hotel and had my meals sent up to me, I could finish it by January 1st, as promised. I said something about the distractions of life in New York, but he said they were nothing to the distractions of life in the country as I lived it.

So for many weeks I was practically in jail and had no chance to do any shooting and often pounded the typewriter all night long and got less and less good-natured. But when the job was finally finished I did not really blame anybody, especially as, on the first day I got out, I met a man who offered to put me up at a pistol-shooting club he belonged to, and another chap who knew Harry Pope.

I had heard about Harry Pope when I was a small boy and dreamed of someday owning a rifle with a Pope barrel. I had been told that Pope was still making barrels, but that it was practically impossible to get a Pope barrel unless you were both an old friend and a fine shot. Pope didn't like to waste one of his barrels on a man who couldn't shoot. There never had been enough Pope barrels for the men who could shoot.

My friend who knew Pope admitted that the chances were I would never succeed in getting a Pope barrel. He knew men who had waited five, ten, even fifteen years for a Pope barrel. But it would do no harm to ask.

6

So Bill and I took the Hudson Tube toward five o'clock one winter evening and got off somewhere in a Jersey factory town and walked several blocks. Bill stopped at a corner and stepped into the street until his back was against a freight car that was standing there, and looked up.

"He's there," Bill said. "I see a light." He took a deep breath and yelled, "Hi, Pope!"

The fourth-story window opened presently and a man with a white beard looked out and saw us and waved his hand. I could see no entrance to the building. But Bill took his stand at the foot of a fire escape enclosed with corrugated iron. I heard somebody coming down the iron stairs.

"Don't tell him I'm a writer," I whispered to Bill.

"No," Bill said, "of course not."

The door opened. "Come in out of the wet," Mr. Pope said.

We climbed three flights of stairs and went into a big room so full of dusty packing cases that we had to pick our way toward the brightly lighted bench at the other end.

Learning of Rifles from Pope
Bill introduced me to Harry Pope, who immediately asked, "Are you the man who occasionally writes stories for *The Saturday Evening Post*?"

I said I was and it didn't matter at all. Mr. Pope had never known a writer who could shoot, but he told me he believed that any man who had the guts could learn to shoot. He took the evening off to show me all sorts of things I wanted to see and to answer my questions, and when, at midnight, Bill and I left, Pope asked me to come again.

I went around the next week and asked him to make me one of his muzzle-and-breech-loading off-hand target rifles, and he said he would. I went to his shop once a week after that and spent hours acquiring rifle lore, and when I came home late for dinner the family never bothered to ask me where I had been. They said, "How is Harry Pope?" I got the rifle in seven months.

I took the gun out to the farm with some misgivings. I knew it would shoot. Mr. Pope had said, when he gave it to me, "It's all right." And then he had shown me the target it had made in his shop test - five shots from the machine rest at fifty feet so nearly in the same hole that a bullet would stick in it. The question was whether I could make the gun shoot.

You can't buy the bullets. You have to cast them, and lubricate them. You have to measure out two kinds of powder just so, checking the measure with a weighing scale down to one-tenth of a grain.

You have to be careful, too, in loading the gun. If you start a bullet down the muzzle and forget to push it all the way down the bore with the ramrod before you fire, you will almost certainly ruin the barrel beyond repair. The mass of burning powder goes up the barrel with high velocity and strikes the bullet a blow like that of a heavy hammer, and the inertia of the bullet is so great that the barrel is expanded, or ringed.

Finally, I had no machine rest; nothing but the hole in the floor where I had intended to put one when my agent interrupted me.

I got a blister casting bullets that covered my entire forefinger. Fortunately, it was my left forefinger and not my trigger finger. I set the powder measure and weighed the charges it threw and reset it and rechecked it with the scale until I got it to drop three grains of smokeless powder from one side into the bottom of the shell and enough black powder from the other side of the measure to fill the rest of the case. I cut wads out of postal cards with a wad cutter on a block of wood with the end grain up. I had a fine eight-power telescope sight by this time. It was a matter of taking pains, shooting muzzle-and-elbow rest, to equal a machine rest.

I went to work, taking pains to select perfect bullets, holding the butt of the rifle delicately and precisely in my arms on top of the bench rest, watching until the cross hairs in the scope quartered the bull precisely, and touching the set trigger with a well-sandpapered finger tip. I got five shots that looked, through the telescope, like a tight group. I went down into the garden. It was a tight group for seventy-five yards. It measured four-tenths of an inch on centers. It was scarcely more than half the size of the best groups I had got with a .22 at that distance.

I was trying it again when a friend dropped in. He watched me put the false muzzle on, set a bullet in place, adjust the bullet starter, hit the plunger a smart blow with the heel of my hand to drive the bullet down through the choke, push the bullet slowly down the bore with the ramrod, and take the false muzzle off. I had the false muzzle tied to a leather thong that hung down from a beam overhead, so I couldn't forget to take it off. My friend watched me prime a shell and hold it under the powder measure while I moved the lever up, and then down. He watched me press a wad down on the powder and look in the open breech to make sure the bullet was there, and finally insert the shell and close the action.

"It's too much trouble," he said.

I pointed to the spotting scope. "Look at the target," I said.

The Election Day Match
He looked at the target. But he still thought it as too much trouble. He thought I was a gun crank. He went away.

The moon was throwing deep shadows on the floor when I remembered that this was an off-hand rifle - a rifle to shoot standing up in the old way. I put up a fresh target. I couldn't see it with the naked eye. It was too dark. But I could see it through the telescope and quarter the bull with the cross hairs. I fired five shots off-hand, the black powder throwing a streak of flame against the dark and the gun booming in the quiet night. It wasn't good shooting. But it was better than I had ever done before off-hand.

My wife came out to tell me we were already late for a dinner. I put the gun in the vise with leather clamps to protect it. I had to clean it, dinner or no dinner.

I put one patch through and cut another from a piece of Canton flannel that had been boiled and washed. I was in a hurry. The patch was too big, and instead of taking it out, I pushed hard on the rod. The patch stuck. I pushed harder. The rod went right through the patch. And then it was stuck for good. I couldn't move it either way. I had done the ultimately inexcusable thing, and Pope was a hundred and thirty miles away.

I gave up trying toward midnight. I stood the rifle up and filled the bore with oil, so it couldn't rust, and the next morning I drove to town.

Mr. Pope never said a word. He polished up a steel rod that fitted the bore and drove that patch out and gently advised me to use absorbent cotton instead of Canton flannel thereafter, and asked me if I had thought of shooting in the annual Election Day match.

9

I knew about the Election Day match. It was first fired in 1893 - a hundred shots off-hand on the German ring target for the championship of New York, open to all comers. It had been fired every year since 1893. The entry list wasn't so long as it once had been. Since the war, young men had taken to shooting prone - lying down on the ground in imitation of military shooting. Few of them could shoot standing up, in the immemorial fashion of riflemen. But it still took as good shooting as ever to win the Election Day match. Only seven different men had won it in forty years.

Of course, I had no intention of shooting in that match. I wasn't in that class. Besides, I was not interested in competitive rifle shooting. I was only interested in scientific rifle shooting - in seeing what a rifle would do, and finding out, if possible, why.

"You mean," I asked, "that I could shoot the .32-40?"

"No," Mr. Pope said, "the range doesn't permit it. The match is limited to .22 caliber."

"I'd like to try it," I said, knowing that the action of my .22 caliber rifle was out of commission, "but I have no gun."

"I'll lend you mine," Mr. Pope said.

So I shot in the Election Day match at that fine-ringed target which so inexorably reveals the difference between one man's shooting and another's. I was more than three hundred points behind the record score of 2275 that won. There were a couple of fellows shooting in the match who were worse. But my eye was on the man who stood next to me through that long afternoon - the man who won. His name was, appropriately, Landrock. He stood there like a rock, holding sixteen pounds of rifle for minutes at a time until, satisfied, he touched the set trigger. I watched his target through my spotting scope. I saw him put three successive shots in the 25 ring, a hundred yards away. The 25 ring is bigger than a dime, but smaller than a one-cent piece.

You can guess the result. It is, I am convinced, a matter of practice. But I think it is a mistake to practice more than three hours a day. The new off-hand .22 rifle that Pope made for me weighs fourteen pounds and three ounces ready to shoot. It doesn't feel heavy. But after about three hours, my shooting falls off. I don't get tired, but I do get careless. And I doubt if you are improving your shooting when you get careless. Golfers tell me that it is seldom wise to play more than seventy-two holes in a single day. It is better to stop while you are still keen to go on. So I limit myself to a hundred and fifty shots a day, or, say, a thousand shots per week. It's foolish to overdo it. There are other things in life than shooting --- unless you are a gun crank.

H. M. POPE - LAST OF THE GREAT GUNSMITHS

No one can say who was the greatest general or the greatest inventor or the greatest athlete. But there is no doubt among experts as to who was the greatest maker of rifle barrels who ever lived. He is a man of 83, known wherever riflemen gather as Harry Pope; or, as he preferred to sign his work, H.M. Pope.

Col. Townsend Whelen, in his book on the American rifle, put it this way: "Harry M. Pope has long held the reputation of being the most skilled maker of rifle barrels in the world.....his product has never been approached by any other maker."

I don't know of any competent critic who would disagree with Colonel Whelen on this point. Certainly Pope would not. I once asked him which men he considered the best makers of rifle barrels.

Pope said: "George Schalck, A.O. Zischang, and George Schoyen - in that order." Then he added softly: "I had it on them because of my education."

You may call that egotism. But it was not the kind of egotism that makes a man think he is better than he is. Pope was better than anybody else and naturally he knows it. He acquired early in life the scientist's regard for the observed fact and he has never been inclined to shade the facts in anybody's favor, even in Pope's favor.

Several yeas ago I found, second-hand, a Pope .32-40 muzzle-loading target rifle. In testing it at 200 yards in the machine rest, I got a ten-shot group which, carelessly, I measured as 1-5/8" from center to center of the two widest bullet holes. I showed this group to Pope the next time I saw him. He was pleased that a rifle he had made more than forty years before was still shooting nicely, but he thought my measurement favored the gun - his gun - somewhat. It isn't easy to measure exactly from one bullet hole to another in a piece of paper. Pope spent nearly an hour with a magnifying glass measuring that target.

"I make it 1.64 inches," he said finally.

One and five eighths inches is 1.625 inches. So I had claimed 1-1/2 hundredths of an inch too much for his gun, and as a matter of course he would not have it.

Such a man has inevitably become a legend. For fifty years the most quoted authority on rifles and rifle shooting in this country, he is also the most misquoted and, I sometimes think, the most misrepresented. Tall tales are told of Harry Pope. He is said to have an uncontrollable temper. I saw a good deal of him over a period of ten years. I spent hundreds of hours in his shop. I went to many rifle matches with him, and he spent a dozen weekends at my place in the Litchfield Hills. I am neither a skilled mechanic nor a fine shot. My only claim on Pope was my interest in rifles. That was all he asked. However much of a pest I've been to him, he has yet to say an unkind word to me. I've never seen him unjustifiably angry with anybody else.

He's a bit testy at times. He is annoyed by men who ask him questions and don't wait for his answer. He despises shoddy work as only a first rate mechanic can. He has no patience with men who lie about what their rifles have done. He is also full of crotchets, many of them practical ones. He has carried for many years a walking stick he cut in the woods, just above where the branch forked. In cutting the stick to length he left an inch or two of the fork. When he wants both hands free he hangs the stick from the lapel of his jacket by putting the short end of the fork through the buttonhole. The stick has no ferrule on the end that hits the ground, so it looks like a brush. When asked why he doesn't put a metal ferrule on the end to protect it, he says, "Because it would be more likely to slip."

His pockets are always full of things that most men wouldn't carry or know how to use if they did. I don't suppose he ever went anywhere without a micrometer caliper, a sharp jackknife, a magnifying glass, a screw driver with four different blades, a watch that gives the correct time within a second or so, and a dozen other things. In cold weather he used to carry a small, flat can with rounded corners and a cloth cover that contained some-

13

thing which would produce heat - a hand warmer. This was not the luxury of a soft man. It was the gadget of a rifleman who knows that when his trigger finger gets cold it becomes insensitive.

The contents of Pope's pockets have often proved disconcerting in argument. Pope is not one to debate ascertainable facts. He prefers to find out what the facts are, and if that requires a micrometer caliper, he has one. I remember when, driving with Pope from Boston to my home in Connecticut after a match at Walnut Hill, I got off the main highway. He and I disagreed about which way we were headed. He told me to stop the car, whereupon he took a compass out of his pocket, walked far enough away so the instrument wouldn't be affected by the metal of the car, and announced that he was right and I was wrong. He did this without the slightest hint of triumph. He was not in the least concerned to prove himself the wiser man. He merely wanted to know which way to go. Since the two of us had different opinions, he referred the question to the standard device for determining the magnetic meridian.

Pope has always taken the same attitude toward more important matters. He was asked, after he became famous, to select the barrels for an American rifle team going abroad to shoot a match. The conditions called for military rifles and at that time the military rifle of the United States was the Krag-Jorgensen. The Krag was made at Springfield Armory which was then, as now, a first-rate shop. However, Springfield was having trouble in keeping the interior dimensions of Krag barrels to specifications. The theory was, as it still is, that a bullet with a hard metal jacket should have the same diameter as the groove diameter of the barrel in which it is shot. The standard diameter of the Krag bullet was 0.308". So was the standard groove diameter of the Krag barrel. But Krag barrels were coming off the machines bigger than .308, sometimes as big as .315. The bigger barrels were not accurate.

Pope went to Springfield with a pocket full of buckshot, a machinist's hammer, a hardwood punch and a micrometer caliper. The superintendent greeted him with courtesy and asked him what he wanted. Pope said he wanted a bench with a vise, a cleaning rod and a rack of new Krag barrels. The superintendent showed him a bench and had a man wheel in a rack of new barrels.

Pope put a barrel in the vise and laid his hat upside down on the bench under the breech end. He tapped a buckshot into the

14

muzzle with his wooden plug, so it filled the barrel to the bottom of the grooves. He pushed his lead slug through the barrel with a cleaning rod, caught it in his hat so it wouldn't be mutilated, and measured it with his micrometer caliper.

"What are you doing?" the superintendent asked.

"Measuring the groove diameter of the barrel," Pope said.

"But you can't do it that way."

"Why not?"

"Because the lead expands when it comes out of the barrel."

"Well now," Pope said, "I never knew that. Let's find out. Have you got a gauge with a hole in it of a known size?"

The superintendent found a gauge with a .300" hole in it. Both the superintendent and Pope checked it. Then Pope drove one of his buckshot through the hole in the gauge and handed it to the superintendent. The slug had not expanded after going through the hole. It measured .300".

The superintendent was an honest man. He admitted Pope was right and he was wrong. When Pope had finished his job of selecting twenty Krag barrels, two for each member of the team, with a groove diameter of .308, the superintendent showed Pope the elaborate and expensive gauge Springfield had been using to measure the inside of Krag barrels. Pope showed him why the gauge was so inaccurate that it could not be relied on to tell the difference between a barrel with a groove diameter of .308 and one of .315.

But the most interesting things about H.M. Pope are how he became the king of rifle barrel makers, a match shot who broke world's records, a hunter who killed twenty-two deer with twenty-two cartridges, and in what ways he was superior to some worthy rivals.

Harry Pope was born in a Vermont village on August 15, 1861. His father, who had made voyages around the Horn and across the Pacific in clipper ships, was killed in a railway accident when Harry was a small boy. His mother died not long after. Harry grew up with his grandparents in Boston, graduated from the Massachusetts Institute of Technology, and went to work not long after in a Hartford bicycle factory.

He was a trifle less than average in height and weight, a dark young man with fine brown eyes, a finely chiseled nose and the long arms that were to serve him so well later. Though not big, he was all bone and muscle, with exceptional endurance, exceptional eyesight and the inner drive of a born perfectionist.

Pope told me that he did his first rifling job when he was a boy in his teens more as a practical joke than as a serious experiment. He was working in a hardware store that sold air pistols and had a range where they could be shot at a target. The pistols were smooth bore. Young Pope rifled one of them by putting a broach spirally through it. The pistol shot so much better than the others that he kept it under the bench for his own use and beat everybody else until his secret was discovered.

But it wasn't until he was in his early twenties that he got seriously interested in shooting and had an unhappy experience that must have had a good deal to do with turning him into a maker of rifles. He joined a rifle club in Hartford and bought a .32-40 Ballard rifle and a bullet mould. It was common then for rifle shooters to cast their own bullets and make up their own ammunition. Many of us do it still. The brass cartridge case is the most expensive part of a cartridge, and it can be re-used many times. In the 1880's the primers, black powder and lead for 100 shots cost less than 50 cents. The club had a 200-yard range. A boy, protected by a bullet-proof wall, signaled the value of each shot back to the scorer in the shooting house, and marked the location of each shot, using a stick with a white disk to mark a shot in the black bull's-eye and a black disk to mark a shot in the outer white.

Pope found he was a poor shot in comparison with the other members of the club. But he expected to learn. It was only when his shooting, month after month, failed to improve that he began to worry about it. A man of another temperament might have reconciled himself to being a dub all his life, but not Harry Pope. Something had to be done about it and no one was likely to do anything about it except Pope.

He worked at a bench in the bicycle shop from 7 o'clock in the morning until 6 o'clock at night. In the days before daylight-saving time it was better to shoot before 7 o'clock in the morning than after 6 o'clock at night during a good part of the year. Pope took to getting up before daylight in order to practice shooting. He packed his targets and ammunition in a trout fisherman's creel and hung it over one shoulder; he hung his rifle by a strap over the other shoulder; then he mounted his high-wheel bicycle and rode to the range. He had time in spring and summer to put

16

up targets, fire ten or twenty shots, get his targets and be in the shop by 7 o'clock. He told me that the ride home was tough because it was all uphill.

Pope was interested enough to continue making his early morning trips to the range several times a week for three years. But it didn't take him anything like that long to find out why his shooting hadn't been improving. He knew little about rifles then. In his innocence he supposed, as many people do today, that when a shot missed the center of the bull's-eye it was wholly the fault of the shooter. It hadn't occurred to him that his rifle was responsible for some of the error. It wasn't a cheap rifle. It was a Ballard, famous for its accuracy. But, looking at the holes in the target paper made by his bullets, he began to doubt. He had never seen the holes before because they were 200 yards away and merely located by the marker with a big disc that could be seen from the shooting house. He was engineer enough to wonder, now that he saw the holes, why they weren't round. They were long, oval holes. In some cases the bullet seemed to have gone in sideways, or, as riflemen would say, to have key-holed.

The holes in the target plainly indicated to Pope that the bullets from his rifle were not flying point on and he guessed a vital fact - which is that bullets that don't fly point on, or nearly so, have no accuracy. His rifle was so inaccurate that no one could do fine shooting with it.

For once the makers of Ballard rifles had made a mistake. They had sent Pope a mould for a long bullet and a rifle with a slow twist, too slow to keep the long bullet travelling point first. The remedy was to get a mould for a shorter bullet.

From then on Pope's shooting improved. But that isn't the whole story. Pope had been infected on those early morning trips to the range by a disease, if you want to call it that, from which he, like most men who have once had the fever, never recovered. He was forever after a rifle crank.

He decided after a couple of years that he wanted a rifle of .25 caliber. No such rifle was made in this country at the time. Pope wrote several manufacturers. One of them offered to make a .25 caliber rifle for $100. He might as well have said $1,000. Pope was married, had a child, and was working as a bench hand for $1.50 a day.

He didn't need a .25 caliber rifle, but it is a characteristic of rifle cranks that they always want something they don't need, that no

17

one has ever made, that costs more than they can afford. Pope's answer was a foot-powered lathe in his backyard shop.

He had never seen a rifle barrel made and there were no books on the subject. He set to work to design the necessary tools and then to make them on his lathe. Some of the tools he made he still regards as better than those in common use. When he had made the tools he made his .25 caliber barrel and fitted it to the action of the Ballard rifle he already had. Thus, in 1887, at the age of 26, Harry Pope turned out his first rifle barrel. It was not a crude job.

To understand what followed, it is necessary to have some kind of picture of what rifle shooting was like at the time. There were several kinds of rifle matches, then as now. Military rifle shooting was largely at long range - at from 600 to 1,000 yards. Few civilian clubs could afford a range long enough. Most civilian shooting was done at 200 yards. Many of the civilian clubs were united under the auspices of the National Rifle Association, whose rules provided that a match rifle must not weigh more than ten pounds, and when shot standing must be held with the left hand so extended that the left arm was free of the body. Pope did all his early shooting under these rules.

But there was another kind of shooting that had been introduced into this country immediately after the Civil War by German immigrants. They used a fine-ringed target, with a center 1-1/2" in diameter, counting 25. The rings were 3/4" apart. That is, each succeeding ring was 1-1/2" larger in diameter than the one immediately inside it. The black of the bull's-eye took in the 18-ring, which was 12 inches in diameter. It was a very different target from the standard American target which many civilian clubs adopted in the late 1880's.

The standard American 200-yard rifle target has a 10-ring 3.39" in diameter, a 9-ring 5.54" in diameter, an 8-ring 8" in diameter, and a 7-ring 11" in diameter. For rest shooting, two rings were added inside the 10-ring, counting 11 and 12. The 12-ring is 1.41" in diameter.

There were other important differences between the Schuetzen clubs and the National Rifle Association clubs. The Schuetzen clubs permitted a free rifle - that is, there was no restriction on the weight or the trigger pull. The Schuetzen rifle, as it is still called, weighs from 12 to 15 pounds, or even more; has double set triggers, which can be made so light that a breath will fire the gun; a double pronged butt plate; and, usually, a palm rest. A palm rest is a wooden ball on the end of a short rod fastened to the fore-end of the rifle. In shooting, a man rests his elbow against his body or, if he has long arms, as Harry Pope has, on his hip bone. It is a steadier position than the extended arm position but not any steadier than the hip rest position without a palm rest in which the rifle is supported on the finger tips of the left hand. The late Dr. W.G. Hudson, whose 100-shot records off-hand with the free rifle on the standard American and the German ring target still stand, did not use a palm rest.

The Schuetzen clubs were large and prosperous. They covered the country from San Francisco to New England. The one in Hartford recently celebrated its seventy-fifth anniversary. There is a league of Schuetzen clubs in Connecticut and in many other states. Every two years the national "bund" of Schuetzen clubs held a fest that lasted a week or more, with a prize list running to $25,000 in gold and an endless list of merchandise prizes in addition. They were smart about that prize list. They didn't want to discourage their thousands of enthusiastic shooters by permitting five or six of the country's best shots to win all the money. So most of the matches at the biennial fest were so arranged that there was a large element of luck in them. Thus they gave one of the big prizes for a one-shot re-entry match which lasted through the fest, a shooter paying a dollar for each entry and entering as many times as he chose. They used a mechanical measuring device for determining down to the last ten thousandth of an inch which shot among the thousands fired, was nearest dead center. The prize was almost invariably won by a lucky dub.

One more detail. It should be obvious that no man shooting in the off-hand or standing position at 200 yards could hit the 25 ring of the German target, the size of a silver dollar, often. Indeed, it was many years before anyone succeeded in making three successive 25's in a three-shot match. It was the Schuetzen custom for the marker at the butt to abandon his usual signalling system when a man made a 25 and to break out the Stars and Stripes, which he waved in front of the target to signify that the ultimate had been achieved.

Pope began to shoot at the Hartford Schuetzen club and to go to matches in the Connecticut Schuetzen league with the new rifle he had made for himself. One day in New Britain, Conn., Pope's turn to shoot came immediately after that of a German twice as big as Pope was. The target was the German ring. Pope fired a shot and the marker signaled a 22.

"Goot, my boy," the big German said. "A twenty-two is a good shot."

The next time round Pope got a 23.

"Fine, my boy," the big German said. "A twenty-three is a fine shot."

The third time around Pope fired and the marker down at the target waved the American flag, signalling a 25. The big German looked at the flag and then at Pope.

"Say," he said, "who the hell are you?"

Pope soon met William Hayes at a Schuetzen match. Hayes, who held the 100-shot record on the German ring target for several years, was a manufacturing jeweler in Newark and an ardent student of rifle shooting. His rifles were made by George Schalk of Pottsville, PA., and he believed them to be the best in the world. Hayes was so taken with young Pope's enterprise and skill in making his own rifle that he set out to help him. He offered to loan Pope one of his Schalk rifles for the winter so he could study it.

"Of course I didn't accept the offer," Pope said, in telling me about Hayes' munificence. "But that's the kind of man Will Hayes was."

But though Pope felt that Hayes' offer was too much to accept, he listened to what Hayes had to say and became convinced that Schalk's system of rifling and loading was more accurate than any other. Schalk's rifles were percussion, or cap lock, muzzle loaders with false muzzles used only to protect the real muzzle in loading. The false muzzles were taken off before firing. Pope went home to make a muzzle-loading barrel with a false muzzle in imitation of Schalk. But Pope was not a man to copy anything, even if it was the world's best, when he saw ways of improving it. He had been doing a lot of thinking about what makes rifles shoot; he had some ideas of his own and he was bold enough to adopt them.

Pope's theory, as he later stated it, was this: "The greatest essential for perfect shooting is to deliver the bullet perfectly from the muzzle. That being done, atmospheric conditions and gravity alone govern its flight; the result is accurate shooting. To so deliver the bullet, it must have a perfect base, and be perfectly centered, and have uniform velocity.

"To illustrate, a group was shot at 200 yards, machine rest, with

20

as perfect bullets as we could select, another (group was shot) with bullets very badly mutilated at the point - these two grouping closely, a three-inch circle holding all. A 3rd group was then shot with bullets very slightly filed on one edge of the base, but otherwise perfect. This caused imperfect delivery, and the group was eight inches in diameter."

Other men before Pope understood why accuracy is obtained only by delivering the bullet perfectly from the muzzle. George Schalk must have understood it. Pope's achievement in coming nearer than any other man ever has to solving the problem was through the design of his bullet, the cut of his rifling, and the exquisite precision of his workmanship.

He was by this time in charge of 600 men at the bicycle factory, and earning an excellent salary. He had the best engineering training of his time. He was in line for a prosperous career. Naturally he hesitated to give up so promising a career in order to become a maker of rifle barrels. But George Schalk died, so there were no new Schalk barrels. Pope was a rifle crank. He quit his job and went to work making rifle barrels.

Never, in the fifty years that followed, did he catch up with his orders. Never, except for a period of about three years when he was employed by the Stevens Arms Company at a salary of $5,000 a year to make Pope barrels under their auspices, did he make a good living. Men who do the finest hand work can seldom charge what their work is worth. But they enjoy, without a doubt, a greater career satisfaction than money can buy.

It took Harry Pope no more than ten years after he made his first barrel entirely on a foot-powered lathe in his backyard shop to become widely known as the maker of the most accurate rifles in the world.

By 1897, when Pope was 36 years old, any match rifleman who wanted the best possible gun went to Pope's shop in Hartford, Conn., to place his order - even though he knew that he would have to wait a long time until Pope could fill orders previously taken.

Forty years later Pope had become a legend. Some friends of his induced him to go once more to the national shooting matches at Camp Perry, where more than sixteen hundred men will enter a single match such as the Wimbledon Cup.

21

When a member of Pope's club, the Manhattan Rifle & Revolver Association, heard of this scheme he said, "If they'd put Harry in a tent and charge twenty-five cents a look and one dollar a question, they wouldn't need the money Congress appropriated for the matches."

They didn't put him in a tent, but Pope spent all his days and half his nights surrounded by shooters eager to ask questions. He was 76 years old; he had begun to look like Santa Claus; but he was still the world's foremost maker of rifle barrels.

The rifles that made Pope's early reputation were muzzle-loaders. They were furnished with a false muzzle and starter so the bullet could be put down the barrel without injuring the real muzzle. But Pope's barrels were fitted to existing commercial breech-loading single-shot actions such as the Ballard, Stevens, Sharps-Borchardt, and the one Pope came to prefer, the Winchester. His rifles had the advantage over the muzzle-loaders of an earlier day using a percussion lock in that the bore could be examined and cleaned from the breach. They could be loaded in three different ways. The bullet could be put down the muzzle and the brass cartridge case containing the powder charge inserted from the breech. Or the bullet could be inserted from the breech into the rifling with a tool made for the purpose, and the charged case put in behind it. Or, finally, fixed ammunition such as that sold by the commercial manufacturers, in which the bullet is seated deep in the cartridge case and often crimped there, could be inserted from the breech.

Fixed ammunition is superior for hunting and war, but it had never produced the kind of accuracy Pope sought with cast lead-alloy bullets. Modern high-velocity rifles using bullets with hard-metal jackets are, as Pope put it, "a different breed of cat", and one he came to later.

Pope guaranteed his rifles of .32 caliber and larger to put ten shots in a 2-1/2" circle at 200 yards. He went on to say he believed his barrels would shoot into 2" at 200 yards when the weather was favorable. It is a matter of common consent among riflemen that Pope did not claim too much. In my own experience, a .32-40 muzzle-loader which Pope made forty-eight or forty-nine years ago will still put ten shots in less than 2" at 200 yards when everything is right, and so will his last muzzle loader, which he made for me about ten years ago.

Pope rifles have often done far better. The late C.W. Rowland, of Boulder, Colorado, a famous bench-rest shot, made many astonishingly small groups with Pope rifles. I don't know of any better 200-yard group than one Rowland made with a .32 caliber Pope. All ten shots break into one ragged hole and the group measures, from center to center of the widest shots, 7/8 of an inch. Every shot would hit a dime.

John D. Kelley, of Williamsport, PA., made a hobby of rest-shooting with Pope rifles. He had one .38 caliber Pope, chambered for the .38-72 case, with which he shot group after group measuring less than 1-1/2".

A young woman, Miss Minnie Schenk, was taught by Kelley to shoot from a rest. She once put five shots from a .32 caliber Pope so nearly in the same spot at 200 yards that all the bullet holes can be completely hidden by a penny.

Harry Pope raised the standard of accuracy that could be got from a rifle higher than it had ever been before.

How did he do it?

All the fine shooting mentioned was done with muzzle loading. Pope did not guarantee his rifles to shoot in 2-1/2" at 200 yards except when muzzle-loaded. When shot with the bullet seated from the breech in the rifling ahead of the cartridge case, the guarantee was 3-3/4". He gave no guarantee of what his rifles would do with fixed ammunition. Cartridges of the kind a man can carry in his pocket were completely out of the picture.

Why should a rifle shoot better when the bullet is loaded from the muzzle?

It will be simpler to answer that question by going back to the problems young Harry Pope faced when he decided to make his first muzzle-loading barrel after meeting Will Hayes of Newark and learning from him why George Schalk's rifles were the best.

Pope's theory was that perfect shooting is the result of delivering a perfect bullet perfectly from the muzzle. He thought that to do this it was necessary for the bullet to have a perfect base, be perfectly centered in the rifle bore, have uniform velocity, and be as little deformed as possible in its passage from breech to muzzle.

The first problem was to make perfect bullets, or bullets as nearly perfect as possible. Most bullet molds were imperfect. They cast bullets that proved under the micrometer caliper to be markedly out of round, with bases seldom truly square with the axis. Pope designed a bullet mold having a cut-off with a bottom plate rigidly connected to it and swinging with it, which, with dowel pins, held the two halves of the mold perfectly in position. Bullets from this mold had square bases and they averaged less than .000,5" out of round. Furthermore, the bullet was poured from the point, bringing any imperfections to the point - which, for fine shooting, is much less important than the base.

Next came the design of the rifling. The process of rifling is one of cutting spiral grooves. In early rifles these grooves were often very narrow, because narrow grooves are easier to cut. Narrow grooves mean wide lands - the lands being that portion of the bore that is left between the grooves. Pope had seen that Schalk's rifling consisted of eight wide, flat grooves with eight narrow lands left in the corners of the octagon. He liked the narrow lands. They displace less bullet metal than wide lands and make muzzle loading easier. But the octagonal form of Schalk's rifling left corners about .008" deep. The bullet had to be big enough to fill those deep corners if it was to make a gas-tight seal, and if the bullet was that big it was (so much oversize that it was) likely to be deformed (in loading). [Words in brackets added by GBL.]

Pope designed his rifling on a radius. That is, his grooves were not flat but rounded on the bottom, so that the corners were only .004" deep, and the middle of the groove had almost no depth. When he had done this, Pope had something that greatly pleased him. He saw that as the eight narrow lands cut into the bullet they would have to do so equally, because the bullet was supported between every two lands by the middle of the groove, thus keeping it central as it upset, or expanded, under the hammer blow of the exploding powder.

He decided on two more refinements of design and one refinement of manufacture. Most rifling has a uniform pitch or twist. Pope preferred a gain twist, that is, one that increases in pitch toward the muzzle. The second refinement of design was choke boring. The choke in a shotgun is all near the muzzle. Pope's choke consisted of a very slight taper from breech to muzzle, hardly more than a thousandth or so.

The refinement of manufacture was in the slightest possible use of the lapping rod. It was customary for most barrel makers to take off the burrs left by the rifling cutter with a lead lap coated with oil and emery. Heavy lapping obliterates the niceties of the original cut. Pope wanted to cut his grooves to his pre-determined shape and he did not then want to spoil this shape by lapping. However, he usually found it necessary to do a little lapping. To distinguish the light lapping he did from the heavy lapping of others, he called what he did "polishing".

No man - at least no man who knew what he was doing - ever designed rifling more difficult to cut than Pope's. And the design was one that had to be executed with unusual precision or its advantages would be lost. However, he had one other nice job on his hands, and that was to make false muzzles.

A false muzzle is a short piece of rifled barrel in which the grooves and lands are precise continuations of the grooves and lands in the barrel on which it is used. It cannot be made by cutting off an inch or so of the rifled barrel. The cut would take away some of the material and thus destroy the exact continuity of grooves and lands. The piece of stock from which a false muzzle is made must be cut off before the barrel blank is bored. It is held in place on the end of the barrel blank with dowel pins and a clamp. Then barrel blank and false muzzle are bored, reamed, and rifled as if they were one piece.

The false muzzle is then removed, knurled, and fitted with a round-headed pin called a blinder pin. The dowel pins of the false muzzle go down for 3/4 inch or so into holes around the real muzzle. They must be so fitted that there can be no lateral movement of the false muzzle. Pope's dowel pins are so precisely fitted that though they push in easily, they pop when you pull the false muzzle off.

The blinder pin serves to indicate which way the false muzzle goes on. It is always at the top of the barrel, or, as a rifleman would say, at 12 o'clock. Its name comes from another purpose. It is intended to cover up the target when the rifle is held in position for firing, if the shooter has forgotten to take off the false muzzle. This scheme worked well enough with iron sights, which are close to the barrel and in line with the enlarged head of the blinder pin. Modern target telescope sights are so high above the barrel that you look over the top of the blinder pin.

Most men who shoot Pope muzzle-loaders sooner or later forget to take off the false muzzle before firing. A friend of mine shot the false muzzle off his rifle three times in five shots while becoming familiar with Pope's system.

Pope's remedy for this sort of carelessness is to tie one end of a shoe string to the blinder pin of the false muzzle and the other end to the loading rack.

The false muzzle is used with a bullet starter. This consists of a cap that fits the false muzzle, with a closely fitted plunger. The inside end of the plunger is shaped to fit the point of the bullet. The outside end has a flattened knob.

In loading you (1) wipe the fouling of the previous shot off the real muzzle; (2) fit the false muzzle on the real muzzle; (3) put a bullet, base down, in the mouth of the false muzzle; (4) fit the starter over the false muzzle with the end of the plunger on the bullet point; (5) hit the knob end of the plunger a smart blow with the heel of your hand, and thus drive the bullet down through the false muzzle and well into the barrel; (6) push the bullet the rest of the way down with the ramrod; (7) take the ramrod out slowly, as otherwise the suction created may draw the bullet part way back; (8) take the false muzzle off and, if it's not hanging by a shoe lace, put it down somewhere so it won't roll off and bend the dowel pins when it hits the floor.

You are then ready to (1) decap a fired case; (2) recap the case; (3) measure the charge of powder into the case; (4) insert a wad in the mouth of the case to keep the powder from spilling; (5) put the case in the breech; (6) close the gun, and (7) shoot.

All this sounds like a lot of trouble to a man who is accustomed to fixed ammunition. Nevertheless, nearly all the better off-hand shots in the United States used Pope muzzle-loading rifles in this way from the middle 1890's up to World War I, and some of them are doing it still. The off-hand records at 200 yards made with Pope muzzle-loaders have never been equalled by men shooting any other kind of rifle. There is just one reason for this and that is the dependable accuracy of the Pope muzzle-loader.

This brings us back to the question of why a rifle will shoot better when the bullet is loaded from the muzzle.

One of the sources of inaccuracy in rifles is the fouling left in the bore by the previous shot. This fouling cuts into the bullet as it passes up the bore and deforms it enough so it does not fly true. When a bullet with a clean sharp base is loaded from the muzzle, it pushes the dirt of the previous shot down to the breech where it can do no harm. To my notion, this is the principal advantage of muzzle loading.

But Pope believes the other advantages are important. He says that when a bullet is seated in the breech "...the lands cutting backward into the bullet drag out burrs behind, leaving an uneven and serrated base. If this bullet is not perfectly centered, these burrs will be longer on one side than on the other. As these burrs leave the muzzle, the gas escapes first from the short side - the result is an uneven and wobbling flight." Finally, Pope says that a false muzzle and starter seat the bullet in exact line with the bore without deforming the base.

A Pope muzzle-loading outfit consisted of the barrel, fitted to the customer's action, false muzzle, starter, ramrod, Pope bullet mold, and Pope pump for lubricating bullets.

One would expect that such an outfit, almost entirely handmade with the most painstaking care by the man who turned out the finest rifle barrels ever produced, would cost a lot of money. Pope explained in his Hartford catalogue of the 1890's that he could not compete with factory work in price. He had to charge more. His price for a muzzle-loading barrel with the complete muzzle-loading outfit was $35. A complete rifle cost from $50 up, depending on the sights and the quality of the stock.

The price seems ludicrously low in 1945. It wasn't as low as it seems now, since money would buy at least three times as much fifty years ago. Nevertheless it was low. Pope raised his prices in time, though they never caught up with the decrease in the value of the dollar. In later years Pope charged $40 for a breech-loading barrel and $65 for a muzzle-loading barrel and outfit. It is plain why the master barrelmaker of all time never got rich. He could not charge what his work was worth. Indeed, he never charged even as much as he could easily have got.

The reason, I think, is that Pope was a rifle crank. He wanted to see his work in the hands of men who could use his rifles' accuracy or at least appreciate it. Few rifle shots have money. A large proportion of them are men working for wages. Pope couldn't, or wouldn't, charge them more than they could afford to pay. Naturally, he was annoyed when a customer took advantage of the situation and sold his Pope rifle for a good deal more than it had cost him.

Pope was behind in his orders from the beginning. He gradually got years behind. This gave rise to some fantastic episodes.

One day a customer complained to Pope that he had waited a year for a Pope rifle, and asked if he could buy the target rifle Pope had made for himself. Pope looked at him indignantly.

"Do you know how long I had to wait for that barrel?" he asked. "I had to wait three and a half years."

On another occasion a rich New Yorker who planned a year in

advance a hunting trip to Africa asked Pope to make him a barrel. Pope had never heard of the man as a rifle shot and he saw no need for a Pope barrel in the rough-and-ready work of shooting lions, but he said he guessed he could do it. The rich man called on Pope again six months later. Pope said he hadn't got around to making the barrel. The rich man thought he saw the light.

"I'll tell you what I'll do," he said. "If you make the barrel before I start for Africa I'll double the price."

"Why, you blankety-blank," Pope said. "What are you trying to do - bribe me?"

Though customers were supposed to wait their turn, there were ways of getting Pope barrels out of turn. I have been accused of using them all. If I did, it was rather the result of the natural innocence of my nature than of any foul design.

Shortly after I met Pope, he told me about the annual Election Day match, which was first shot in 1892 and has been shot every Election Day since. The match originally called for 100 shots off-hand at 200 yards on the German Ring target. Members of accredited clubs all over the country shot the match on their home ranges and wired their scores to New York. Since most of the 200-yard ranges in the United States have been cut up into building lots, the match is now shot at 100 yards with .22 caliber rifles on a target slightly less than half the dimensions of the 200-yard target.

Only eight or nine men have won the match in more than fifty years, and their names read like a roster of American off-hand shots: Fred Ross, Michael Dorrler, H.M. Pope, W.G. Hudson, Arthur Hubalek, Paul Landrock, Arthur Elliott - though there were some first-rate men who are not included, such as D. W. King, W.H. French, L.P. Ittel, J.E. Kelley, I.P. Hansen, Adolph Strecker, and A.H. Pape. It was in an Election Day match that Dr. Hudson made the world's record score of 2301 for 100 shots on the German Ring target.

I asked Pope if I could attend the match. He said I could shoot in it - that it was open to all comers. He did not, however, approve of my rifle, which was by another maker. He insisted on loaning me his own .22 caliber free rifle. I shot a poor score and Pope realized how badly I needed a Pope rifle built to fit me. He made me one.

I took up pistol shooting. Pope made a Pope barrel for my

pistol.

I wanted to shoot at 200 yards off-hand. Pope made me a .32-40 muzzle-loader.

Then I discovered that Pope had a .25 caliber high-velocity barrel he had made for Franklin W. Mann, the author of **The Bullet's Flight from Powder to Target.** Mann died before Pope could deliver the barrel, and it had never been chambered. Pope agreed to let me have the barrel and began to make chambering reamers for it.

Subsequently I stopped in at Major Anthony Fiala's outfitting store in downtown New York to look at a Ballard rifle I had bought by mail and asked to have sent there. I was prying the lid off the box when a tall and handsome stranger walked in.

"A Ballard," he observed. I nodded.

"I have a Pope-Ballard," he said. "So have I," I said.

I have two Pope-Ballards," he said. "So have I," I said.

The handsome stranger looked a little grim: "I have three Pope-Ballards," he said.

"So have I," I said.

The tall stranger looked me up and down. "I know who you are. You're the so-and-so who's had Harry tied up all summer with that .25 caliber gun of yours so nobody else can get anything done."

The life of a Pope customer was often difficult, and customers often made Pope's life difficult, especially when he was shooting. He usually fired 200 or 300 shots at the target every week and he became a good shot when he was still in his twenties. But it took him longer to become a champion off-hand shot than it did for him to become the king of rifle-makers. He reached his peak as a shooter about 1901, when he was 40 years old, after fifteen years of shooting, and set out to break the 50- and 100-shot records at 200 yards on the Standard American target.

He was going well against the fifty-shot record when, in his fourth 10-shot string, a shooter asked him a question that required a thoughtful answer. Pope was in the act of loading his rifle, but he paused to answer the question. When he fired his next shot he knew by the sound, and everybody in the shooting house knew, that he had fired without putting a bullet down the

29

barrel. Under the rules the shot was scored as a miss. It cost Pope 10 points. However, he dropped only 3 points on the other nine shots of his fourth string and went on to drop only 4 points in his final ten shots. Despite his mistake of firing a shot without a bullet in the gun, he had made a new record of 467 on the Standard target. Forty-five of Pope's 50 shots that day were in the 9 ring or better. The 9 ring is 5.54 inches in diameter - smaller than the saucer of a coffee cup. In other words, Pope was hitting saucers nine times out of ten at 200 yards.

Pope's record for 100 shots on the Standard American was 917. It was beaten by Dr. W.G. Hudson, who made the present record of 921.

Pope was a target shot, but he loved to hunt. He told me once some things he had read about the incredible amount of game in this country when it was first invaded by white men. He finished by saying, "You and I were born too late - we should have lived by the rifle."

I'm sure that Pope would have liked living by the rifle, and I was flattered that he included me as one of his own kind. Pope did his first deer hunting with a lever-action repeating rifle. He was not the kind of hunter who enjoys pumping shot after shot in the direction of a running deer, hoping to hit by accident. Pope liked to place his shot precisely. He found that a repeating rifle was no use to him. It didn't occur to him to make a rifle for himself - probably because he'd have had to wait too long to get it. He chose a Winchester single-shot chambered for the .30-40 cartridge, the one used in the US Army Krag. The list price was $20. Pope added an ivory-bead front sight and a Lyman rear sight, tuned up the trigger pull, and bought some factory cartridges with soft-nose bullets. The rifle had a 30-inch barrel and weighed nearly ten pounds. It would seem long and heavy to most deer hunters (then or today). It did not seem heavy to Pope, who was used to shooting a thirteen-pound target rifle and who knew that up to a point, the heavier a rifle is, the better it holds.

Pope killed twenty-two deer, one of them an elk, with twenty-two shots from this rifle. The twenty-third deer was down when Pope came up with it, but it was still alive. Pope had to use a second cartridge on it.

Two things happened during Pope's career which promised to make his muzzle-loading rifles obsolete. The first was the increasing success of the arms makers in the use of bullets with hard metal jackets and smokeless powder, a combination that eventually produced velocities two and three times as great as those obtainable with black powder. Our Army adopted the Krag rifle in 1892 and its successor, the Springfield, in 1902. The commercial arms companies began putting out rifles for the new ammunition in the middle 1890's.

The new rifles did not approach Pope muzzle-loaders in accuracy. Pope was interested in finding out what could be done with jacketed bullets at high velocity. He made a .30 caliber single-shot rifle on a Sharps-Borchardt action. He wanted more power than that of the Krag cartridge, so he chambered the rifle for the .38-72 case necked down to .30 caliber.

He used commercial jacketed bullets, but, taking a leaf from his experience with lead-alloy bullets, he modified their shape so less metal would be displaced. He made a swage with which he reduced the body of the long 220-grain bullet to bore diameter and left a base band the full groove diameter. With this rifle and his reformed bullets Pope made a ten-shot group at 200 yards measuring 15/32" from center to center of the two widest shots. Thus he achieved fine accuracy with jacketed bullets before either the commercial manufacturers or the Army's experts were able to do so.

Soon Pope was making .30 caliber rifles for long-range military shooting. When an American team beat a British team in a long-range match, the British protested the win on the ground that the Americans weren't using military rifles, but rifles with Pope barrels. I don't know the rights of the protest, but I'm sure the British were licked before they started.

Pope had to abandon most of the refinements of his early rifling in making barrels for jacketed bullets at high velocities. A metal-jacketed bullet cannot be loaded from the muzzle. The force required would be too great. A jacketed bullet is not easily deformed by the fouling of the previous shot and smokeless powder leaves but little fouling. Pope cut his smokeless barrels with five grooves instead of eight, with wider lands to take the punishment of jacketed bullets.

The other event that threatened Pope's supremacy was World War I, which almost finished shooting with the Schuetzen free rifle off-hand at 200 yards. Match rifle shooting increased rapidly after 1918 but most of it was small bore shooting in the military prone position. A man who knows how can shoot a rifle almost as well in this position as he can from a bench rest. The prone shots soon discovered that their rifles weren't too good. They demanded more accurate .22 caliber target rifles. Many of them went to Pope, and he did not let them down.

The late E.C. Crossman, in his book **Small-Bore Rifle Shooting,** credited Pope .22 caliber rifles with shooting average groups 0.2" better at 100 yards than the best of the commercial target rifles. That was in 1927. Since then the ammunition manufacturers have greatly improved the .22 long rifle cartridge. Match ammunition in this caliber made just before the present world war was incredibly good. Commercial makers of .22 caliber target rifles studied Pope's rifles and went to work. I doubt if their average product is equal to Pope's average. But it is probable that any large manufacturer could choose (i.e. *select*) .22 caliber target rifles from the production line that will equal any Pope .22 still in use.

What was Pope's permanent contribution to the science of rifle-making?

He was not an inventor in the ordinary sense. He was rather a man who took what he found and improved on it. There was probably little that was wholly new in Pope's muzzle-loading system except the design of his rifling. Pope's finger lever was an adaptation of one he saw on an old rifle that hung in a restaurant where he used to go to lunch. Pope's set triggers were merely Ballard or Winchester double set triggers rebuilt so the front trigger cannot kick back in firing, and thus retains its clean sharpness indefinitely.

Pope retained always, in spite of his training at the Massachusetts Institute of Technology and his craftsmanship, a trace of the handy man. He liked to use the simplest means. His work was done with little - too little. Thus in the ten years when I visited his Jersey City shop so often, I never saw him use any power tool except a lathe he had bought for $125. His rifling machine was built out of a similar lathe. He had to use power in drilling his barrels, but he refused to use power in rifling. He moved his rifling head forward and back by traversing the lathe carriage, patiently turning the crank by hand and making a cut of .002,5" in fifty passes. He said that since he couldn't get inside the barrel to watch the rifling cutter, he had to depend on feel to know what was happening. He couldn't feel if the rifling head was power-driven.

He cared little about the outside appearance of a rifle. One of his famous rifles was known as the "dogfight gun" because it was so hard-looking. Pope had never taken the time to polish or blue the outside of the barrel. It still shows the marks of the lathe tool. But it shot so well that fellow members of the Manhattan Rifle and Revolver Association were always borrowing it to shoot their scores with.

In spite of his apparent indifference to the appearance of things, Pope's work had distinction of design. If you will set beside a Pope design - a bullet, for instance - a similar design by any other maker, you will at once be struck by the clean character of Pope's work.

My own notion is that though some of the things Pope did were superior because of the theory behind them, most of them owe their superiority to Pope's superb workmanship.

However that may be, Pope will live as the last of the great gunsmiths. Not that we shan't have fine gunsmiths in the future. We have some splendid ones who will be at work again as soon as the war is over. But the opportunity for another career like H.M. Pope's is probably gone forever.

Experts are divided as to whether modern rifles with machine-made barrels shooting jacketed bullets at high velocity are as accurate as Pope muzzle-loaders, with their delicate handmade rifling and lead-alloy bullets. One expert says you can't beat a Pope muzzle-loader up to 200 yards with any high-velocity rifle and the next expert says you can. I set out some years ago to settle this question for my own private satisfaction, but so far I have shot only 4 high-velocity rifles and only 3 Pope muzzle-loaders. The result is still in doubt.

There is no question that the high-velocity rifle is superior in accuracy at long range. And there seems to be no question that jacketed bullets do not require the delicate rifling Pope designed for lead bullets, or the precise workmanship with which he carried out his design.

Harry Pope gave up a most promising career in manufacturing to make fine rifles, thus condemning himself to a small income for life. Does he regret, at 83, the choice he made as a young man?

I don't think so. I well remember what he once said to my wife. Although my wife is a grand person, she is not much interested in rifles, and prefers the music of Beethoven to that of a Pope .32-40 muzzle-loader. Pope had been at our house for several days. As we finished dinner on the last night of Pope's visit, my wife said, "Harry, don't you ever talk about anything but guns?"

33

Pope lit his cigarette with deliberation, and said, as if he were rendering final judgement on his own life - and incidentally putting my wife in her place - "All the pleasure I ever got out of life I got out of making and shooting guns."

(I thought it was Pope who said, after returning from a visit to Springfield Armory, "Now *there* is a gun shop!". However, I was mistaken. Lucian Cary reported that comment as coming from an un-named employee of the Winchester plant, in connection with his (Cary's) own questioning of John Garand, designer of the famed M1 Garand. Cary had the opportunity to visit Springfield, and discuss with Mr. Garand and the people at Springfield, the Garand rifle, which at the time had recently emerged from the battle grounds of WWII; Cary had asked the Springfield people if they had found the M1 a difficult rifle to make. The answer was that no, they had not, and they had in fact just finished making about 3 million of them. Cary's comment (to the reader) was that they had spent about 30 or 40 million dollars on tooling - the implication being that with unlimited funds to make the job possible, virtually any difficulty ought well to have been ironed out.) G.B.L.

Harry Melville Pope was born August 15, 1861. He died on October 11, 1950, at the age of 89.

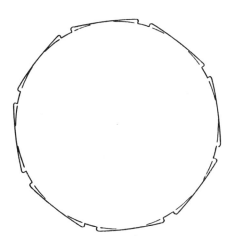

34

THE RIFLE CRANK

One hot afternoon last summer just after the hay was cut I heard the unmistakable crack of a high-powered rifle. It is a sound we often hear in November, in spite of the fact that deer are protected in Connecticut; but it is a sound we don't often hear in July. Even those who are agin the law hesitate to kill deer in hot weather when you can't keep the meat.

I went up the woods road to see what was going on. After a quarter of a mile I found a big Snyder-Farquharson of mature years parked in the barway that leads to the upper meadows. There is something especially impressive about a middle-aged Snyder-Farquharson. A bootlegger might drive a new one, but a middle-aged one somehow implies respectability.

I looked up the slope of the meadow. There was nobody in sight. I started in toward the rise of ground that divides that meadow into two parts. I felt that it was really worse for a man who drove a Snyder-Farquharson to kill deer illegally than for a man who drives a flivver. At the top of the meadow I looked down. Just below me, a large man sat on a rock with a rifle across his knees. He was gazing across the valley at the opposite slope through a pair of field glasses. I could see nothing across there but a meadow that had been in clover hay.

The man wasn't glad to see me, but he was polite about it. He was a good deal like his car - large, heavy and mature. He was wearing shooting spectacles made of some special greenish-yellow glass.

"I suppose I'm on your land," he said.

I'd intended to say something about that part of it. But I didn't.

35

I was too much interested in his rifle. It was years since I'd had my hands on a fine rifle.

"Do you mind letting me see that gun of yours?" I asked.

He extracted the cartridge from the chamber and handed me the gun. I guessed that it weighed twelve pounds. It was a bolt-action rifle with a telescope in micrometer mounts on the barrel, double-set triggers, a stock with a cheek piece and a pistol grip, and a broad leather sling. It was all plain blued steel and dark oiled walnut without ornamentation. But it was a work of art. Every detail had been thoughtfully worked out and patiently executed by the kind of workmen that aren't supposed to exist any more. I handed it back reluctantly.

"It's a beauty," I said. "You must have taken a great deal of trouble to get exactly what you wanted."

"Yes," he said.

Evidently he didn't want to talk. But I had to know more about that rifle. And after all, it was my meadow. I persisted in asking questions.

"I didn't know," I said, "that the Germans ever put out micrometer mounts for their rifle telescopes."

"They don't," he said. "I got these mounts from a fellow in Pittsburgh who makes optical fire-control instruments for the Navy.

I went on asking questions until I learned that he had begun with the action of an Army Springfield and combed half a dozen states for the rest. The barrel had been rifled by a man in Michigan who makes a specialty of that sort of thing; the stock had been made by a man in the Adirondacks, out of a piece of walnut he'd imported from England; the set triggers had been made and fitted by a mechanic in the Marine Corps; and a shop in New York had tooled the firing pin and fitted a special spring to speed up the lock.

Finally I asked to see the cartridge. The brass shell was marked .30-06 - which is shorthand for the .30 caliber Army cartridge - but the bullet - a bullet jacketed with gilding metal up to an exposed lead tip - was plainly smaller than .30 caliber.

"I didn't know they made a cartridge like this," I said.

36

"They don't," he said. "I loaded that myself."

"Weighing each powder charge on a chemist's balance and measuring each bullet with a micrometer gauge, and all that sort of thing," I said.

"Exactly," he said.

"Is it accurate?" I asked.

"I've made some six-inch groups at five hundred yards," he said. He made a gesture toward the opposite hillside. "How far do you think it is to that big squarish rock over there?"

I guessed it was between four and five hundred yards. He nodded. "I make it four hundred and twenty-five through the scope," he said.

"You mean you can measure distances with that scope?"

"I've got marks on the perpendicular cross hair," he said briefly. He took up his field glasses and studied the clover field.

By that time, of course, I knew what he was hunting. There is only one wild animal in the world for which anybody carries a twelve-pound rifle with precisely adjustable telescope sights and a high-velocity load.

"There," he said. "He's come out again." He handed me the field glasses. I had some trouble in focusing them. While I turned the adjusting screw he got down behind the rock he'd been sitting on. He put his hat under the barrel of the rifle as a cushion. He thrust his left arm through the loop in the rifle sling. I got the glasses focused and found the mark. Across on the opposite hillside a woodchuck sat up in the clover to look and to listen, as a woodchuck will.

I glanced down at my friend with the rifle. He had got himself into a comfortable position. He set one trigger and his finger found the other. He took a deeper breath than usual and slowly expelled the air from his lungs as the muzzle steadied on the mark. I looked through the glasses. The woodchuck had dropped on all fours to eat clover. For half a minute we waited. Then the woodchuck sat up and turned his head sideways to look and to listen. The rifle cracked beside me.

"I got him," my friend said triumphantly.

37

We walked slowly back to his car. "I suppose," I said, "that you've spent the spare time of a year to accomplish that."

"The spare time of ten years," he said. He patted the stock of his rifle. "This isn't my first woodchuck rifle. I've had five others. And of course I began shooting with a little .22 repeater. After a while I wanted better sights, and then a better trigger pull, and then more weight in the barrel, and then a better fitting stock, and then more power. It leads you on and on. Perfectly ridiculous how particular you get."

"Absurd," I said.

"Only," he said, "Daniel Boone couldn't have done it. He couldn't have seen well enough with open sights to aim at a woodchuck four hundred yards away and he couldn't have depended on his rifle to hit at that distance."

The obvious answer was that Daniel Boone wouldn't have bothered about so trivial an animal as a woodchuck. But there was no use being unpleasant about it.

Another Willing Victim...
"I had supposed," I said, "that the old fashioned rifle crank had ceased to exist."

"Not at all," he said. "There are ten times as many rifle cranks as there used to be. And there will be still more. The high schools and the colleges have taken up rifle shooting all over the country. Last summer a nineteen-year-old girl from South Dakota and a fourteen-year-old boy from Chicago shot as members of the American team in the annual match with the British for the Dewar trophy. Rifle shooting is having a boom in this country."

I went home thinking how ridiculous it was to go in for twelve-pound rifles and telescope sights and set triggers and loading by hand in order to hunt the inoffensive woodchuck. But about a week later my wife reported that the woodchucks were eating all the string beans in the garden. I bought a little .22 repeater and lay in wait, early in the morning. A woodchuck appeared and walked down between the rows of string beans, nibbling daintily first at one side and then at the other. He wasn't more than twenty-five yards away. I got him.

But the next woodchuck was fifty yards away, and I never knew whether I hit him or not. He disappeared in his hole. I got some better sights for that .22 and had a gunsmith lighten the trigger pull. With these improvements I killed a marauding woodchuck at fifty yards. I took to looking for woodchucks that weren't marauding.

I can see what is going to happen. I'll come to telescope sights, and then to a heavy barrel, and then to set triggers, and then to a stock made to fit me, and then to a larger caliber. A .22 bullet really isn't big enough to stop a charging woodchuck. And my avowed object will be stopping woodchucks. The real lure will be that of putting bullets closer and closer to dead center at longer and longer distances.

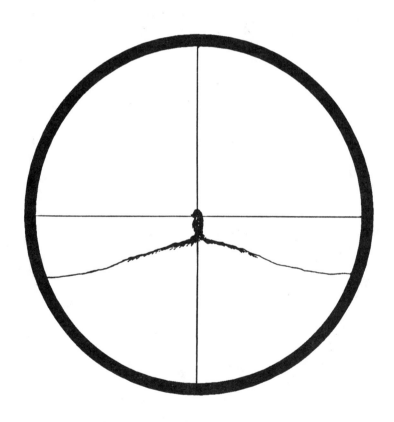

THE BIG-GAME HUNTING OF RUFUS PEATTIE

It may be that any man who does what Rufus Peattie did for more than thirty years is a hero. Every September, for more than thirty years, Rufus Peattie faced a class of boys and knew that it was his task to lead them, stumbling and reluctant, through that history which begins, without preliminary flourish or preamble, *Gallis est omnis diviea in partes tres*.[1] And after doing it over and over again, for more than thirty years, he was still patient and helpful, and only occasionally indulged himself in gentle sarcasm at the expense of a boy who did not, after who knows how many meetings, recognize the ablative absolute.

But Rufus Peattie would never have been known to the world that reads newspapers as a hero if it had not been for a fortuitous circumstance. It was as if coincidence, which is said to have a long arm in works of fiction and is known to have an even longer arm in the actual lives of men, reached out and touched Rufus Peattie on the shoulder and said, "Come with me." And Rufus Peattie went.

Rufus Peattie went and greatly astonished the generations of boys who had sat under him in second year Latin at the Parker Hall School and who referred to him lightly as Old Pete and thought of him as a mild, insignificant little man with no interest in anything more adventurous than the dative case.

He was a mild little man, and he was perennially interested in the attempt to teach boys to read Caesar's Commentaries in spite of a growing conviction that he was not really succeeding in doing it. But Rufus Peattie had his dreams, like everybody else. He had read tales of Daniel Boone and Davy Crockett and Custer's last stand and hunting grizzly bears in the Rocky Mountains, and of the mighty Samuel Baker, who, on occasion, in a tight corner, used a double four-bore rifle shooting fourteen drams of black powder and a lead ball weighing more than a

40

quarter of a pound.

Rufus Peattie knew that he could never hunt big game. He had read that there was no truly dangerous game in North America. And how can a Middle Western school teacher go to Nairobi and hire a safari to go into the Lake Tanganyika country, where lions are as common as alley cats on the island of Manhattan? But though he could never do it, Rufus Peattie could dream about it and read books about it. He collected a small library on big game hunting and rifle shooting, and subscribed to a magazine devoted to shooting and said nothing, never even to Maud.

Rufus Peattie was more than forty years old when he surprised and delighted himself by marrying Maud Thomas, who taught algebra and geometry in one of the local high schools. They bought a second-hand flivver and as soon as the school year was over they drove to New England and saw the ocean for the first time, and charming old villages with wide, elm-shaded streets. They were enchanted by the intimacy of the New England landscape - by the small, irregular fields enclosed by thick stone walls, by the green hills, with bits of woodland, with white birches against hemlocks, and by the white houses with small paned windows and big chimneys and gardens of hollyhocks and delphinium and phlox, with rows of large, old gnarled apple trees.

They missed the way one afternoon, after they had turned toward home, and found themselves on a back road. Rufus drove on with a Middle Western faith that a poor road must eventually lead to a better road. They came, after five miles, to an abandoned farmhouse. It was a small salt-box house built around a big chimney, with a row of sugar maples in front of it.

Rufus stopped the car. They sat looking at the house and then, of one accord, they got out to explore.

"There's lilac in the dooryard," Maud said. "And I think I see a rosebush."

She looked through all the windows of the first floor in turn while Rufus looked into the succession of sheds at the rear of the house. He found a grindstone in a heavy handmade oak frame, neatly mortise-and-tenoned together, and a workbench with a vise, and half a dozen old-fashioned planes of beech and cherry. One of his dreams was to have a workshop and tools.

"Look, Rufus," Maud said when he walked back toward the house - "look through this window."

41

They stood peering through a tiny pane into the dusky room.

"Did you ever see a sweeter fireplace?" Maud asked. The house had never been an elegant one. But the chimney breast was neatly panelled. And the fireplace, of stone and brick combined, was one of those wide, high shallow New England fireplaces designed to heat a room in wintry weather.

"And look at the floor," Maud said. "How wide the boards are."

They turned and looked at the view. To the north the house faced a little meadow, inclosed in stone walls. Beyond was a piece of woodland, with clumps of white birch and hemlock and oak and maple and beech. To the east, there was a small orchard of old apple trees.

"Do you suppose," Maud said, "... do you suppose we could buy it?"

"We'll ask," Rufus said.

He turned the flivver around to go back the way they had come. Maud sat looking over her shoulder. "It's perfectly sweet," she said. "It's what I've always dreamed of having. And we could do it, too, Rufus. We could drive East as soon as school is out every year and stay until September, and I could have a flower garden and you could go around in overalls all summer."

The flivver sputtered and would have died on the hill. Rufus remembered to shift gears. As he did so, a little animal with horns and long, slender legs jumped lightly into the road. It stared at them a moment as if debating whether to do battle, and turned and leaped lightly over the stone wall on the other side of the road, waving a white flag at them.

"Oh," Maud cried, "what was that?"

"A deer," Rufus Peattie said. He had never seen a deer before, but he knew.

"Good heavens," Maud said, "a wild deer?"

"Yes," Rufus Peattie said, with an exulting heart, "a wild deer - a buck."

"You haven't said you really liked the house, Rufus," Maud said.

Rufus nodded grimly. "I'm going to buy that place if it takes my last dollar," he said.

42

The real estate agent grumbled. The house was ninety miles from nowhere. Their nearest neighbor would be half a mile away. Did they know what a country road was like in spring when the frost came out of the ground? He could sell them a better house right in the village. They got the little house and sixty acres of meadow and woodlot for twelve hundred dollars, and bought some furniture at a country auction and moved in for the few remaining weeks of their vacation.

Before they left for Illinois they engaged a neighbor to plow and harrow and plant a garden for them as early in the spring as the weather permitted. Maud studied the seedsmen's catalogs that winter and ordered plants sent on from a nursery - tomatoes and hollyhocks and cabbages and petunias and onions and delphiniums and cauliflower and Canterbury bells and peppers and phlox and her favorite vegetable, broccoli. Rufus Peattie read his shooting magazine every month with an almost feverish interest. He did not buy a rifle. He felt foolish about it. He felt that his hobby would seem a little ludicrous.

They drove back in June as happy and excited as a young couple making their first home. Rufus lived in overalls and wore an old felt hat and patched the roof and puttied the windows and fitted screens and cut the grass and hoed the garden. Maud made curtains and painted woodwork and acquired a cat to discourage the mice and attended all the auctions for twenty miles around in search of rush-bottomed chairs and tavern tables and andirons.

It was almost always cool enough in the evening for an open fire. They sat in front of a fire of wild cherry or hard maple after dinner and watched the small, dancing flames with that agreeable, that almost luxurious, fatigue that comes of doing a day's work with your hands. The yellow cat lay on the hearth and purred. And nightly they decided to put off doing the dishes until morning and went to bed at nine o'clock and were up again before six in their eagerness to work on the place.

Maud discovered, one evening when she went to gather vegetables, that some animal had been eating the new heads of broccoli as fast as they formed. Rufus watched at intervals the next day from the open workshop window. In the late afternoon he discovered the marauder. A fat woodchuck came out of the stone wall at the end of the garden and sat up to look and to listen. Rufus waited. The woodchuck walked down the rows without pausing at the cabbages or the new peas. He sat up again suddenly, his head cocked alertly on one side. Rufus stood still beside the window. The woodchuck was apparently satisfied there was no danger. He took a nip of broccoli. He ate broccoli with evident relish, standing almost upright on his hind legs to reach the heads, and pausing every minute or so to look anxiously around.

Rufus drove to town the next morning and bought a little .22 rifle such as is made for boys. He tried it out when he got home, shooting at an envelope tacked to a board. He hadn't shot a rifle since he was a boy, and not much then. But he had learned a good deal by reading. He knew you couldn't snatch at the trigger when the sights came on the paper and expect to get off the shot before they swung off again. The act of snatching threw the sights off the target. He knew you had to pull the trigger slowly, putting on almost enough pressure to fire the rifle, and then as the sights swung on, you added the last ounce. The trigger pull of the little rifle was rough and heavy; the barrel was much too light; the stock was too small. But taking great pains, Rufus Peattie found he could hit the envelope two or three times out of five at a distance of fifty feet. He noticed that his bullets struck a little low and a little to the right. He did not trust his skill sufficiently to try knocking the front sight over, and the rear sight was not adjustable. He would have to remember and allow for the error in the sighting.

He waited in the late afternoon by the workshop window. The woodchuck came out for the evening meal exactly as he had before. Rufus rested the muzzle of the rifle on his window sill and his elbows on the workbench, and waited. The woodchuck reached the broccoli and began to eat. Rufus aimed at the woodchuck's head and drew the front sight down in the notch and held his breath, and tried to pull slowly, without disturbing his aim. The woodchuck disappeared as the rifle cracked.

Rufus walked down into the garden. He had been so sure he was going to hit. He hoped to find the place were the bullet had cut the dirt. He was startled pulling aside the broccoli, to find the woodchuck on his back. The little bullet had slipped through just above the shoulders, breaking the spine and killing instantly.

Sir Samuel Baker was not more triumphant when he brought a charging elephant to his knees with that four-bore field piece of his, which would have knocked any lesser man off his feet with its recoil, than Rufus Peattie was at stopping the woodchuck in his tracks. He had forgotten to aim high and to the left. He had failed to hit the woodchuck in the head at twenty yards. But he had killed his game with one shot.

Rufus Peattie drove all the way to Springfield the next day to find a man who could fit an aperture sight, adjustable for elevation and windage, and refine the trigger pull. And then he set to work to learn to shoot. He learned more rapidly than most, having grasped the fact that nearly all the skill in rifle shooting is in pulling the trigger.

It is contrary to instinct to pull a trigger slowly, deliberately, without moving the hand, without changing the pressure of its grasp on the rifle, and without flinching at the explosion, while all the time the front sight bobs to either side and above and below the bull. The peculiar control necessary to let the shot off must be acquired by long and earnest practice. The rest is knowledge.

Rufus Peattie came back the second summer with a .22 target rifle weighing nearly ten pounds, with finely adjustable sights and a full pistol-grip stock - an instrument of precision. He learned that summer to shoot in the prone position, with a sling; and sitting with his elbows supported on his knees; and finally, with a muzzle and elbow rest.

He was fascinated by rest shooting. He knew his rifle was capable of putting ten successive shots in a circle the size of a dollar at a hundred yards; and often, in a smaller circle. It had done that in a machine rest when the maker tested it. Rufus built a solid table on posts set two feet in the ground, with a heavy notched board at the forward end in which to lay the rifle muzzle. He sat in a chair beside the table, resting his body against the table with both his elbows firmly supported. The rifle would seem to be almost without tremor. Rufus would hold his breath and slowly press the trigger and hold the sight after the bullet had left the barrel, and still he could not put ten shots in the ten ring. He sent the rifle away then to be fitted with a telescope sight and waited impatiently for its return.

He was amazed, sighting with the telescope, which magnified eight times, at how much tremor there was at the bench rest. But he could see what he was doing. He made his ten shots "possible" on the third day - ten shots in the ten ring. And shooting thus, with a rest and a telescope, he learned how tricky a game he had chosen. He learned that you had not only to let the shot off correctly, you had also to hold the rifle in the same way each time, with the same firmness, or else your shots scattered more widely.

That summer Rufus Peattie shot a goshawk at a hundred and twenty-five paces and discovered, in trying to shoot woodchucks at longer ranges, that he needed something more powerful than a .22, and with a flatter trajectory.

He acquired during the winter a target rifle of a generation ago, a Ballard with double-set triggers. When you set the lock by pulling the rear trigger, the merest flicker of the finger on the front trigger fired the rifle. The Ballard action had been fitted with a muzzle loading barrel by the American craftsman, Pope. You loaded the bullet through a false muzzle with a special tool, and pushed it home with a rod. Then you put the primed shell, with a wad of blotting paper over the powder to keep it from spilling, in the breech. It was a great deal of trouble. It was quite unsuited to hunting. But it did make sure that the bullet was correctly started in the rifling, concentric with the bore.

Rufus Peattie learned to make bullets in the mold that came with the rifle, and, discarding all but the perfect ones, to lubricate them. Once that summer he fired ten successive shots at a hundred yards that would all have hit a dime. He was a confirmed rifle crank.

In ten years, with a new rifle every year or two, Rufus Peattie became an accomplished rifleman. He knew how to find out what a rifle would do, and how to make it do its best. He learned all the things you had to watch to get fine results. He grew more and more meticulous as he began to use high-velocity rifles with jacketed bullets. He weighed his powder charges on assayer's scales. He weighed his bullets and checked their diameter with a micrometer caliper and spun them for concentricity.

He got used to handling and to carrying on long walks a rifle that weighed twelve or thirteen pounds. He learned to kill crows at two hundred yards and woodchucks at three hundred, and never shot at them unless they were far enough away to make it difficult. He privately gloried in the fact that his hobby had no practical use. He was like a golfer who ignores tournaments and plays only against bogey. He had no interest in the military, being by temperament and principle a pacifist. He increasingly regarded rifle shooting as a laboratory experiment in which, with rifles to which the most skilled mechanics have devoted their most earnest effort, one may, by taking infinite pains, approach perfection, but never attain it.

After ten years the little salt-box house sat in the middle of a green lawn, with borders that bloomed from early June to the first hard September frost, with a kitchen garden as nearly weedless as may be. Maud had furnished the house with pieces of maple and cherry and pine such as country cabinetmakers built in the days of Duncan Phyfe - pieces that no museum would have looked at twice, but pieces that would have brought a fancy price in Madison Avenue. Rufus repaired them and waxed them and polished them. The New England community had not so much accepted them as come to take them for granted.

Rufus walked one sunny summer evening, when most of the hay in the neighborhood had been cut, to the top of the knoll west of the house. He was wearing overalls and a blue dungaree jacket to which Maud had sewed large pieces of sheepskin according to his instructions. There was a sheepskin pad on each elbow; and another on his right shoulder, where the rifle butt rested; and a fourth on his upper left arm where the sling came.

Rufus laid his rifle down beside him and surveyed the meadow below through a pair of binoculars. There was nothing in sight. He fired a shot at a stone two hundred yards away merely to dirty the barrel. He disliked the first shot from a clean barrel. It usually goes high.

He sat studying the meadow with his glasses for fifteen or twenty minutes. Then he saw a woodchuck come out to feed. He guessed the distance at two hundred and twenty five yards. He put down the binoculars and picked up the rifle and got into the prone position with his left arm through the sling and his elbows on the ground. The rifle had been a pet for two summers - a Government Springfield action which he had had fitted with a heavy .25 caliber barrel, and a full stock, and a telescope. He noted the elevation. He turned the micrometer elevating screw one click - enough to raise the bullet an inch at that distance. There was apparently no wind - not a breath.

He had settled down into position. His finger was on the trigger when he heard the sudden drumbeat of a big car coming at high speed. The woodchuck scuttled for his hole. Rufus Peattie rolled to the right, enough to get his arm out of the sling. He saw the car coming down the hill. It was a big closed car. It hit the flat at sixty or seventy miles an hour. Rufus Peattie reflected that if the driver didn't take his foot off the gas he would never make the curve.

The car didn't make the curve. One wheel struck a stone. The car didn't crash or overturn. The driver managed to get it back on the road and bring it to a skidding stop. It wasn't a hundred yards away. Four men got out and looked at the wheel. Two of them had guns. Rufus Peattie recognized the odd shape of the guns. They were sub-machine guns. Rufus Peattie regarded those guns with contempt. They were deadly enough at close range, of course - spraying pistol bullets as one sprays water from a hose - but they were not instruments of precision. They had coarse sights and their recoil made them jump all over the place. You couldn't hit a woodchuck at forty rods with one - not in a hundred shots.

The men suddenly abandoned the car and ran across the meadow toward the woods. Rufus Peattie got to his feet and started downhill toward the abandoned car. As he walked he opened his rifle. The magazine was empty. He used the rifle as a single loader, not caring to subject his precisely loaded cartridges to the jar of being racked through a magazine. But now he filled the magazine and put a cartridge in the chamber and set the safety.

A smaller car came hurtling down the hill. Rufus saw a man in a blue uniform on the running board. A third car was coming behind it, and a fourth. They all came to violent stops at the big, enclosed car with the dished wheel. A dozen farmers surrounded the big car. Two of them had pitchforks. One man had a crowbar. Another had a shotgun. The policeman had his revolver.

They all yelled at Rufus. They yelled, "Which way did they go?"

Rufus pointed up the meadow toward the woods. The four men had already gained the woods. They were out of sight.

The policemen and the rest started out across the meadow.

"Here!" Rufus yelled, "Spread out! Spread out!"

Nobody paid any attention. Rufus saw young Hiram Morton and grabbed him by the arm. "What's happened, Hi?" he asked.

"They're New York gangsters!" Hi Morton gasped. "They came down Main Street and shot a fellow on the sidewalk and they killed Bennie Owens! I was right behind them! They had machine guns!"

There was a sudden burst of shots from the woods. Bullets threw up little spurts of dust fifty yards ahead of them. The crowd

48

halted, clustering together.

"Spread out!" Rufus Peattie yelled. "Spread out! They can't hit you with a machine gun if you spread out!"

The policeman suddenly dropped his revolver and clasped both hands to his stomach and groaned.

Rufus Peattie stopped and picked up his revolver. "Here, Hi," he said, "shoot at them."

Rufus Peattie dropped flat on his stomach and pushed the safety off as he went down and thrust his arm through the sling and laid his cheek against the stock. He could see the man who was shooting as plain as could be through the scope. He was steadying the submachine gun against a tree and firing. The cross hairs in the scope quartered his face, swung off, as a rifle will, even in the prone position, and swung on again. Rufus Peattie pulled as they swung on. The machine gun ceased abruptly.

Rufus Peattie got up, slamming the bolt home. "Get that policeman to a hospital quick," he said, and started out across the meadow, his rifle cradled in his arms.

There was another machine gun out there, he knew. But he was not afraid. He was no more afraid of being hit by a submachine gun in the hands of gangsters, who had never learned to shoot except at the shortest ranges, than he would have been of being struck by lightning in a summer thunderstorm. When he reached the edge of the woods he stopped to listen. He could hear them crashing through the brush. They hadn't got far. They'd probably run in a circle. They didn't know the woods. They were going down hill toward the swamp. If they got through the two miles to the state road they'd hold up the first passing car and take it away from its owner and perhaps shoot him. But even if they knew the direction, they wouldn't find their way quickly.

Rufus Peattie cocked one eye at the sun. There was a good two hours of daylight left. There was plenty of time. And he knew every rock and tree and laurel thicket in these woods.

He walked on with his rifle cradled in his arm, and paused now and again to listen. When he could no longer hear them, he proceeded cautiously. He might not have seen a head raised above a fallen log ahead if he hadn't known that old hemlock log so well. He stepped behind a thick sugar maple just as the submachine gun spoke. He heard bullets spat to his right. He took off his hat and peered around his tree. A submachine gun bullet

49

wouldn't go through the maple he stood behind. But a bullet from his .25 caliber would go right through that rotten old hemlock log as through so much butter.

He raised his rifle. The head was gone. The three of them broke and ran. Rufus Peattie did not fire. There were too many trees; and a high-power target scope is not the thing with which to take a quick shot at running game. The field of view is too small.

Rufus Peattie trudged on. They waited for him between two great boulders. Rufus knew those boulders well. He ducked behind a tree, sat down and reset his elevation for the shorter distance. He got into the old Gun-Sling Dave position with the rifle cradled across his knees. They won't let you use it at the target any more. They say it isn't really sitting. They say it's just as steady as the prone. Rufus Peattie hunched himself along until he could see the rock. He could see the muzzle of the submachine gun lying on top of the rock. It wasn't more than a hundred yards. He thought he could hit the muzzle at that distance and put the gun out of action. But as the cross hairs steadied down the machine gun barked. And when it barked it jumped up and down on the rock. No man could have hit that mark, less than an inch in diameter, when it was jumping that way.

Rufus Peattie shot at the face of the rock behind them. He knew there wasn't much chance of a hit by ricochet. But he thought the bullet would break up against the granite, and send pieces of bullet jacket and pieces of granite flying like bird shot around their heads.

The answer to his shot was a yell. They ran, dropping the machine gun. Again, there were too many trees, and the target telescope was too slow. Rufus Peattie shook his head. He wished he had a Springfield sporter with a hunting scope. He trudged on after them. He must keep his eye out for the third man. There had been only two behind the rock.

He came on the two in the swamp. They were mired knee-deep beside the brook. They turned and fired at him with automatic pistols. Rufus Peattie shot off-hand. It wasn't more than seventy yards. He aimed deliberately for the shoulder of the nearest one. He plugged him neatly through the shoulder. The other man threw up his hands.

"Throw your guns in the brook," Rufus Peattie said.

They did so.

"All right," Rufus Peattie said. "March back and give yourselves up."

He watched them start. He stood watching them. The fellow who was unhurt walked on ahead and did not help his comrade who had a bullet through his shoulder.

One more, Rufus Peattie thought. *And he's the wisest one.*

He walked on as cautiously as if he were stalking a deer. He walked on until he came to the woods road. There he paused and cogitated. If this fourth man had found the woods road, he'd be hurrying on. But he'd be stopping every now and then behind a laurel thicket to look back. He'd be ready to shoot. And at fifty yards he might be dangerous. Rufus Peattie crossed the woods road and walked along beside it. He walked on until the woods road ran into a high meadow. Rufus Peattie stood looking at the other side of the meadow, where the woods began again. The fourth man was waiting there.

Rufus Peattie raised his rifle. It wasn't more than three hundred yards. He could have shot the man. The fellow would never have known what hit him. But it didn't seem sporting. It didn't seem the kind of thing one did. Rufus Peattie stepped out into the open and held his free hand cupped beside his mouth and yelled.

"Do you surrender?"

The answer was a burst of pistol fire. Rufus Peattie raised his rifle. It wasn't fair, but what else could you do?

The reporters from New York got in before midnight. They told Rufus Peattie who the four men were and why they had put their erstwhile comrade on the spot, and demanded a statement. Rufus Peattie told them briefly what had happened.

"Let's get this straight," the young man from the World said. "You regard machine guns as nothing at all?"

"They were submachine guns," Rufus Peattie said.

"Submachine guns, then," the young man said. He had an odd, ironic smile.

"It's a matter of distance," Rufus Peattie said. "Of course, they're dangerous at short range. They're like a sawed-off shotgun loaded with buckshot. At forty yards they're murderous. But not

51

at two hundred!"

"I see," the young man said. "So you had no hesitation in walking right into machine-gun fire."

"You don't understand," Rufus Peattie said. "In the first place, they weren't regular machine guns. They were submachine guns, firing pistol ammunition. And the men who were using them weren't experienced shots."

"How do you know?"

"Oh," Rufus Peattie said, "how does anybody know anything? They couldn't be. Where would a New York gangster have a chance to try out a submachine gun at two hundred yards?"

"What about the fourth man?"

"He was shooting an automatic pistol, at three hundred yards," Rufus Peattie said.

"You knew nobody could hit you with a pistol at that distance?"

"Oh," Rufus Peattie said, "I wouldn't say that nobody could. Some fellow in the Marine Corps who's shot a lot and knows where to hold might have hit me. But no gangster could."

So the reporters wrote an ironic story, in which they made it appear that Rufus Peattie was a hero.

It was just as bad when he got back to Illinois. The alumni of the Parker Hall School insisted on giving him a dinner. And when he tried to explain that a submachine gun was not an instrument of precision, that no one who knew would ever be afraid of one except at short range, they howled him down with delighted howls.

But he must have taught them something about Caesar's Commentaries. The watch they gave him at that dinner was engraved with a legend. This watch was made to say that Rufus Peattie was a gentleman and a scholar, and entitled to remark, with his favorite author, Julius Caesar, "Veni, vidi, vici."[2] Which is a way of saying, "I, too, have hunted dangerous game."

       1. "All of Gaul is divided into three parts...."
       2. "I came, I saw, I conquered."

THE MADMAN OF GAYLORD'S CORNER

It was a long time ago. It was a long time ago, when there were no radios and no motor cars and no state police and no newspapers printing photographs brought in by airplane from the scene of the crime. It was almost fifty years ago, when J.M. Pyne was young.

J.M. Pyne sat beside the driver of a spring wagon of a summer afternoon with his rifle in a canvas case between his knees. He had hired the wagon to take his trunk and a chest of tools and a box of groceries from the railway station at Winchester four miles up into the New England hills to the place he had rented near Gaylord's Corner. The driver, being a man with a beard, and a native of the region who had returned to it after travels as far west as Indiana, conceived himself as one of wide experience and his passenger as a boy.

He asked a good many questions, but only now and then paused to hear the answers J.M. Pyne gave him.

He chuckled to himself at odd intervals, as if he possessed some secret source of amusement which he might reveal if he chose. But he made no secret of his astonishment at young Mr. Pyne's purpose in renting the old Barnes place.

"You aim to make gun barrels!" he said.

"Rifle barrels," J.M. Pyne said.

"You figur' to sell 'em to one o' these factories?"

"No," J.M. Pyne said. "I'm going to make them for individual customers."

The driver wagged his head. "I dunno where you expect to git customers way up here in these hills," he said. "You won't have a neighbor 'side of two mile."

Young Mr. Pyne hadn't quit his job in the Hartford bicycle factory without misgivings. He had a wife and a small son to look out for. So far, he had made rifle barrels as an avocation, in the spare time he found after working ten hours a day in the factory. He suspected he was moving to the country because he liked the country. But he had a few dollars in the bank and orders enough to keep him busy for several months. He had sent a small advertisement to Mr. Gould's weekly, *Shooting & Fishing*, in Boston, announcing that he was prepared to make and fit target barrels of superior accuracy. The great George Schalk of Pottsville, in Pennsylvania, was dead. There was room for a new man. There was always room for a new man if he could make rifles that shot better than other men's.

The old Barnes place had a furnished house, a good barn, and a shop with water power. It was the sort of one- or two-man farm and factory that was once to be found every mile or two on every brook in southern New England. J.M. Pyne had got it for ten dollars a month. His overhead would be but a fraction of what it would be in Hartford.

"Used to be," the driver said, "there was good enough farms hereabouts, and people to farm 'em. But nowadays the meadows are all growin' up to brush. Everybody's gone West. When I was as young as you be, they were all goin' to Californy to dig for gold. They been goin' ever since. When 'tweren't one thing 'twas another."

They approached a crossroad, with a small church and a cluster of white houses looking onto an elm-shaded green. This was Gaylord's Corner. The driver pointed with his whip.

"Yonder, at the store, they got some right good hard cider."

"I'm in a hurry," J.M. Pyne said.

The driver wagged his head sadly. "Just as you say," he said. He turned his horses into the road that led downhill. He flicked the nigh horse with his whip. "Giddyap."

The plodding animals began to trot, their feet throwing up little spurts of dust that united to form a trailing cloud behind the wagon. They lumbered, after fifteen minutes, across a wooden bridge over a brook and drew up at a small white house built around a central chimney.

J.M. Pyne sat a moment gazing at the place. There were lilac bushes as high as the eaves on either side of the front door, and to one side a dozen old apple trees, and beyond, a towering sugar maple with no branches near the ground. A woodchuck raised himself upright, his head cocked sidewise above the long grass as he looked and listened. He dropped suddenly and scuttled for his hole.

J.M. Pyne got down from the wagon and unlocked the kitchen door. The place had the musty smell of a house that has long been closed. But it was clean and neat. He stood his rifle in a corner, making sure that it would not fall and bend the delicate windage screw of the front sight, and went out to help the driver get his boxes out of the wagon.

When they had got everything inside, they stood beside the wagon. J.M. Pyne gave the driver the two dollars they had agreed on. The driver put the money in a worn leather pouch with drawstrings. He drew the strings tight and wrapped them round the neck of the pouch and stowed it deep in a back pocket. When he had completed this ceremony, he jerked his thumb at the house.

"Nice place," he said. He added, with meaning, "To look at."

The Ghost of Abel White
The house and the barn and the tall sugar maple were making long shadows on the grass - shadows that reached almost to the brook. The sun was going down. It was warm and still and peaceful. J.M. Pyne looked off across the brook, across the marsh, to the wooded hills half a mile away that rose tier on tier to the north.

"I like it," he said.

The driver took out a plug of tobacco and a pocketknife. He cut slivers from the plug and stowed them in his cheek.

"Son," he said sententiously, "son, you ain't afraid to sleep here?"

"No," J.M. Pyne said.

"You might be," the driver said. "You might be, if you knew more about this place."

"If I knew what?" J.M. Pyne asked.

"Ain't nobody told you nothin?" the man demanded.

"No."

"This place is haunted."

J.M. Pyne smiled. He believed in his micrometer caliper, with which he could so easily do something that none of the old-time rifle makers, not even George Schalk, could do - he could measure to a ten-thousandth of an inch. J.M. Pyne did not believe in ghosts.

"That's why there ain't nobody livin' here," the old fellow continued. "Ain't been for ten year. The ghost of young Abel White druv out ever' man that's tried to live here ever since."

J.M. Pyne waited impatiently. He wanted the man to get through and be gone.

"You see that big sugar maple yonder? That's where young Barnes shot young Abel White. The coroner's jury called it an accident. But the way I heard it, they was both sweet on the same girl."

"And how," J.M. Pyne asked, "do they know that the ghost is the ghost of young White?

"Because he's so tall and he has to duck to come in the kitchen door. Young Abel was like his father, and old Abel was six feet four."

J.M. was not impressed with this piece of reasoning. But there was no use in arguing with a man who believed in ghosts.

"If I was young," the old fellow said, "I'd find some other place."

"I don't take much stock in ghosts," J.M. Pyne said.

The old fellow put one foot on the hub of a front wheel and climbed up to the seat of the wagon and gathered up the lines.

"Mebbe you don't now," he said. "Mebbe you will before many nights." He backed his team, cramping the wheels so he could turn his wagon around. He got the wagon turned around. The horses pricked up their ears and started out toward home. The driver turned and shouted over his shoulder, "You can't say I didn't warn you!"

A Quiet Evening

J.M. Pyne explored the place as long as the light lasted. He remembered every detail of it from his first visit a month earlier. But he wanted to see it all again. He wanted to make sure he could get a full two hundred yards from the shop window for testing rifles.

He went into the house when it was dark and lit the kerosene lamp in the bracket on the wall and built a fire in the kitchen stove. He had bread and butter and coffee and some thin slices of round steak. He pounded the steak with a hammer and rolled it in flour and fried it in butter with some onions.

When he had eaten, he set the lamp on the table and got out paper and pencil. He had an idea for a rifle action that would combine the strength of the Sharps, with its solid-steel breech-block sliding in a steel mortise, and the camming motion of the Ballard, which pushes a cartridge home. He sketched the parts over and over again. He lay awake with the problem for half an hour after he went to bed. He heard the sad monotonous cry of a whippoorwill outside. He heard a patter on the floor over-head. He guessed it was the patter of a chipmunk. He heard the stairs creak, as if someone were stealing down them. He remembered the old man and his talk of ghosts, and smiled. Old houses did creak when it was quiet enough to hear the sound. Old men and old wives liked to believe in ghosts. He went to sleep.

A Rifle's Roar

J.M. Pyne was up at daylight the next morning. He had a lot of work to do before he sent for Mary and the baby. He worked all day repairing the gate that let the water onto the wheel for the shop's power. He scarcely paused, except to eat a couple of sandwiches, for twelve hours. Then he went to the well and drew a fresh bucket of water and drank thirstily. He was aware sud-denly of being tired. He walked slowly out toward the big sugar maple, wiping his sweaty face with a big blue-and-white ban-danna handkerchief. He stood under the big maple tree, looking at the marsh and the green hills beyond. His foot struck some-thing in the long grass. It was a piece of old iron. He stooped to pick it up and, stooping, saved his life.

As he bent down, he heard the distant roar of a gun, and a bullet struck the tree behind him with a solid thunk.

J.M. Pyne was on the other side of the tree in two strides. He peered around the trunk of the tree, exposing scarcely more than an eyebrow. He could see no sign of the man who had fired the shot. He looked higher. He could see nothing in the green hills beyond the marsh. A gun as loud as that must use a lot of powder, and yet there was no smoke.

J.M. Pyne could only guess where the shot had come from, remembering the sound. He asked himself whether he had heard the shot before he heard the bullet strike. A bullet would start with a velocity of fourteen or fifteen hundred feet a second. That was a good deal faster than sound. But after a couple of hundred yards, the bullet would be going slower than sound. He couldn't remember which he had heard first - the sound of the shot or the thunk of the bullet. But he knew that the sound of the gun had come from a long way off.

It was, of course, an accident that the bullet had come so near to hitting him. Some farm boy a mile away had shot at a hawk high in a tree, not thinking it mattered where his bullet came down in that half-deserted country. But what would a farm boy be doing with a rifle that made so great a noise?

J.M. Pyne kept the tree between himself and the distant hills as he retreated to the house. He got his rifle out of its case and set the windage at zero and the elevation at two hundred yards. It was the first rifle he had made for himself and the only .25 caliber rifle in America. It was a light rifle, weighing less than ten pounds to conform to the Massachusetts rules for off-hand matches, and it shot a light charge. But J.M. Pyne loaded it with confidence. He knew what the little rifle would do. He knew you didn't need a heavy charge to stop a man - not if you put the bullet in the right place.

He got back to the shelter of the big sugar maple and watched and waited. He waited till dusk. Then he waited a little longer, until he was sure no one at a distance could see him well enough to shoot at him, before he went around in front of the tree. He found the bullet hole a trifle higher than his heart. It had been made, he saw, by a big bullet. The green wood would have closed around the path of a small bullet. He was able to thrust a wire a full two inches into the hole. He was astonished at the angle. He guessed the angle at more than thirty degrees. That bullet had come a long, long way. It must have come from the wooded hills yonder.

J.M. Pyne got a brace and bit, and a chisel. The maple was

green and tough. He had to bore several holes, and cut away a good deal of wood to get the bullet out without digging into it, but he got it. It was the biggest bullet he had ever seen. It weighed something like a quarter of a pound.

He took the bullet into the kitchen and lit the lamp and got out a magnifying glass and his micrometer caliper. The nose of the bullet was mushroomed. The base was not much deformed. He measured the diameter of the base with the micrometer caliper. It measured .6823. He knew, because it had no cannelures for grease, that it had been patched with paper.

Two-Piece Bullet
He saw a hairline around the bullet - the line of a joint. It had been made in two pieces. He picked up the magnifying glass. There was no doubt about it. The bullet had been cast in two parts and swaged together. He tested first the butt and then the forward portion with his fingernail. Even to so rough a test, the butt was softer. The butt had less tin alloyed with the lead than the forward portion.

J.M. Pyne knew the type of rifle from which that bullet had come. He had never seen such rifles, but he had heard about them. And knowing the type of rifle, he could guess some things about the man who had fired the shot. He wasn't a farm boy shooting at a hawk high in a tree.

The rifle must be of the type that Berdan's sharpshooters had taken into the Civil War. They'd been given something easier to carry a few months after they went in. But they had gone in carrying rifles made for the peculiarly American sport of double-rest shooting. The lightest of their guns weighed twenty pounds and many of them weighed forty pounds. But none of them shot a bullet as big as the one J.M. Pyne held in his hand. The rifle that fired that bullet must be the great-grandfather of double-rest rifles. It must weigh fifty pounds or more. Not even John L. Sullivan could shoot it off-hand. You had to have a rest.

J.M. Pyne got a fire going in the stove and cooked a slice of ham and a couple of eggs. He hardly knew what he was eating. He was thinking too hard. The man who fired that rifle must have known what he was doing. He must have known where his bullet was going. He would be that kind of man. And if he knew where his bullet was going, he was trying to kill J.M. Pyne.

J.M. Pyne was awake before dawn the next morning. He got up and looked out. The stars were still shining. He got into his clothes and cooked himself a solid breakfast of ham and eggs. He made two sandwiches and put them in the side pocket of his dungaree jacket. He got his compass and five cartridges and picked up his rifle.

He crossed the brook and, skirting the marsh, set out for the hills that began half a mile away. The wire in the bullet hole had pointed slightly east of north. He thought he could find the spot from which that bullet had come. He paused as he entered the woods and changed the elevation of his rear sight to that for 75 yards. He knew where to hold, with that setting, for anything between point-blank and a hundred yards. He had carried the little rifle many a mile and shot crows and hawks and wood-chucks with it.

The woods were the typical New England sort, of hemlock and beech and oak and birch, and an occasional great chestnut with branches as thick as the trunks of other trees, and an under-growth of laurel.

J.M. Pyne went slowly, in order to go quietly and to miss nothing, as if he were hunting deer, and paused often to watch his back trail. It was useless to hunt deer in such a forest while the leaves were on the trees. You could see only a few yards ahead in that thicket of greenery, with only an occasional splash of sunlight coming through a gap in the foliage aloft. A deer scented you and heard you long before you were near enough to see him. You wouldn't see so much as his white flag as he bounded off. A man, J.M. Pyne reflected, had poor ears and no nose at all. A man was easier to hunt. But unlike any other animal to be found in the New England woods, he might turn and hunt you.

J.M. Pyne climbed a steep slope with outcropping ledges of granite. He consulted his compass. He must, he guessed, be somewhere near the line of the bullet's flight to the sugar maple tree. But he could see nothing to the south. He could not see so much as a bit of roof on the old Barnes place.

He turned again north. He went down a little pitch and began to climb the second ridge. The woods were hot, with little clouds of minute insects that got in his eyes.

He paused at the summit to wipe his face with the big blue and white bandanna handkerchief. He was, he thought, nearly a mile from the old Barnes place and several hundred feet above it. But he couldn't see it.

60

He made a circle of a mile or so in diameter, and then a smaller circle, and then a still smaller circle. He came finally to a comparatively open space on a knoll higher than the rest of the ridge. The forest was creeping in. But he saw that the land had once been fenced and cultivated. He found the place where the house had been. The lower part of the big stone chimney was still standing in the middle of a stone-walled cellar with a white birch tree four inches in diameter growing beside it. He guessed it must be thirty years since that house had burned down.

He saw, farther on, the old barn. It was much farther away from the house than was common in New England. The wide doors in the middle had come off their hinges and lay on the ground; the mow door above was gone too. But the barn, built of heavy timbers mortised and tenoned together, was little out of square.

J.M. Pyne sat down in the wide doorway and rested. He hadn't had much luck. He hadn't found a place from which a man could have fired that shot. He looked about for a likely tree to climb. He didn't see a likely tree. He stood up. He saw that the ladder to the hayloft, made of heavy rungs let into two posts, was still intact. He laid his rifle down, thought better of it, and carried it in his left hand as he climbed to the loft. The loft was empty except for an old three-legged bench made of a slab. J.M. Pyne walked to the hay mow door, looked out and swore softly. He saw a bit of roof in the valley three-quarters of a mile away. He saw a clear space at the foot of the big sugar maple. It must be more than a thousand yards! But he could see clearly the open space in front of the tree where he had been standing late the afternoon before, when he had so fortunately stooped to pick up the piece of old iron. He stood now at the place from which that bullet had come.

J.M. Pyne turned and examined the bench. One end was higher than the other. One end was as high as an ordinary table. He explored the shadows of the hayloft and found a balk of wood such as would be sawn to split into stove wood. He set the balk of wood on end beside the bench and sat down. He no longer had any doubt.

The Rifle
He walked around the walls of the loft, kicking into a loose bit of old hay here and there. He found nothing. He could just reach the broad top of the plate on which the rafters rested. He walked along the wall, feeling the upper surface of the plate. It was deep in dust and seeds. He felt his way along. He felt a wooden box.

He got the balk of wood and stood on it so he could see. It was a long, heavy box. He raised the lid.

The rifle lay in a compartment of the box made to fit it. It had a full-length telescope sight. J.M. Pyne lit a match and stood staring at the contents of the box. The rifle was as clean and unscarred as the day it was made, and the long octagon barrel was as thick as a man's arm. He saw the false muzzle and the bullet starter and the muzzle brace and patches and caps and bullets and an enormous flask of powder. He picked up the false muzzle and one of the bullets and a patch, and got down from his perch. He stood in the mow door examining the false muzzle and the patch.

He had heard of the cross patch, but he had never seen one before. It was like a Greek cross, cut from tough bank-note paper. The false muzzle was recessed to take the patch. You put the patch on the false muzzle, centering it; you centered the bullet on the patch and pushed it part way down with your fingers, and adjusted the starter. You hit the starter a hard clip with the heel of your hand and drove it down through the muzzle and pushed it the rest of the way home with a ramrod. The butt of the bullet had to be soft, or you could never have driven it through the false muzzle. The patch was cut so precisely to size that the arms, bending up alongside the bullet, exactly enveloped it without overlapping - the eight edges butted.

J.M. Pyne climbed up on the balk of wood. It took all his strength to lift the rifle out of the case from that position. He guessed the gun weighed well over fifty pounds. He got it down without falling or letting it drop, and laid it on the bench and sat down beside it and looked through the telescope sight. He could see the open space in front of the big sugar maple. The scope was not brilliant. It was too high-powered for so small an objective. But he could quarter the trunk of the maple tree with the cross hairs.

J.M. Pyne carried the rifle out to the haymow door in order to see it in a good light. He knew that it was the work of a fine craftsman. But he could find no maker's name. He stood the rifle up on its butt plate while he thought what he should do.

He could disable it easily enough. He could fix it in a few minutes so its owner would never fire it again. But he could not bring himself to ruin so fine a rifle. He wanted rather to study it. He wanted to measure the bore, and especially the false muzzle, with soft lead slugs, to find out exactly how the rifling was cut and how much choke it had. He had never made a false muzzle. But he was going to make a false muzzle.

It was harder to get the rifle back in its box than it had been to get it out. But he managed it. He put everything back just as he had found it and picked up his own rifle and climbed down the ladder. He guessed by the sun that it was an hour and a half or so after noon. If the man was coming back to shoot again, he'd wait until late afternoon, until the wind had died down. Even with a bullet that weighed a quarter of a pound, you were at the mercy of the wind at long range.

The Rifleman
J.M. Pyne went down the slope, hunting for a spring or a brook. He found a tiny brook and drank. He sat down on a boulder and ate his sandwiches. Then he went back up the slope and found a place where he could hide, but from which he could keep an eye on the wide doorway of the barn. He sat down to wait. He waited hour after hour. But toward sundown he heard a stick crack. He looked up, as alert as a wild animal. He saw a very tall, gaunt old man striding toward the barn. J.M. Pyne got to his feet, his rifle cradled in his arms.

"Hi," he said.

The old man turned and waited. He had a lean brown face over white chin whiskers. He was dressed more like a townsman than a farmer. He wore a gray suit and a white shirt with a low linen collar and a black tie.

"Who are you?" he asked, with the air of one who had the right to know.

"My name," J.M. Pyne said, "is John Pyne. Am I trespassing?"

"You're on my land," the old man said. "I'm Abel White."

J.M. Pyne stood still and hoped his face gave no sign of his surprise. He did not know what to say. He wasn't going to be driven off. But he hoped he wouldn't have to defy the old man just yet. He wanted to know more than he already knew. He wanted to know why. He saw that Abel White was staring at the rifle he held cradled in his arms. The man was a rifleman. He would want to know about that rifle. He would want to take it in his hands. J.M. Pyne waited.

Abel White broke the silence. "What kind of a gun is that you have?" he asked.

J.M. Pyne opened the breech of his rifle and took out the cartridge and handed the rifle to Abel White.

"Ballard," Abel White said. He held the muzzle up and looked through the barrel. He turned and gave J.M. Pyne a quick, appraising glance. "What caliber is that?

"Twenty-five caliber," J.M. Pyne said.

"They don't make .25 caliber rifles," Abel White said.

"I make them," J.M. Pyne said.

Abel White gave J.M. Pyne another quick glance. "You made this rifle?"

"I made the barrel," J.M. Pyne said.

Abel White looked through the barrel again. "Eight grooves," he said.

He put the rifle butt down and J.M. Pyne noticed that, instead of putting the butt directly on the ground, he rested it on his foot, like a man who respected rifles.

"The lands are very narrow," Abel White said. "They're little more than knife edges."

"Yes," J.M. Pyne said. "Narrow lands displace less metal and so deform the bullet less."

"You think that is an advantage?" Abel White said.

"It's difficult to control the deformation of a bullet," J.M. Pyne said. "And unless it is deformed the same way every time, you get wide shots. So the less deformation the better."

Abel White stared at J.M. Pyne as if he were a stranger from Mars.

"You know something about rifles," he said.

"Yes," J.M. Pyne said. "I do."

Abel White handed the little rifle back.

J.M. Pyne cradled it in his arms without reloading it.

"Son," Abel White said, "I've got a rifle here that you ought to see. It's one of Horace Warner's double-rest rifles - the biggest one Horace ever made."

He led the way into the barn and up the ladder to the loft. He was so tall he could lift the rifle off the plate without getting up on anything. He laid the rifle on the bench and got out the false muzzle and the starter and a bullet and a patch.

Muzzle-Loaded Bullet
"You talk of deforming the bullet," Abel White said. "The way to deform it least and center it perfectly in the bore is to load it from the muzzle. Nobody has ever got the accuracy from a breech-loaded bullet that can be got from a muzzle-loaded bullet. And nobody ever will."

He demonstrated deftly the false muzzle, the cross patch and the bullet starter while J.M. Pyne listened. The man seemed to have forgotten everything but the joy of explaining the niceties of fine shooting to a young man who could appreciate them. But he hadn't forgotten everything. He paused in his talk and took a little spyglass out of his pocket and went to the loft door. He trained the spyglass on the old Barnes place.

J.M. Pyne started involuntarily when Abel White turned around. He was no longer the same man. J.M. Pyne had never seen a madman before, but he knew this man was mad. He knew before he spoke again.

"I almost got him yesterday," Abel White said.

J.M. Pyne stood quite still. His rifle wasn't loaded. Abel White was old. But he was powerful. He was eight inches taller and fifty pounds heavier than J.M. Pyne, and he was crazy.

"You almost got him?" J.M. Pyne said, softly.

"Young Barnes," Abel White said.

"Why do you want to get young Barnes?" J.M. Pyne said.

"He murdered my son," Abel White said fiercely. "He shot him down in cold blood, and the coroner's jury said it was an accident. Everybody knew he murdered young Abel. But I knew he'd come back, like any other man with the blood guilt on his hands. He came back last summer, and I was waiting here. I put a bullet within a foot of his head. I waited for him every afternoon for two weeks after that. But I must have scared him off. I

65

had to go home to York state. But he's back now. I saw him yesterday. I almost got him yesterday."

"You missed him?" J.M. Pyne said.

Abel White nodded. "It's two hundred and twenty rods," he said, "I know. I got it by triangulation within six inches. It's easy to miss a man at two hundred and twenty rods. That gun is the best long-range rifle ever made. I told Horace Warner I wanted a rifle that would break them into the same hole at eighty rods, and he made it. But it won't stay on a man's body at two hundred and twenty rods - not quite. And the slightest change of wind is enough to make you miss."

J.M. Pyne nodded. Two hundred and twenty rods was more than twelve hundred yards. A thousand yards was the longest range at which rifle matches were ordinarily shot. The Wimbledon Cup called, originally, for thirty shots at a thousand yards, on a three-foot bulls-eye. No man had ever made the possible score in shooting for the Wimbledon Cup. It took a good rifle to put four bullets out of five in a three-foot bull's-eye at a thousand yards in calm weather. You had no chance to do it in a breeze.

Abel White picked up that fifty or sixty pound rifle and put it back in its box. He put everything back. J.M. Pyne followed him down the ladder. He saw that the man was himself again. His madness was like a nightmare that had passed. J.M. Pyne doubted if he remembered it or how completely he had incriminated himself.

Abel White held out his hand. J.M. Pyne shook his hand.

"Take my advice," Abel White said. "Make muzzle-loaders. Breechloaders are all right for rough-and-ready work like hunting. But you'll never get the finest shooting out of a breech-loaded bullet."

"I'm going to make muzzle-loaders," J.M. Pyne said.

It was after dark when he got home. He sat for an hour after supper trying to find a way out. He was, he felt, perfectly safe as long as he kept away from the space in front of the sugar-maple tree. That space was the only space that Abel White could see. But Abel White had to be stopped.

J.M. Pyne realized suddenly why he had seen no smoke when Abel White shot at him. He had fired from inside the barn loft.

The smoke had mostly stayed inside the loft. And by the same token, Abel White had not seen his victim stoop just in time. Abel White had touched the set trigger, and instantly the cloud of smoke from the muzzle of his rifle had obscured his vision. He couldn't see much for a few seconds. It would take the bullet about four seconds to go twelve hundred yards.

Pyne's Preparations

J.M. Pyne got a lantern and went out to the shop to see what he could find. He found some wire. He nailed one end of the wire to the house and stretched it as tightly as he could over a branch of the maple tree. The lowest branch was high, but he tied a piece of iron to a string and threw it over the branch and pulled the wire after it.

He went back to the shop then and made a pulley with a kind of trigger release. He had only odd pieces of metal to work with. He had to bend them cold. But by midnight he had something that worked.

He walked to Gaylord's Corner the next morning and got two balls of twine. He led four lengths of twine from the house to screw eyes in the maple tree and back again. Then he went to work to construct a frame of lath, with joints like a man's knees and elbows. He dressed his framework neatly in an old suit of clothes and tacked a hat on top with the brim turned down to conceal the lack of a face. He had it all done early in the afternoon. He had to wait several hours to try it.

At sundown he hung the scarecrow on the wire and attached his lines. He had one line to each knee and one to the neck and one to the trigger release of the block. He ran the scarecrow out on the wire and tried out his lines. He had, in effect, a puppet. He could make it look very much like a man walking. It would pass for a man at twelve hundred yards, even through a telescopic sight.

The Last Shot

He pulled his creation out into the space in front of the big sugar maple. He let it stand there, within a yard or so of where he had stood two days before when Abel White had shot at him. He waited, his heart pounding. And then he heard the shot. He heard the great rifle roar high up on the hill three-quarters of a mile away and the vicious thunk of the great bullet against the maple tree.

J.M. Pyne made the puppet thrash madly and fall over and lie still in the long grass.

He waited five minutes and made himself wait five minutes more.

Then he gently drew in the puppet. Abel White hadn't missed. The bullet had gone through the middle of the puppet's body.

J.M. Pyne got out his little rifle and loaded it and started for the barn on the knoll. It was only three-quarters of a mile as a bullet flies, but it was a long way around the marsh. It took him twenty minutes. But he made it. Abel White had finished cleaning his rifle and was oiling the bore. He was humming softly to himself as he worked. He looked up at J.M. Pyne.

"I got him," Abel White said. "There wasn't enough wind to make a ripple in the marsh grass. I held dead on and I got him."

J.M. Pyne helped get the rifle and the case and the tools down from the loft. They put the rifle and all the things that went with it in the case. Abel White stood gazing down at the rifle. It was easy to see he loved it.

"Mr. Pyne," Abel White said, "the rifle has done its work. I shall never shoot it again." He was smiling happily. He looked benignly on J.M. Pyne. "Would you accept it as a gift?"

J.M. Pyne stood there, staring at Abel White.

"I'd like to have it," J.M. Pyne said. "I'd like to see what it would do, and then I'd like to find out why."

"Then," Abel White said, "it's yours. You're the only man I know who'll appreciate it and take care of it."

He shook hands with J.M. Pyne.

"You had better get a horse and wagon," Abel White said. "That gun is heavy."

J.M. Pyne nodded. But he didn't hire a wagon. It cost money to hire horses and a wagon. And the only man he knew in Gaylord's Corner who had horses and a wagon for hire was a garrulous old fellow who talked of ghosts. J.M. Pyne did not believe in ghosts. He got a wheelbarrow. He got that great rifle home by himself.

THE OLD MAN WHO FIXES THE GUNS

T. Ballentyne got the news of a morning in May.

He sat there staring at the telegram and getting angrier. The thing had happened before. Another man would have said it happened every spring about this time, and expected it. But T. Ballentyne the Fourth, who spent his life in knowing what is happening in the world and what is about to happen, as the head of a great banking firm must, had gone on believing that this year, in this school, T. Ballentyne the Fifth would take seriously the task of preparing himself to become in his turn the head of T. Ballentyne & Co.

The night letter, as always, was tactful. Headmasters did not summarily dismiss a Ballentyne. This one, in California, merely said that the boy agreed it was better for him to leave the school at once. Of course, if Mr. Ballentyne preferred, he would keep the boy until the final examinations.

"Ledyard," T. Ballentyne said to his secretary, "wire Tim to come home. Wire the school."

"Yes, sir," Ledyard said, and stood waiting.

T. Ballentyne sat drawing squares and circles and triangles on a sheet of paper. He wasn't given to scribbling meaningless things. He only did it when he was puzzled. He couldn't imagine what the boy had done. He never had learned exactly why a school thought it better for his son to leave. The headmaster never said that Tim was a liar and a thief, or openly defiant or stupid. On the contrary, the men who wanted to get rid of him admitted that he was forthright and intelligent. They said he didn't seem to care; they said he wouldn't co-operate; they said he was undisciplined. T. Ballentyne the Fourth always felt they could say more if they would. But when he pressed them, they said the main thing was that the boy wouldn't study anything he didn't like and the things he did like were always, by a coincidence, outside their particular school's curriculum.

T. Ballentyne reflected that Tim was nearly 18. He was old enough to be entering college and he wasn't halfway through prep school. T. Ballentyne the Fourth had entered Harvard at 17. He had taken a doctor's degree at Bonn when he was 23. He couldn't remember that he had ever been too young to know there was more glory in being the head of Ballentyne & Co. than in being President of the United States. He hadn't done just as he pleased. He had begun, by the time he was 12 or 14, to do what he had to do in order to succeed his father. But at 18 Tim was still a child - still playing with toys and dreaming boyish dreams of being an engineer or an aviator. He had built a toy motorcar the spring he was fired from Groton and been arrested for doing 70 miles an hour in it. He had built a glider the spring he was fired from St. Mark's and made a 7-minute flight in it before his father wired them to stop him.

"His mother has always babied him," T. Ballentyne said to himself. "Even I have been too easy with him. He has no guts."

"Ledyard," T. Ballentyne said, "we're going up to the Bridge tomorrow. Tell Tim to meet me there. Get a tutor. Have him come up on Sunday."

"Yes, sir," Ledyard said. "I'll see that the house is opened."

T. Ballentyne the First had built the place at Miller's Bridge in the Berkshire Hills before the Civil War. The Ballentynes had called it the Bridge ever since. They hadn't used it much for two generations and not at all for 10 years. It was too far away from everything, but it held more of the Ballentyne tradition than any other house.

T. Ballentyne drove himself and Ledyard the next day. T. Ballentyne liked driving a car, especially when he was annoyed with the world. He hated airplanes. He had never been in an airplane. He felt that a man as important to the world and to Ballentyne & Co. as himself would be a fool to use airplanes. He often drove hard.

He had a late lunch in the long dining room at the Bridge. He went into the library afterward with Ledyard and some work. He looked up, as he dictated, at the portraits of the Ballentynes: T. Ballentyne the First, his great-grandfather; T. Ballentyne the

Second, his grandfather; T. Ballentyne the Third, his father. His own portrait would hang there soon. There was a fellow in New York painting it.

His reflections on the glory of the Ballentynes were interrupted by the sound of a rifle shot, so loud and so sharp that it seemed just outside the open window.

Opening Shot
"What was that?" he asked. He really meant, "What man would dare to fire a rifle outside the Ballentyne windows?"

There was another shot before Ledyard had time to answer. They both listened for a third shot. It came promptly. They counted 10 shots, at intervals of half a minute, before the shooting ceased.

"I'll go and find out about it," Ledyard said.

Ledyard came back in 10 minutes. "The gardener says it's the old man who fixes the guns."

"What?"

"He's a gunsmith who bought the old mill down the brook and set up shop, 8 or 10 years ago. He's been living there alone ever since, although it's a mystery where he gets any work to do."

"That's a mile from here," T. Ballentyne said.

"Almost a mile in a straight line and two or three miles by road. The gardener says the sound comes up the brook. That's why it seems so close."

"Call up Judge Horton and have the fellow stopped," T. Ballentyne said.

But Judge Horton wasn't at all sure the fellow could be stopped, except, of course, on Sunday.

The shooting began again - 10 more shots at regular intervals.

"I'll stop him," T. Ballentyne said.

He wasn't ordinarily a vindictive man. He almost never used the power that was his in petty ways. He was a little ashamed of his own anger. But he disliked guns as much as he disliked airplanes. He told himself he had good reason to dislike guns. His best friend had been killed by a careless fellow sportsman on a

71

grouse moor in Scotland. Besides, you couldn't have a racket like that going on.

They drove down to the old mill. T. Ballentyne stopped the car beside a galvanized-iron mail box on a post. The name on the box was J.M. Pyne. The mill was little more than a large shed, gray with age. It stood across the brook below an old stone dam. T. Ballentyne got out of the car and crossed the brook on a narrow, swaying footbridge and knocked on the door of the mill. He got no answer. He knocked again, more sharply. He heard somebody call "Come in." He opened the door.

He saw the old man with a white beard at a bench under a bank of windows at the opposite end of the shop. The old man did not look up. T. Ballentyne picked his way around boxes and over a pile of round steel bars. When he got near the bench he saw that a window at the end of the bench was open. A rifle lay in some sort of fixture, its muzzle out of the window. Beyond - a long way beyond, across the meadow at the rear of the shop - he saw something he guessed was a target, and beyond that a sand bank.

"How do you do, Mr. Pyne," T. Ballentyne said.

The old man raised his head and looked at T. Ballentyne over his glasses. He was wearing two pair of glasses.

"My name is Ballentyne," T. Ballentyne said. He held out his hand.

"Pleased to meet you," the old man said, shaking his hand.

"I heard you shooting," T. Ballentyne said. "At first I thought it was just outside my library window."

The old man bent over a small piece of steel he had in the vise and peered at it with a magnifying glass. "I was testing a .30 caliber in the machine rest," he said.

T. Ballentyne looked about the shop. It was full of things of no value. He looked at the littered bench. It held layer on layer of cigar boxes and pasteboard boxes and tin boxes in a crazy pile - the accumulation of years. He looked at the old man. He had a slip of oilstone in his right hand and a magnifying glass in the other. He was trying to stone the bit of steel in the vise. He was obviously poor. He must be hard put to it to find work. T. Ballentyne did not wish to take advantage of one so weak.

"I'd like to buy this place of yours," T. Ballentyne said.

72

The old man looked up sharply. "What for?"

"I don't like shooting."

"There's no danger whatever," the old man said.

T. Ballentyne made a gesture toward the rifle with its muzzle out of the window. "How far will a gun like that shoot?" he demanded.

"Four or five miles."

"Well, then!" T. Ballentyne exclaimed.

"The bullet travels only a few inches in the sand back yonder."

"What happens when you miss the sand bank?"

"I don't miss it."

"But suppose that you did miss it."

"Why suppose something that can't happen?" the old man asked.

T. Ballentyne tried hard to be genial. "I would like to make it worth your while to move."

"You can't," the old man said.

T. Ballentyne smiled. "I see you don't know who I am."

"I know who you are," J.M. Pyne said. "But you can't make it worth my while to move." He made a gesture at the bench, at the shop. "It would take me 6 months to straighten up every-thing, and label it, and pack it, and move it into a new place, and get so I could find anything."

"I'll pay you 6 months' income."

The old man stared fiercely at T. Ballentyne. "No," he said.

"And three times what this place cost you."

"No," the old man said. "How many times do I have to tell you? No."

"But Mr. Pyne -" T. Ballentyne began again.

"I'm too old to care about money," Mr. Pyne retorted. "I'm inter-ested in time. I haven't got time enough left to do half the things

73

I want to do. If you can give me three times as many hours in a day as there are now, and three times as many days in the year as there are now, I'll talk business with you."

He bent his head again over the small piece of steel in the vise and picked up his magnifying glass. T. Ballentyne knew that he was dismissed.

Young Ballentyne Arrives
Tim Ballentyne arrived at the Bridge Saturday night. His father was in the library. His father was plainly astonished.

"When did you leave?" his father asked.

"About five minutes after I got your wire."

His father stared at him. "You came by plane."

"Yes, sir."

"You know I don't want you to travel by plane."

Tim said nothing. He had learned long since that the less you said the better off you were. It didn't pay to argue with headmasters or with your father. You merely got in deeper.

His father talked at length about the absurdity of traveling by airplane, then abruptly changed the subject to one Tim cared even less to discuss with him.

"How do you account for your failure this time?" his father asked.

Tim Ballentyne shook his head. "I don't know how to account for it."

"You didn't really study."

"I did at first," Tim said. "I didn't do much these last weeks."

"You didn't have the guts to stick it out."

Tim would have liked to tell his father exactly how it was. He always started in, determined to do himself proud and get ready for Harvard, as his father wished him to do. His resolution always flagged. By spring he was planning something he wanted to build. And once he started to make the drawing, he thought of nothing else. He stayed up later and later making drawings. He went to bed at dawn and failed to make his morning classes.

74

"You're going to spend the summer up here," his father said. "You won't have a car to drive. You'll have a tutor. I'll come up every other weekend to see how you're getting on."

"Yes, sir."

His father talked a lot before he talked himself out. The hard thing was that Tim sympathized with his father in spite of himself. His father once again made him feel the glory of the Ballentynes, made him wish to carry it on, like his father, and his grandfather, and his great-grandfather and his great-great-grandfather. At such moments he felt he could do the things his father wished him to do. But mostly he knew he never could.

The tutor arrived next day. His name was Johnson. He was all right. Tim Ballentyne knew there were only two sorts of tutors - the rare sort that is determined to make good with your father by getting you through at least one college-board examination, and the usual kind that is just as ready to loaf as you are. He guessed that Johnson was the usual kind, but he wasn't sure.

Tim's father left on Monday morning. Tim spent four hours with Johnson while Johnson found out what he would have to learn in order to pass college boards.

They were sitting around the library after lunch, a little discouraged with each other, when they heard a rifle shot. They heard 10 shots, half a minute apart.

Tim got up and strolled toward the door.

"If you don't mind," he said, "I'll take a walk. I haven't seen this place since I was about 7 years old."

Johnson obviously didn't mind. Tim made his way down the brook, mildly curious about the shots. He stopped at the mill pond and sat down on a rock and lit a cigarette. He couldn't see any hope for the summer. There was a girl on Long Island he had been writing to, but there wasn't much chance of seeing her.

Tim finished his cigarette and walked out to the road. He saw the mail box and the name, "J.M. Pyne". Tim stared at the name. It might be that it was the J.M. Pyne he had read about and heard about.

He went into the mill and saw an old man doing something to a lathe.

"Don't talk to me now," the old man said. "I'll be with you in a minute."

Tim stood silent and watched. The old man had a small grinder rigged on the lathe, and he was grinding a reamer. He took a minute cut and picked up a magnifying glass and the micrometer and measured. Then he took another tiny cut. He worked for 15 minutes, with a curious intentness, before he threw off the belt and looked up.

"I had my head full of figures just now, some of them to four places, and I couldn't talk without losing them. What can I do for you?"

"Why," Tim said - "why, you're J.M. Pyne, aren't you? I mean you're the famous rifle maker?"

"I make rifles," the old man said, "and so far as I know, I'm the only J.M. Pyne who does."

"I heard about you at school last year, in California. I was shooting on the school rifle team, and the coach used to tell us stories about you and how you used to shoot."

J.M. Pyne gave Tim a cigarette and took one himself. "What's your name?"

"My name is Ballentyne - Tim Ballentyne."

J.M. Pyne studied Tim over the top of his glasses. He had an odd little smile. "H'mmm," he said. "Do you shoot?"

"Not what you'd call shooting," Tim said. "I was high man on the school team. We shot four positions - prone, kneeling, sitting and standing."

"What did you make standing?"

"I was averaging about 88 toward the last," Tim said.

"Hard pull?"

"Yes, sir," Tim said, "and a prone stock."

"Military shooting," J.M. Pyne said. "It's all right in its way. But it isn't as much fun as off-hand shooting with a gun that's made for it."

"I've never even seen an off-hand gun," Tim said.

Mr. Pyne got a gun out of the corner. It was a long heavy rifle with double set triggers. It had a palm rest and a pronged buttplate and a stock that looked as if it had been chopped out with a hatchet. He handed the rifle to Tim and got out a bag. He took a telescope out of the bag and fitted it on the rifle.

"Now," J.M. Pyne said, "put that up and see how it feels."

Tim put the gun up and tried the set triggers. The stock looked like a makeshift. But it wasn't a makeshift. It was right.

"I'd love to learn to shoot a gun like that," young Ballentyne said.

"There's no reason you can't," Mr. Pyne said.

Tim looked at him. "You mean you'd make me a Pyne rifle?"

"Well," Mr. Pyne said, "I didn't say that. I've got work piled up here for two or three years. But you can come down here and shoot that rifle all you like."

"You mean that?" Tim said.

Mr. Pyne took a couple of 100-yard targets from the bench. "Tack these up down yonder," he said. "You'll see the place - a hundred yards is at that frame halfway down."

Tim ran out of the shop and down the meadow and tacked up the targets and ran all the way back.

"The first thing you've got to learn is not to run when you're shooting," J.M. Pyne said. "Sit down until your heart gets back to normal."

He found a box of .22 long rifle cartridges.

"Now," he said, "I'm going to stand behind you and watch you. If I touch you on the shoulder, put the gun down without firing it."

Tim put up the gun. He couldn't hold the crosshairs on the black. He couldn't hold on the paper. He was too conscious of the fact that J.M. Pyne was watching him. He felt a touch on his shoulder. He started obediently to put the gun down and touched the set trigger in doing so. The bullet struck the ground halfway to the target.

"The great thing is not to pull any bad shots," J.M. Pyne said. "That's what it is to be a rifle shot. People brag about one shot they made. But one shot is nothing. It's mostly luck. What you've got to learn is to make a fair shot every time you pull. And after that, to make a good shot every time. The center shots will take care of themselves, if you never pull a bad one."

Tim shot for an hour under J.M. Pyne's coaching, learning to put the gun down when he failed to get a good hold before he began to feel short of breath.

"There's no use trying to outhold your wind," J.M. Pyne said. "You've got to hold your breath when you're shooting, and you can hold it only so long before the gun begins to wobble farther and faster. When that happens, you've got to put the gun down and rest a minute and take a couple of good deep breaths before you try again."

"Do you think I might make a rifle shot?" Tim asked.

"It's a matter of guts," J.M. Pyne said. "You learned to shoot prone first; and usually when a man learns to shoot prone, he never has the guts to learn to shoot well off-hand. It is so much harder and takes so much longer."

"Would it be all right if .... if I came again tomorrow?" Tim asked.

"I don't know why not," J.M. Pyne said.

"I'm afraid it's an imposition - taking your time."

J.M. Pyne smiled. "I've got plenty of time for anybody who's really interested to learn."

Tim's Education
They talked about getting an education a couple of weeks later, when Tim had had a dozen lessons in off-hand shooting. Tim told J.M. Pyne about the tutor.

"You mean you haven't passed in your studies?" J.M. Pyne asked.

"Only about half the time," Tim said.

"Well," J.M. Pyne said slowly, "there are a lot of people wasting their time trying to get an education. They'll never get it because they aren't capable of it. But I wouldn't have said that you were one of them. What college are you going to?"

"Harvard," Tim said.

78

"What are you going to be?"

"A banker," Tim said.

"What would you like to be?"

"An engineer," Tim said.

"Why don't you be one?"

"I can't," Tim said.

"Can't?" J.M. Pyne said. "Can't. That's what they said to me when I was a boy. 'You can't be an engineer!'" He paused, remembering the past. "I graduated from M.I.T. before I was 21."

"I'd like to go to M.I.T.," Tim said.

"How are you in mathematics?"

"I haven't had any to speak of," Tim said.

"If you don't take to mathematics," J.M. Pyne said, "maybe you're wise not to try to be an engineer."

He changed the subject abruptly. He talked about the first rifle he had ever made and how he had designed the tools, never having seen any rifling tools.

Tim walked slowly back to the house to his dinner with Johnson. He said almost nothing during dinner.

"Johnson," Tim said afterward, in the library, "could you teach me algebra?"

"Yes," Johnson said, "I think I could take you as far as prep schools ever go, if I had the books."

"If you'll make a list," Tim said, "I'll order the books."

J.M. Pyne was reading a copy of *The American Rifleman* when Tim arrived at the mill a few days later.

"I see," he said, "they're having an old-time off-hand match at Walnut Hill next month. I used to shoot at Walnut Hill 30 or 40 years ago. It's almost the only famous old club that's left. It used to be full of rifle cranks."

"Are you going?" Tim asked.

"I'd like to," J.M. Pyne answered. "But I don't see how I could take the time."

"I'd like to go," Tim said. "I'd like to see a real off-hand match."

"It's at 200 yards," J.M. Pyne said. "You'd have to shoot a bigger rifle than the .22. You'd have to shoot a .32-40."

Tim looked at J.M. Pyne in amazement. "They wouldn't let me shoot in a match like that."

"The match is open to all comers."

"But I'm just learning to shoot."

"How do you expect to learn to shoot in matches if you don't shoot in 'em? Don't you know match shooting is harder? Don't you know you've got to fight the nervousness that comes with competition?"

"Well--" Tim said.

"If we go, you'll shoot," J.M. Pyne said.

"All right," Tim said, "we'll go."

J.M. Pyne got out the mould and started the plumber's furnace; he cast some bullets for the .32-40, greased them in a brass pump, and showed Tim how to load the gun. He insisted on Tim's following an exact ritual, putting the bullet through the false muzzle and ramming it home and leaving the loading rod in the bore until he was ready to insert the case loaded with powder into the breech.

"If you don't make a habit of doing it just so every time," J.M. Pyne said, "the time will come when somebody'll come up and talk to you while you're loading and you'll forget and leave the bullet near the muzzle, where the starter puts it, instead of ramming it down, and then, when you shoot, you'll ring the barrel. The charge of burning powder goes up the barrel so fast that it's practically a solid. If it hits a bullet near the muzzle, something has to give. And it's mostly the barrel that gives. It won't burst, but it'll expand so much that it won't shoot any more."

Tim got some practice with the .32-40 every day after that. The noise bothered him at first. It was so much louder than a .22. But he got used to it. He could almost stay in the 6-inch black at a hundred yards with it. He could put 9 shots out of 10 in the black.

There was no convenient railway route from the Bridge to Boston. Tim had no car. He decided they'd have to go on a bus. They'd have to get up early on Sunday morning and catch a 6 o'clock bus.

Tim had a telegram from Ledyard Saturday evening, saying his father was driving up to the Bridge Sunday morning. Tim decided not to wire back that he was leaving early Sunday morning. He wrote a note to his father and left it on the library table. He told Johnson to explain.

He couldn't go to sleep. He lay awake wondering what he'd do if he forgot and fired the gun with a bullet up the muzzle. You couldn't replace a Pyne barrel if you spoiled it, the way you could replace a friend's car if you wrecked it. Then, suddenly, he knew that the noise which so annoyed him was the alarm clock beside his bed.

J.M. Pyne was standing out by the mailbox with the .32-40 in a canvas case, and a bag containing the false muzzle and starter, the re- and de-capper, cleaning cotton and the little kit of tools he had with him wherever he went. They had to carry it all of a mile.

Walnut Hill

It was noon when they got to Walnut Hill. They walked into the clubhouse, and somebody recognized J.M. Pyne, and in two minutes he was surrounded. They shook his hand and slapped his back and asked him a dozen questions simultaneously.

Tim looked about for a place to put the gun. He saw his father sitting in a corner. His father must have driven hard.

"I got your note," his father said stiffly.

"I'm sorry you don't like this," Tim said, "but there's no harm in it."

"No," his father said. "There's no harm in it. But you're still playing with toys. When you take a day's vacation, you choose to take it with an ignorant old man. I'd rather see you associating with your superiors."

Tim set his rifle up in the rack beside the loading table and laid out the tools and fastened the loading flask. A young chap came up and introduced himself.

"You came with Pyne, didn't you?" he asked.

"Yes," Tim said, "I did."

"You know him well?"

"We're good friends," Tim said. "We live next door to each other."

"Listen," the young chap said, "could you say something to him for me? Could you help me get a Pyne barrel?"

Tim introduced somebody to J.M. Pyne every 15 minutes on that plea. He was besieged by people who knew only that he had arrived with J.M. Pyne. It was hours before he could get a chance to load the gun, and when he did, young men stood three deep around him, watching him, asking questions. Few of the younger men had ever seen a Pyne muzzleloader before. But they had all heard of Pyne muzzleloaders. They wanted to know all about Pyne muzzleloaders.

Tim watched himself. His hands trembled so he fumbled. He couldn't ruin the barrel. He had to load it correctly. He got it done at last. He went outside to the shooting stand. All the young men rushed to the window to watch his shot.

He raised the gun. The bull looked no bigger than a half dollar. His knees trembled. There was no reason his knees should tremble. No one expected or asked that he shoot well. And this was only a sighting shot, not a shot for record.

The gun moved so fast across the target that he couldn't get a hold. One minute the crosshairs were off the paper and next moment they were passing across the little bull's-eye 200 yards away at 60 miles an hour. He had to snatch at it. It was his only chance. And then he remembered. In the act of touching the trigger, he put the gun down and waited and took long deep breaths. When he put the gun up again, he got a fair chance. The crosshairs hung for an instant in the black. He touched the trigger and the gun boomed, and half a second later he heard the thunk of the bullet in the sand bank behind the target. The marker came up. At least he was in the black. "An 8," the scorer said.

He went back to load again. His father was close behind his stand. He saw a man he remembered to have seen somewhere coming toward his father with hand outstretched. He must be some important person. He looked like the sort of man who sat on boards of directors with his father.

"Why, Timothy," the man said to Tim's father, "they tell me you came over with Pyne."

"Not exactly," T. Ballentyne said. "My son--"

"But you know him, Tim. And I want you to help me. I want you to introduce me to him and tell him you would consider it a personal favor if he would make me a Pyne barrel."

Tim stole a glance at his father. Tim's father was looking at the man as if he thought him crazy.

"George," T. Ballentyne said, "if you want a rifle barrel, tell the man to make you a barrel."

Tim stole another glance. George was shaking his head.

"You don't understand," he said. "You can't tell J.M. Pyne to do anything. J.M. Pyne does what he pleases. He mostly pleases to make barrels for his friends. That's why he charges so little."

"Double his price," T. Ballentyne said. "It won't make any difference to you."

"Tim," George said, "do you know what happened to a friend of mine who tried that? He ordered a Pyne barrel a year ahead of time. He was going to hunt lions in Africa. He went to see Pyne after 6 months to ask how his barrel was coming along. Pyne said he hadn't got around to it. My friend knew he could make the barrel in a week if he wanted to. He said to Pyne 'If you get that barrel finished before I start for Africa, I'll pay you $100 for it, instead of $50.' And Pyne looked at him and roared, 'Are you trying to bribe me? Get out of here!'"

Tim loaded the rifle and went out to fire another shot. He had fired his first 10 shots for record when he saw J.M. Pyne coming toward him with a determined stride. He had to be determined to get away from the rifle cranks who surrounded him.

"How's it going?"

Tim shook his head. "I can't keep them in the black."

"Knees wobble?" J.M. Pyne asked. Tim nodded.

"I know," J.M. Pyne said. "I've been there. The only thing you can do about it is to take your time and be careful. Wait it out. If you don't get a good hold when the gun is moving slow enough so you can get the shot off clean, wait. Remember what the old fellow said: 'All things come to him who waits, provided he knows where to wait for 'em.'"

Men were at both Mr. Pyne's elbows, dragging him away. Tim set his teeth. He went out to fire the first shot of his second string grimly. Then he remembered - you couldn't be grim. You had to relax. You had to take it easy while remaining fiercely determined not to snatch at the trigger when the gun was swinging fast, not to press it until you got a good hold.

He was sorry when it was over. He felt he was doing better. He wished the match were longer. He wished it were 100 shots. He thrust his score ticket in his pocket. J.M. Pyne would never see that. Fortunately, J.M. Pyne was completely surrounded by admirers. He would have no chance to ask what score Tim Ballentyne had made.

They drove to Boston in his father's car for dinner with several gun cranks. When they started for home, Tim noticed that his father was most respectful to J.M. Pyne. Tim sat in the back of the car with the Pyne .32-40 muzzleloader beside him. He was fond of that rifle. The stock had never been finished. The bluing was worn off the barrel. But the inside was a precise work of art.

M.I.T. Beats Harvard
T. Ballentyne the Fourth took a quick look over his shoulder at his son as he drove out of Boston. The boy was asleep with his arm around the rifle.

"Mr. Pyne," T. Ballentyne said, "I want to apologize. All I had heard of you when I came to complain about your shooting was that you were the old man who fixes the guns. I didn't understand."

"Naturally," J.M. Pyne answered, "you didn't know who I was. You aren't a rifleman. But we both like your boy."

T. Ballentyne stared for along time at the road ahead, trying to find the right words.

"A friend of mine was there today," he said. "He's a pretty big man. He asked me to ask you if you would make a barrel for him."

"Your son introduced him to me," J.M. Pyne said. "He wants a

.30 caliber barrel for a hunting rifle. He wants to kill a moose. I'd like to oblige him, but there wouldn't be much sense in it. Maybe a Pyne rifle will shoot a little closer than a factory barrel, but you don't need it for moose. A moose is such a big mark you could hardly miss him if you can shoot at all. Most any gun that has power enough is all right for rough-and-ready work like shooting a moose. I've shot moose and elk and many deer, and a factory rifle was always good enough for me."

"I see," T. Ballentyne said. "You really don't care to make rifles for men who aren't crack shots."

"I know people say that about me," J.M. Pyne said, "but it isn't so. Take your boy. He doesn't know it yet, but I've got a barrel for off-hand work almost finished for him. All I've got to do is brown it and put the telescope blocks on. I tried it out yesterday in the machine rest. It shoots like a house afire."

"You mean Tim can't shoot, but you're making a barrel for him anyway?"

"Of course he can't shoot ..... yet. He hasn't been shooting long enough. You can't expect to shoot off-hand in a few weeks or a few months. It takes a few years. No, Tim can't shoot --- but you ought to see him try."

"I didn't have much chance to watch him today," Pyne went on. "But I've got a copy of his score in my pocket, and by studying it I can tell pretty well what was happening to him from shot to shot. It was his first match, and he had match fever so bad he could hardly load his rifle without dropping something on the floor. He was pretty wild some of the time. But he'll learn. He has the guts."

"You think that the boy is all right, Mr. Pyne?"

"Yes," J.M. Pyne said, "the boy is all right. He'll be an engineer, and a good one."

"What makes you think he'll be an engineer?"

"Because that's where his heart is."

"Maybe that's why he isn't getting along in school," T. Ballentyne said. "Maybe he doesn't want to go to Harvard."

"You tell him he can go to M.I.T., and see what happens. My guess is he'll go to M.I.T. anyway. But it would be nicer for you both if you told him he could."

T. Ballentyne knew that he had to do it. He couldn't bear to give up his ambition for his son. But he knew he had to. He hated airplanes. And Tim would be designing airplanes and flying them. But there was no way to stop him.

"I had hoped," T. Ballentyne said, "that Tim would see - well, what I'd call the glory of carrying on Ballentyne & Co."

"There's more than one kind of glory in this world," J.M. Pyne said. "You have your kind of glory. The boy has to find his."

"From what I saw at Walnut Hill today," T. Ballentyne said, "I know you have your kind of glory. They told me you were one of the greatest rifle shots who ever lived."

"Well, you see," J.M. Pyne said, "I always liked to shoot."

FORTY ROD GUN

Young Ballentyne didn't know, in the beginning, what J.M. Pyne meant by "a forty-rod gun" or "string measurement" or "the bud". He had never heard of Enoch Worden or Adam Vondersmith. The plan he formed, as J.M. Pyne talked about the old days, was innocent. He did not mean to start a war.

Young Ballentyne went to J.M. Pyne's shop that wintry afternoon as he always did when he got back to the Bridge for a day. He saw a car standing in the snow by the mailbox and knew that J.M. Pyne had a visitor.

J.M. Pyne opened the door himself. Young Ballentyne saw that J.M. Pyne's white beard was freshly trimmed. It gave his patriarchal head a roguish air. J.M. Pyne introduced young Ballentyne to the visitor.

His name was Walcott and he had something to do with a sportsmen's magazine. Young Ballentyne stood silently by while J.M. Pyne continued his talk with Walcott. You always stood up when you visited J.M. Pyne because J.M. Pyne was always standing. He was seventy-five, but he had stood at bench and lathe all his life. It never occurred to him to sit down to talk.

Walcott was asking if it was true that modern high-power rifles would shoot better than old-time ones.

"At long range," J.M. Pyne said. "They have more power to buck the wind."

"I've read," young Ballentyne said, "that a Springfield .30/06 will beat an old-time black powder rifle at any range from fifty feet to a thousand yards."

J.M. Pyne looked at him. "Yes," he said. But young Ballentyne knew from his tone that he didn't mean "Yes." He meant, "So you believe that, do you?"

"Of course," young Ballentyne said, "he didn't mean the Springfield service rifle or a National Match Springfield. He meant a Springfield with a heavy barrel - a bull gun."

J.M. Pyne went to a cabinet of small shallow drawers and took out three heavy cards about the size of cabinet photographs.

He put one of the cards on the bench and laid a steel rule across the group of bullet holes in the center of it and picked up his magnifying glass. He said the group measured an inch and nine sixty-fourths on centers. The other two groups measured within a quarter of an inch the same. There wasn't a shot in the whole thirty but would have hit a half dollar.

J.M. Pyne picked up the cards in one hand and held them out. "You can't beat that," he said.

"Those groups," Walcott said, "were shot at two hundred yards?"

"Yes," J.M. Pyne said.

"With a Pyne muzzle-loader?"

"Yes," J.M. Pyne said. He looked at the cards as if it did him good to see again the shooting one of his rifles had done. "John Kelly shot them with a .38 I made for him, with a toggle-joint starter that would put anything down the barrel, and a twenty-power scope." He looked up at Walcott. "That," he said -- "that was a gun. I wish I had it now. I tried to get it back when John Kelly died, but somebody else got there first."

"So," young Ballentyne said, "you think a Pyne muzzle-loader would beat a Springfield bull gun up to two hundred yards."

"Up to forty rods," J.M. Pyne said, "shooting double rest, shortest string to count, I'd rather have a gun like the one I made for John Kelly."

"There are men who wouldn't agree with you," Walcott said.

"There are a lot of men who don't know as much about rifles as they think they do," J.M. Pyne said. "In the old days, they would have had to prove their notions in competition. In the old days, men got together and shot double rest at forty rods, and when they got through they knew which gun was best."

J.M. Pyne put the John Kelly targets back in the drawer of the cabinet. Then he stared fiercely at Walcott.

"Where do you think the old-time rifle makers got their reputations? By talk? No. They made their reputations at the target."

"I don't even know who they were," young Ballentyne said.

J.M. Pyne turned on him. "You never heard of Billinghurst or Horace Warner or Norman Brockway?" Young Ballentyne shook his head.

"You ought to have," J.M. Pyne said.

"Were they better than the men who came after?"

"They didn't know some of the things we found out later," J.M. Pyne said.

"Was any man in your time as good as you were?" Walcott asked.

Young Ballentyne was embarrassed to hear Walcott ask that question. But J.M. Pyne was not embarrassed.

"I am an engineer," he said. "I went to M.I.T. I had the edge on them."

He turned and leaned his back against the bench and took off both pairs of glasses and wiped the lenses carefully.

"There was one man who made me hump myself," he continued. "He was a young German whose father came over in '48 and settled in Pennsylvania. He and I both worked for a while in Enoch Worden's shop in Vermont. He was the most stubborn, pigheaded, obstinate cuss I ever knew. His name was Adam Vondersmith.

J.M. Pyne paused, remembering the past. Young Ballentyne and Walcott waited patiently for him to go on.

"If he hadn't been so pigheaded he would have been as good as I was," J.M. Pyne said. "He wouldn't admit anything. I beat him in a rest match, shooting lubricated bullets against his paper-patched ones. He wouldn't admit that the lubricated bullet was as good. He said I won because I was a better judge of wind than he was. There's nothing you can do with a man that's pigheaded. We had an argument one morning and Vondersmith lost his temper. I was sort of exasperated myself. Enoch Worden fired us both - Vondersmith went his way and I went mine. I never saw him but once after that. We didn't speak. That was fifty years ago."

"Is Vondersmith still making rifles?" young Ballentyne asked.

J.M. Pyne shook his head. "I don't know," he said. "If he's still alive, he must be pretty old. He was a year older than I was."

"Did you know," Walcott asked, "that Enoch Worden is still living?"

J.M. Pyne turned sharply. "No," he said. "He can't be."

"He is," Walcott said. "My grandfather knows him. They used to shoot in the rest matches at Vernon, in Vermont. Worden retired 30 years ago. But he's still living in some little town in Massachusetts."

"Enoch Worden must be nearly a hundred years old," J.M. Pyne said.

"He's ninety-five," Walcott said, "but he's as smart as ever."

"If he is," J.M. Pyne said, "he's pretty smart."

"We've got to stage a double-rest match at forty rods under the old rules," young Ballentyne said to Walcott, after they left J.M. Pyne. "I'd like to see J.M. Pyne beat some of these birds who think a Springfield bull gun is the last word in accuracy."

"I'm afraid we couldn't stir up much interest in such a match," Walcott said. "The men who shoot bull guns are so sure their rifles are better than black powder guns that they wouldn't bother to come out and prove it."

"Suppose there was money in it. Suppose there was a thousand dollars up as prize money?"

"That would be different," Walcott admitted.

"I think I can get my father to put up the thousand dollars," young Ballentyne said.

They planned it standing there in the snow outside J.M. Pyne's shop. Walcott said he would start a controversy in his magazine about the relative accuracy of black powder rifles and modern ones, and when the argument got bitter, he would announce the match for the Fourth of July. He was sure his grandfather would bring Enoch Worden to the match. They would make it an event. They would hunt out all the old-time riflemen who were still alive. They might even find Adam Vondersmith.

Young Ballentyne was starting his car when Walcott called out to him.

"Listen, Ballentyne," he said. "What if J.M. Pyne doesn't win?"

"But he will," young Ballentyne said.

Young Ballentyne drove home, and as he drove he was not so sure. Old men were prone to exaggerate the achievements of the past. J.M. Pyne was an old man now.

Young Ballentyne learned, after writing a good many letters, that Adam Vondersmith had a shop near Williamsport, in Pennsylvania. Young Ballentyne got up of a morning in spring to drive down there. He came, late that afternoon, to a neat white house with a shop built alongside it. He knocked at the shop entrance and got an answer. He opened the door and walked in. A bell tinkled overhead. He saw a rifling machine, and, beyond, at a bench under a bank of windows, a tall old man with a white beard.

Young Ballentyne saw that the old man was wearing three pairs of glasses, one in front of the other. He had a graver in his hand, and on the bench was something that looked like a twenty-dollar gold piece.

"It is not, I believe, forbidden by these new laws," the old man said. "I engraved that gold piece thirty years ago to put in the head of a cane I gave an old friend. Now his widow wishes also I should engrave the date of his death and a few words for her son, to whom she gives it."

Young Ballentyne gave the old man a proof of the program for the double-rest matches at forty rods and asked him to read it.

"It is goot," he said when he had finished. "It is now many years since I have seen so much prize money offered. In the old days, I have known it to be more. Once my old friend, Will Hays, took the prize money for the Schutzenbundesfest home in a satchel, so no one could steal it. The satchel was very heavy. The sum was twenty-five thousand dollars!"

"Twenty-five thousand dollars!?"

"Ja, for one veek of matches and maybe one t'ousand shooters."

Adam Vondersmith gave the program back to young Ballentyne and picked up his graver.

"I came to ask you if you would shoot in our match," young Ballentyne said.

Adam Vondersmtih looked up sharply. "Ach Herrje," he said, "I do not shoot any more."

"We would like very much to have you," young Ballentyne said.

"No," Adam Vondersmith said. "I vill not shoot."

"I drove all the way from Boston to ask you."

"Today you drive from Boston? You must be tired," he said. He laid down his graver and called out, "Sophy! Sophy!"

A little pink-cheeked old lady appeared at the side door. Adam Vondersmith spoke to her in German.

"Ach, du lieber Gott!" she said. She turned to young Ballentyne. "So, you come by Boston already. I have coffee and Kuchen."

Adam Vondersmith took off his apron. "I also vill have coffee and Kuchen," he said.

Young Ballentyne followed Mrs. Vondersmith through the side door of the shop, through a kitchen of amazing neatness, and into the dining room. He sat down at the dining room table with Adam Vondersmith while his wife ran back and forth, bringing the coffee pot from the kitchen range, and hot milk and slices of cinnamon cake and coffee cake.

She waited on them, refusing to sit down. Young Ballentyne wondered how J.M. Pyne could have contrived to quarrel with a man as gentle as Adam Vondersmith. But it was plain that he was immovable. Young Ballentyne had no hope of persuading him to change his mind and shoot in the match.

"Mr. Vondersmith," he said, "did you ever know a rifle maker named J.M. Pyne?"

Adam Vondersmith leaned forward. "Ja," he said. "I know him - that Johnny Pyne." He turned to his wife and spoke again in German.

Little Mrs. Vondersmith threw up her hands. "Ach, due lieber Gott!" she cried. "That man! So hot-tempered! He vas crazy!

He vould have killed my husband if Mr. Vorden had not stopped him!"

"No," Adam Vondersmith said with sudden violence. "No, he vould not have killed me. I vould have killed him."

"What happened?" young Ballentyne asked.

Adam Vondersmith thrust his chin out at young Ballentyne. "Do you know anything about shooting?" he demanded. "Do you know what a pinhead is?"

"Yes," young Ballentyne said, "it's a tiny bead on a thin stem, used for a front sight."

"So," Adam Vondersmith said. "Do you also know what an aperture front sight is?"

"It is a small ring through which you see the bull's-eye."

"So," Adam Vondersmith said. "That is how it started. We are talking about sights that morning. Johnny Pyne says he has found out a pinhead is the best of all front sights. I say I do not think so. I tell him I think the aperture is more better." He paused to throw his hands wide. "Which is so - and everybody knows it is so. But you cannot tell Johnny Pyne anything. No matter how I explain to him why the aperture is more better than the pinhead, he says the pinhead is better. Pretty soon he gets crazy mad and curses me for a pigheaded Dutchman, vich I am not. I am High German. So I tell him he is one dumbhead Yankee, vich is the truth. And I see he has my hammer, and just before I hit him we hear a roar behind us, and we turn, and it is Enoch Vorden. But when he is mad he has a voice like an Old Country drill sergeant.

"'Stop!' he yells. And we stop. Enoch Vorden says he has had enough of us. We are through. But we can only leave separately, and not together, because he vill not let us kill each other."

Adam Vondersmith shrugged his shoulders.

"That is vot happens. Me and Johnny Pyne have worked together at the bench for one whole year, but we never speak to each other again. Vot can you do when a man has such a temper? You can do nothing vith such a man."

"Wasn't Pyne a good workman?" young Ballentyne asked.

"Donnerwetter kreuzmillion!" Adam Vondersmith yelled. "Did I say he vas not a good vorkman?" He leaned forward and fixed young Ballentyne with his blue eyes. "I vill tell you something - that Johnny Pyne is not only good. He vas the best rifle maker in the whole vorld."

"I've always heard that he was good," young Ballentyne said.

"Ach! What you hear people say! What does that mean! Macht nichts aus! They know nothing. Nothing. But me, I know. I can put a soft-lead slug in the breech and upset it so it fills the grooves, and push it through the barrel, and tell you how good the man who made it vas. When I have put a slug through a Pyne barrel, I know this is the end - this is as far as man can go."

"Mr. Pyne has promised to shoot in our match," young Ballentyne said.

"But how vould he?" Adam Vondersmith asked. "He is an old man. He is almost as old as I am."

"Just the same," young Ballentyne said, "he has promised to shoot."

"Ach, Herrje!" Adam Vondersmith cried. "You are telling the truth?"

"Yes," young Ballentyne said, "I am telling the truth."

Adam Vondersmith brought his fist down on the table so hard that the coffee cups jumped out of their saucers.

"Then I also vill shoot," he said. "And I vill beat him. I have the rifle to beat him."

"That's the spirit, Mr. Vondersmith," young Ballentyne said.

"My boy," Adam Vondersmith said, "you vill see something. And Johnny Pyne vill see something - something he does not expect."

Young Ballentyne drove back to Boston and M.I.T., and wondered, as he drove, what Adam Vondersmith had in reserve. He seemed so sure he had the gun to beat J.M. Pyne.

Young Ballentyne stopped for J.M. Pyne before daylight that Fourth of July. He had a hundred miles to drive, and he wanted to be there early.

94

He and Walcott had spread out the thousand dollars in prize money so it would do the most good. They had allotted two hundred and fifty dollars for each of three ten-shot matches - one hundred dollars for first place, seventy-five dollars for second place, fifty dollars for third place, and twenty-five dollars for fourth place. That left two hundred and fifty dollars. They had agreed to give the two hundred and fifty in one lump sum to the man who made the best score in all three matches.

"I wish," J.M. Pyne said - "I wish I had my John Kelly gun. That toggle-joint starter pushed the bullet down so gently there was no upsettage. There is some upsettage when you hit the starter a blow with the heel of your hand. There's got to be. And it can't always be the same."

Young Ballentyne parked his car at the range and got out J.M. Pyne's rifle and his shooting bag.

J.M. Pyne made a gesture toward the rifle. "I'll carry that."

"I don't mind," Ballentyne said.

"I mind," J.M. Pyne said. "I want to carry my own gun - as I have for fifty years."

Young Ballentyne had to give him the rifle. J.M. Pyne hung the rifle over his shoulder by the strap on the canvas case and trudged toward the shed where the loading stands were and the long line of benches for double-rest shooting. J.M. Pyne did not get far before he was stopped by friends who wanted to shake his hand and wish him well. Young Ballentyne saw that the shed was already crowded. He hurried on. He had to find Walcott and arrange to close the entries at ten o'clock. It seemed to him that every man there had a Springfield bull gun. He saw a dozen Marines. He knew how well the Marines shot at Camp Perry.

Young Ballentyne was so busy making up lists of shooters and assigning them to relays that he had no chance to see what J.M. Pyne was doing. And then he heard a shout and looked up and saw Adam Vondersmith coming down the line with a rifle in a case over his shoulder.

Young Ballentyne stood up to watch. It was J.M. Pyne who had shouted.

"Why, Adam," J.M. Pyne was saying, "I'm glad to see you."

"I'm glad to see you, Johnny," Adam Vondersmith was saying.

"I'd have been glad to see you any day for fifty years."

You knew from the sound of their voices, from the way they continued to shake hands, that they meant what they said. It was touching to see the two old men making friends again.

"Adam," J.M. Pyne was saying, "I never had anything against you. It was foolish for us to quarrel over a thing like that. You know it was foolish, and by this time you know you were dead wrong about the pinhead. You know an aperture is no good except when the light is just right."

"Johnny," Adam Vondersmith cried, "you are wrong; you are wrong."

"Adam," J.M. Pyne said earnestly, "you've never used a pinhead that was right. When a pinhead is right, it looks the same size as the bull. You put the top of the pinhead at the bottom of the bull, and the pinhead and the bull make a perfect figure 8, and if you're sighted in, you've got a center shot."

"You are yust the same as effer, Johnny!" Adam Vondersmith yelled. "Nobody can tell you anything! You know it all! You think, you Shafskopf, that because a pinhead..."

"Adam," J.M. Pyne broke in, "you're wrong about the simplest principles of optics. You don't know..."

"Donner und blitzen!" Adam Vondersmith yelled. "I know what everybody knows - that an aperture is the best sight that.."

"You pigheaded Dutchman," J.M. Pyne interrupted. "You don't listen to what I'm telling you."

Men stood round and listened and marveled at the passion with which they argued. Young Ballentyne thought it would never end. And then he saw a little old man with chin whiskers coming down the line on the arm of a slightly younger man. The little man walked in carpet slippers, with a stick in his free hand. His head was completely bald. His upper lip was clean-shaven. But his lower lip, his chin, his cheeks wore the most luxuriant whiskers young Ballentyne had ever seen. Young Ballcntync knew who he was - who he must be.

Enoch Worden walked straight up to J.M. Pyne and Adam Vondersmith.

"Boys!" Enoch Worden said to those two old men. "Boys!"

They did not hear him.

"You don't understand plain English," J.M. Pyne said, shaking his finger in Adam Vondersmith's face.

"You Dummkopf," Adam Vondersmith said. "You vas always crazy."

Enoch Worden's mouth set in a grim line above his chin whiskers. Enoch Worden raised his stick and rapped J.M. Pyne hard across the shins, and almost in the same motion he walloped Adam Vondersmith.

J.M. Pyne and Adam Vondersmith reached for their shins, as any man will when he's struck there. They reached for their shins and forgot each other and saw Enoch Worden, and seeing him, they were no longer privileged old men. They were boys again in the presence of the boss.

They bowed to Enoch Worden. They gave him the deference that courteous youth gives to old age. They shook Enoch Worden's hand; they told him how well he looked; they reminded him of his great past.

But again Enoch Worden shut his mouth in that thin line. He raised his stick. "You've talked enough, you two," he said. "Now get to work." He waved his stick at two Marines ensconced at rest benches with Springfield bull guns and telescope sights. "Look at that," Enoch Worden said. "Are you two going to stand there chattering when you've got that to beat?"

A bull gun spoke just then. A bull gun spoke and the hills rattled.

Enoch Worden raised his head. "Are you two going to let a man with a thing like that beat fine rifles?"

"No, sir," J.M. Pyne said meekly.

"Ach, Herrje," Adam Vondersmith exclaimed. "I am making again a fool of myself."

Young Ballentyne took J.M. Pyne's shooting bag to him. J.M. Pyne got his telescope sight out of its cloth bag. Young Ballentyne pulled the .32-40 out of its case. And while J.M. Pyne put the telescope in place and turned up the screws tightly, young Ballentyne laid out the boxes of bullets, the primers, the false muzzle and the starter.

97

"I guess," he said to J.M. Pyne - "I guess you're ready to fire a fouling shot."

But J.M. Pyne was not listening. He was staring at Adam Vondersmith, three yards away at another loading bench.

"Do you see what he's got?" J.M. Pyne demanded.

Young Ballentyne looked across at Adam Vondersmith. He was fitting a strange implement to the false muzzle of his rifle - an affair with two metal arms opposite each other.

"Don't you know a toggle-joint starter when you see it?" J.M. Pyne said. "The son of a gun has got my John Kelly gun."

"Well," young Ballentyne said, trying to think of something soothing to say to J.M. Pyne, "well ---"

"I waited until John Kelly had been buried a week before I wrote his widow that I wanted to buy back that gun. I thought it was only decent to wait a week. But that Dutchman didn't wait a week."

"At least," young Ballentyne said, "it means he admits a Pyne rifle is better than anything that he can make."

J.M. Pyne waved his hand at the range. "Look," he said.

The long red silk ribbons that he preferred for wind flags were lifting clear of the posts on which they hung. The long red ribbons were snapping in the gusts.

"He never was a good judge of wind," J.M. Pyne said. "He can't beat me today - not even with my own forty-rod gun."

J.M. Pyne prepared his target. He pasted a long strip of white paper across the top. Then he got out the little steel rule he always carried, and measured off three inches from the center toward the top, and put a black target paster, perhaps three-quarters of an inch square, on that point.

"That's my bud," he said.

"Your aiming point," young Ballentyne said.

J.M. Pyne put a row of target pasters clear across the top of his target, each one inch from the next.

"That's my wind gauge," he said. "If the wind is blowing the bullet three inches to the left, I'll hold on the third paster to the right from the center, and so on."

Young Ballentyne called the first relay and walked down to the butt with the men who were going to shoot. He saw them tack up their targets. He saw that Adam Vondersmith was using a red wafer of the sort that's put on legal papers for a bud. There was a fellow who used four pasters marking the corners of a square. But J.M. Pyne was the only man who had a wind gauge on his target.

Young Ballentyne took up his post behind a big spotting telescope when they got back from the butts. There were sixty men on the line, and J.M. Pyne and Adam Vondersmith were the only ones who were shooting old-time rifles. The relay got impatient waiting for J.M. Pyne and Adam Vondersmith to load. A big Marine with a Springfield bull gun sat beside his rest bench and muttered, "Come on. Come on." But he had to wait until Enoch Worden called, "Time."

Rifles cracked all along the line when Enoch Worden gave the signal. Young Ballentyne looked over at J.M. Pyne. He saw that the old man was holding his fire. He was watching the wind flags. Young Ballentyne saw the wind flags stiffen in a gust. J.M. Pyne threw up his head. Enoch Worden called out, "One minute to go." Young Ballentyne wondered if J.M. Pyne would ever shoot. Enoch Worden called out, "Thirty seconds to go." And still J.M. Pyne waited. Enoch Worden called fifteen seconds. And still J.M. Pyne waited. Young Ballentyne saw the wind flags dip. He saw the wind flags drop. And then J.M. Pyne's rifle spoke. It sounded like a .22 after the crashes of the bull guns. It sounded so slow - go bang! How could it ever compete with the power and speed of modern military rifles?

Young Ballentyne looked into the big spotting scope to see where J.M. Pyne's shot had struck. J.M. Pyne's first shot had taken out the center where the diagonals crossed as neatly as if the target had been lying on the bench and he had used a wad-cutter.

Young Ballentyne swung the scope to look at the other targets. Adam Vondersmith had a shot half an inch from dead center. The big marine had done as well. Not one man in ten was more than two inches from center with his first shot.

There was no way to tell which man had won until they had brought the targets back and Enoch Worden had measured them. Enoch Worden took a clean strip of paper and laid it on a target and measured from the center of it to the center of a shot hole, and made a mark; then he put the mark on the center of the target and measured to the center of another shot hole, and so on, adding automatically the sum of the deviation of the shots from center.

Young Ballentyne hung over Enoch Worden's shoulder to watch him. But he could not stay. He had to get another relay going. He didn't know who had won until he heard somebody shout. He turned and saw them pounding J.M. Pyne on the back, and knew that J.M. Pyne had the shortest string. He saw J.M. Pyne walk back to his loading stand, and went over.

"Who got second?" young Ballentyne asked.

"Vondersmith," J.M. Pyne said. "He should have won that match. His elevation didn't vary half an inch. But he had his shots strung out with the wind. He never was a judge of wind."

"Who got third?" young Ballentyne asked.

J.M. Pyne jerked his thumb at the big Marine who had been so impatient while he waited for J.M. Pyne and Adam Vondersmith to load their old-time guns.

"My string was five and three-quarters," J.M. Pyne said. "Vondersmith had six inches. That Marine had six and one eighth inches."

Young Ballentyne learned, late in the afternoon, that J.M. Pyne had won the second ten-shot match. He went over to congratulate J.M. Pyne. But J.M. Pyne was not smiling.

"What's the matter?" young Ballentyne asked.

"Firing pin broke," J.M. Pyne said.

"But surely you can borrow a firing pin."

"There are only two single shot rifles on this range," J.M. Pyne said. "One is mine and the other is Vondersmith's. You wouldn't find a firing pin that would fit my gun within a hundred miles."

"At least," young Ballentyne said, "you've won two of the three matches."

"I've lost my chance for the third match and for the main prize -

for the shortest string in all three matches."

"I'm sorry," young Ballentyne said. "I'm afraid that means a bull gun is going to win."

"No, it doesn't," J.M. Pyne said. "You wait and see."

Young Ballentyne saw him walk slowly over to Adam Vondersmith's loading stand. Young Ballentyne started that way and paused. He was near enough to hear what they said.

"Adam," J.M. Pyne said huskily -- "Adam, I'm out of it. I've broken the firing pin of my rifle. It's up to you. The rest is up to you."

"Johnny," Adam Vondersmith said, "I'd give my right arm to win this match."

"You don't have to do that," J.M. Pyne said. "You only have to do what I tell you to do."

"Was ist das?" Adam Vondersmith cried.

"You're a poor judge of wind," J.M. Pyne said. "You always were. What you've got to do in this last match is line up your gun and wait until I touch you on the shoulder. When I touch you - pull."

Adam Vondersmith glared at J.M. Pyne and the veins knotted in his temples.

"Donner und blitzen!" he exploded. "You think you can teach me how to shoot?"

"It wasn't my idea," J.M. Pyne said. "It's what Enoch Worden says."

Adam Vondersmith opened his mouth to speak, thought better of it, and swallowed hard. "So," he said in a low voice - "so it shall be."

Young Ballentyne watched them as they worked together, a little awed by their intensity. Adam Vondersmith loaded the John Kelly gun while J.M. Pyne stood by. Adam Vondersmith laid the John Kelly gun on the rest bench, the muzzle just so, and waited, his eye at the telescope sight. J.M. Pyne stood behind him, watching the wind. After three, four, sometimes almost five minutes, J.M. Pyne was satisfied that the wind was the same as for the last shot. He touched Adam Vondersmith on the shoulder and the John Kelly gun spoke.

They had to score the last targets by lantern light. The sun had gone down and the moon had come up, and still Enoch Worden sat at a table with clean strips of paper and a pencil, measuring string after string. Men stood five deep behind him, watching and waiting. Enoch Worden saved Adam Vondersmith's target till the last. Men who had shot bull guns nudged one another when they saw it, not willing to believe their eyes. Enoch Worden took a silver dollar from his waistcoat pocket and laid it on the target. It covered all the shots.

Enoch Worden measured the target with great care. The string came to four and one-quarter inches, meaning that the average deviation for ten shots from center was less than half an inch.

Enoch Worden stood up and found his stick and smiled. "Adam Vondersmith has won the third ten-shot match," he said. "He has also won the grand prize for the shortest string in three matches -- in the whole thirty shots."

"But for your gun, I could not have done it, Johnny," Adam Vondersmith said to J.M. Pyne. "It is really you who von this match."

"Thank you, Adam," J.M. Pyne said. "If I couldn't win myself, I'd rather see you win."

"I could not have von without your gun," Adam Vondersmith said, "and maybe I could not have von without you there to keep me from shooting on the wrong vind. I never vas a goot judge of vind. I admit it. That is why you beat me fifty years ago, shooting your lubricated bullets against my paper-patched ones. That is why you make scores with a pinhead that I could not make with the aperture, vich is so much better."

"You pigheaded Dutchman," J.M. Pyne said. "You ---"

He got no farther. Enoch Worden swung his stick sharply -- swish, swish! J.M. Pyne reached for his shins, and so did Adam Vondersmith.

"That will do," Enoch Worden said. "Don't you know you've won? Don't you know you've beaten these fellows who thought a bull gun was better than a handmade rifle? Don't you know it took you both to do it? Can't you see it's time to quit and be friends?"

102

JOHNNY GETS HIS GUN

Johnny had to piece the story together from what they told him and what he overheard. His father and mother never told him any more than they could help. He heard his mother tell his father that she didn't want her son to grow up scared.

Johnny was eleven years old then. He knew a great deal more than they supposed he did. He knew those men had shot his father that day in Chicago because his father was the only eyewitness the state's attorney had. The two men in plain clothes who had been assigned to protect his father had died that day. One of the newspapers said they had died as bravely as policemen usually died.

Johnny's father had been in the hospital for months. The surgeons had taken four submachine gun bullets out of his father's body. But his father had recovered.

Johnny knew what his mother feared most. If they ever caught the two murderers who had got away, his father would have to testify against them, too. That was why the state's attorney had urged his father to go away somewhere. Johnny heard his father and mother discussing what they ought to do, when they thought he was asleep. His mother said they ought to pack up and drive to her father's place in the North Woods and stay there for a year.

"I suppose," Johnny's father said, teasing her - "I suppose you think I'd be safe there because your father would protect me. If anybody who looked bad came along, the old man would out with his trusty rifle and pot him."

Johnny's mother ignored the gibe. She was in earnest. "Father is seventy-five," she said. "I don't believe he shoots any more. I'd feel safe up there with him because it's so far from a city. I'd feel that city killers would never find their way up there."

"It isn't likely they'll ever try to find me."

"You know what the state attorney said."

"The state attorney believes in melodrama."

"Perhaps he does," Johnny's mother said. "But if you're afraid, you're afraid whether it's reasonable or not. I'm afraid."

"You'd be bored to death up there in the woods," Johnny's father said.

"I wouldn't. I'd love it. I'd love to see that Father gets the right things to eat and that he doesn't work hard. And you'd like Father. He's an artist, too."

Johnny could hear his father get up and walk back and forth. He must be weakening.

"You'd get a lot of work done," Johnny's mother said, "with nothing to distract you."

"At least," Johnny's father said, "there wouldn't be any cocktail parties. There wouldn't be any rich women you have to flatter because they might buy something."

That first night at his grandfather's place, Johnny lay awake in the dark loft over the sitting room and listened to the wind in the pine trees and the distant roar of the brook over the dam, and wished he hadn't asked to sleep there. He had asked to sleep in the loft because you climbed a ladder to get there, pushing up the trapdoor with your head.

Johnny listened to the strange sounds and thought he heard a car coming, and was afraid. He knew it couldn't be the men who had promised to get his father. He knew it was just the wind in the pine trees. But he was afraid. He knew pretty much how the men would look. He had seen the sketches his father had made from memory. His father did that sort of thing with a touch of exaggeration, so you knew the person quicker than you ever would from a photograph.

But after that first night Johnny forgot to be afraid. He was too much interested in his Grampa and his Grampa's shop. There was no school within twenty miles and no neighbor within ten miles. Johnny's mother taught him arithmetic and geography and English every morning, while his father painted. After lunch Johnny was free. Grampa never came in to lunch, no matter what Johnny's mother said. He took a couple of sandwiches and a small tin of coffee with him when he went out to work in his shop in the morning. After lunch Johnny ran the hundred yards down the road to his Grampa's shop. He usually stayed there until dark.

You wouldn't think much of the shop unless you knew. The shop stood beside the brook, below the little mill pond that furnished power for the lathe. The shop was one big room, with a bank of windows along one whole side over the bench, and a chimney in the middle. It looked as if it were full of junk. But if you were a rifle crank you knew better. If you were a rifle crank you knew it was full of treasures. If you were a rifle crank you knew that Grampa made the most famous rifle barrels in the world - match barrels.

He wore two pairs of glasses now, and used a magnifying lens in a brass mount besides, when he wanted to read the micrometer. But he made match barrels, rifling them by hand, just as he had rifled them for fifty years, to meet the only test he had ever recognized - the way they'd shoot in a machine rest.

If the rifle shot the kind of groups Grampa thought a rifle ought to shoot, he'd put it in the vise and get out the die. He'd line up the die on the left side of the barrel, near the breech, and strike it a smart blow with the hammer. When he took the die away you'd see the name on the barrel, in small Roman letters, cut sharply in the steel: J.M. Pyne.

Sometimes if it was a .22, it wouldn't shoot. Grampa would threaten to wrap the barrel around the anvil. Grampa would curse .22's. Grampa would say with passion that he hated .22's. But he never did wrap the barrel around the anvil. When he cooled off he went to work on the action. He'd make a new firing pin. He'd change the mainspring. It was the ignition that made the trouble. Grampa always worked twelve hours a day. But when he had a .22 that wouldn't shoot, he'd work seventeen or eighteen hours. He'd work far into the night under a battery of gasoline lamps.

Johnny learned to keep still when a .22 wouldn't shoot. Johnny would get one of the bound volumes of *Shooting and Fishing* from the stack against the chimney and curl up on the cot and read. One afternoon, in a volume thirty years old, he came on an article about a new world's record for 100 shots at 200 yards off-hand. There was a picture of the target with the bullet holes in it. The name of the man who had made the record was J.M. Pyne.

Johnny took the volume and laid it open on the bench beside the vise and pointed to the target.

Grampa looked at the target - a long look. Then he looked at Johnny over his glasses. Grampa's beard was white and his shoulders were stooped with more than fifty years of bending over his work. But there were moments when his brown eyes sparkled with mischief.

"I used to shoot," he said.

"Don't you ever shoot any more?" Johnny asked.

"Not often," Grampa said. "My left wrist is half crippled."

"You can't shoot at all?"

"I wouldn't say that," his grandfather said. "I can still pull one plumb if I have to. But I can't shoot hundred-shot matches any-more. My wrist won't hold out for more than a few shots."

Grampa bent again over his vise. He was working on the tip of a trigger where it engaged the sear, with a smooth, hard, oilstone. He'd take three or four strokes with the slip of stone and pause to look at the work through the magnifying glass.

"I wish I could see you shoot," Johnny said.

"I'd have to stop and cast some bullets for the .32-40," Grampa said, "but I could shoot a couple of shots with the hunting gun. I'd like to be sure it's sighted in. A deer might come along this fall."

Johnny got a target and ran outdoors and down the range. He tacked the target on the frame in front of the log butt at 100 yards. Grampa had the spotting scope set up, and the shooting port open, and the hunting gun out when Johnny got back.

The hunting gun was a plain .30-40 single-shot rifle with an ivory bead in front and an aperture sight on the tang. There was a row of punch marks on the stock. There were twenty-two punch marks without a break. That meant twenty-two deer in twenty-two shots. The twenty-third mark was double. That meant it had taken a second shot to kill the twenty-third deer.

Johnny looked down the range. The black of the target was six inches in diameter and contained the eight, nine and ten rings. The ten ring was two inches in diameter. The black looked awfully small to Johnny. What if Grampa couldn't hit the black? What if he couldn't hit the paper? He was an old man now. He was thirty years older than he'd been when he'd made that world's record.

"You take the spotting scope," Grampa said, "and when I've called my shot, you tell me what I've got."

Johnny put his right eye to the spotting scope and watched Grampa out of the corner of his left eye. Grampa raised the rifle and put his cheek against the stock, and his body straightened and the weariness went out of his shoulders. He held his head high as he peered through the aperture of the rear sight. The roar of the rifle startled Johnny. He hadn't known it would be so loud or come so quickly.

"I pulled it high at twelve o'clock," Grampa said.

Johnny looked wildly over the white part of the target above the bull's-eye. He couldn't find the bullet hole.

"It isn't in the white," Johnny said.

"No," Grampa said, "I didn't say it was a wild shot. It's a nine at twelve o'clock."

Then, staring through the scope at the black, Johnny saw the break in the ten ring at twelve o'clock.

"It's a ten!" he cried.

"It shouldn't be," Grampa said. "I pulled a nine."

Grampa reloaded the rifle. This time Johnny watched through the scope while Grampa aimed, and when the rifle roared, Johnny saw the hole leap in the black, taking away part of the little white 10 in the center of the black.

"It's a ten!" Johnny cried. "What is it you call it when it's exactly in the middle?"

"A pinwheel," Grampa said.

He put the rifle in the vise, with the leather jaw liners, and pushed a pledget of absorbent cotton through the bore with a cleaning rod.

Johnny watched him. He seemed pleased with himself, but not at all excited.

"Could I ever learn to shoot like that, Grampa?" Johnny asked.

"I had a bit of luck," Grampa said.

"Luck?!" Johnny said.

"Yes," his grandfather said. "I pulled the first one for a nine and I got a ten. That's luck. I pulled the second one plumb and got a pinwheel. It's always luck when you get a pinwheel. That rifle won't shoot that close - it's good for about just under two inches at a hundred yards. So when you pull one plumb and get a dead-center shot, it's luck."

"I bet you could get a ten any time you wanted to," Johnny said.

"No," Grampa said. "But I can pull one plumb if I have to. I wouldn't be very far from the ten ring if I needed a ten."

"Grampa," Johnny asked again, "could I ever learn to shoot like that?"

J.M. Pyne oiled a pledget of cotton and swabbed the bore of the rifle.

"I've always said that any man who had the guts could learn to shoot off-hand," he said. "But nowadays they haven't the guts. Nowadays they all learn to shoot lying on their stomachs and resting their elbows on the ground, and all trussed up in a sling strap, military fashion. And when they try to shoot standing up and can't make more than half a score, they quit and go back to the prone position, so they can hit something."

"I'd like to learn to shoot off-hand," Johnny said.

Grampa took the hunting gun out of the vise and stood it up in the corner.

"The trouble is," Johnny continued, not without guile, "Father thinks I'm too young to have a gun."

Grampa glared at Johnny. "What," he demanded, " - what does he know about it?"

Johnny thought that was the moment to say nothing.

"I haven't a rifle in the shop that's light enough for you to shoot," Grampa said. "Even the hunting gun weighs close to ten pounds."

"I know," Johnny said, "I'll have to wait until Father will buy me a light rifle."

"I'd rather trust you with a rifle right now than most of the men who go deer hunting. You know more about rifles just from being around my shop and asking questions."

He got his flashlight and crawled under the long workbench. Johnny waited hopefully. It looked impossible to find anything in that shop, with everything piled hit or miss. But Johnny had never known Grampa to fail.

Grampa emerged at last. He had a light rifle barrel in one hand.

He put the barrel in the vise and wiped it out. Then he took a soft lead slug and pushed it slowly through the bore. He caught the bullet in his cap as it came out of the muzzle. He studied the slug with the magnifying glass and measured it with the micrometer.

"I'm two or three years behind with my orders," he said. "That's why I moved up here in the country, so my customers couldn't bother me. They have to write to me to complain, and I don't have to read the letters. And now I'm going to lose another week while I fix up something you can shoot."

"I know you oughtn't to do it," Johnny said. "Only--"

"Only you hope I will."

"I do want a rifle," Johnny said. "I want to learn to shoot."

"You needn't worry," Grampa said. "You're going to learn right here in this shop, and nobody but you and I are going to know anything about it."

Grampa cut a piece off the end of the light barrel where it had a tight place in it, and lapped out the bore. He rechambered it, and fitted it to an action, and lightened the hammer and adjusted the trigger pull. He made a stock and a forearm, and found an old vernier peep sight.

After that, Johnny had a lesson in off-hand shooting every afternoon. Johnny learned things about rifles through a long northern winter. Chicago seemed very far away.

Johnny's father went to New York for two weeks in March about an exhibition of his pictures. The only train he could get back on stopped at Wood's Junction, forty miles away, at three o'clock in the morning. Johnny's mother planned to start out the evening before to meet him. The road was still frozen, but a good deal of it was so rough you couldn't drive more than ten miles an hour over it.

Grampa had an ulcerated tooth. Johnny's mother decided she'd have to start after lunch and take Grampa to a dentist. They might get some sleep at Wood's Junction while they waited for the train.

She asked Johnny if he'd mind spending the night alone in the house. Johnny said of course he wouldn't. He was twelve years old now.

"We could take you with us," his mother said.

"Who would keep the fires going?"

"That's true," she said. You had to feed wood fires.

"I suppose it's all right," she said. "We'll be back here by seven o'clock in the morning unless the train is late. But if anything should happen to you, I'd never forgive myself."

"What could happen to me?" Johnny asked.

"The only thing I'm afraid of is fire," his mother said.

"I know how to tend fires," Johnny said.

"I know you do," she said.

Johnny saw that she had lost her fear of the men who had promised to get his father. They had been living at his Grampa's for almost a year, and nothing had ever happened.

Johnny got no chance to speak to Grampa alone before they left.

He wanted to ask for the key to the shop, so he could shoot his rifle, but he could not ask in front of his mother. He had to occupy himself carrying in wood after they had gone.

When it began to get dark, Johnny lit the big oil lamp on the sitting room table and put fresh wood in the chunk stove. He turned on the drafts in the kitchen stove and cooked himself a dish his grandfather called yellow jackets. He cut up two cold, boiled potatoes and browned them in a pan with strips of bacon and broke eggs over them and stirred the whole. After supper he sat down beside the big lamp with Fremantle's Book of the Rifle. For once, he could stay up as late as he liked.

Now and again he looked up and listened. He wasn't afraid. He knew there was nothing to be afraid of in the North Woods. He bent again over his book. He read on and on.

Suddenly he found himself listening like a wild animal. He thought he had heard a car coming in the distance. Of course, it was just the wind in the pine trees outside. But he listened. And, listening, he knew it wasn't the wind. It was a car coming. He jumped up and went into Grampa's bedroom and looked out. It was dark in the bedroom and darker still outdoors. He saw the headlights of a car in the dark. The car was coming pretty fast, considering the road. The lights lurched from side to side.

The car stopped and turned in. Johnny watched with his nose against the cold windowpane. The car was a big sedan. Two men got out of the car. They came toward the house.

Johnny waited until he heard them on the porch. Then he opened the door and asked them in. They came in, stamping their feet. There was still some snow on the ground.

"Well, bub," the tall man said, his back to the chunk stove, "where's your folks?"

"They're away," Johnny said.

"They'll be back tonight, won't they?"

"No," Johnny said. "Not till tomorrow."

"The reason I'm asking," the tall man explained, "is that we're tired and hungry and we're lost. We thought we might get a meal here and put up for the night."

"I guess you can do that," Johnny said. You didn't turn strangers away in the North Country. Even if you didn't like them, you gave them a meal and let them stay the night. "I could give you ham and eggs and fried potatoes and coffee," Johnny added.

"Fine," the tall man said. He took off his hat and coat. He wasn't bald. The other man took off his hat. He wasn't bald either. One of the men Johnny's father had sketched for the state attorney was bald. His hat had fallen off that day in Chicago and revealed him as completely bald.

Johnny found the ham and the eggs and peeled some cold, boiled potatoes. The short man cooked the ham and eggs while Johnny found bread and butter and set out plates and knives and forks on the kitchen table. The tall man got a bottle of whisky out of his overcoat pocket. They drank half a tumblerful of whisky apiece and poured out more, and ate like hungry men.

When the two men had eaten, they went out to their car. Johnny watched them from the dark bedroom window. The tall man had a flashlight. He held the light while the short man got something out of the rear of the car. Johnny saw that he had a gun. He handed the gun to the tall man and got another gun. The tall man locked the door of the car. He tried the other doors to make sure they were locked too.

Johnny ran back into the living room. He was putting wood in the chunk stove when they came in. He took a look at those guns and tried not to betray his interest.

They put their guns in the corner of the sitting room. Johnny saw that one of them was a Springfield Army rifle and the other was what the Government called a light machine rifle, though it was twice as heavy as a Springfield and was only light when compared with a machine gun. You could come by a Springfield honestly enough, but the Government did not sell the light machine rifle to anybody. Johnny had never seen one before. But he knew the gun by the pictures he had pored over in Grampa's shop.

"We've been hunting," the tall man said. He nodded toward the rifles and smiled at Johnny.

It was all right to say you were hunting in March, if you needed the meat. No native would report you to the game warden for killing a deer out of season. But city men with a big car had no business hunting deer in March. And did they think he was so stupid as to believe that anybody would hunt deer with anything so heavy and clumsy as the Government's light machine rifle?

"I guess I'd better show you your room before I go to bed," Johnny said.

"All right, bub," the tall man said. Johnny noticed how tired he was. His eyes were bloodshot. He looked as if he hadn't slept for days. His face was a kind of dirty gray.

Johnny showed them the spare room. It had two beds.

"The stove doesn't heat much in here," Johnny said. "But there are plenty of blankets."

"You haven't got a telephone?" the tall man said.

"No," Johnny said. "The nearest telephone is at Johnson's."

"How far is that?"

"It's twelve miles from here," Johnny said. The tall man nodded.

Johnny showed him how to turn off the drafts of the chunk stove before he went to bed, so the fire would smolder all night instead of burning out. Johnny said good night politely and climbed the ladder into the dark, cold loft. He found his flashlight on the shelf beside his bed. He took off his shoes and rolled under the covers and listened.

The two men sat at the sitting room table and talked. At first their voices were so low Johnny could not distinguish the words. He put his ear close to a stud at the head of his bed. He could hear a good deal better. The two men were drinking whisky, and as they drank, their voices grew louder. Johnny could hear every word they said. But some of their words puzzled him.

"This place would make a good refrigerator." Johnny recognized the short man's voice. He had hardly said a word all evening, but he was talking freely now.

The tall man disagreed. "You don't know country people, Al," he said. "They've got nothing better to do than watch a stranger. The country gets hot fast."

They got nasty with each other as they drank. They reminded each other of things. They had a long argument about where they would go in the morning. The tall man got impatient.

"Listen, Al," he said, "as soon as we bump this guy off, we're going to Buffalo - to Joe's."

Johnny lay there, his heart pounding. At last they went to bed. Johnny heard them arguing about the drafts in the chunk stove, and then they went into the bedroom.

Johnny waited. He had no way of telling time. He waited until he was sure he had waited an hour, and then he waited some more. He put his flashlight in his pocket and crawled on his hands and knees toward the ladder. It was slow going because so many of the boards creaked. He opened the trapdoor and listened. He could hear a snore. He listened until he heard two distinct snores. He went down the ladder backwards, in his stocking feet.

The corner where they had stood their guns was empty. They had taken their guns into the bedroom with them. Johnny turned the lamp low and stole to the open bedroom door and listened. He got the flashlight out of his pocket and took a quick look inside the room. They had gone to bed with their clothes on.

They had each hung a .45 Government automatic pistol on a bedpost. The holsters were the kind that hang under your armpit.

Johnny stole back into the kitchen, and shut the door, and lit the bracket lamp. It was cold in the kitchen. Johnny turned on the drafts and, taking great pains not to make any noise, put some kindling on the coals. It was one o'clock by the alarm clock on the shelf. He ought to make Johnson's in three hours, even in the dark. Ole Johnson had a car as well as a telephone. He'd get word to Wood's Junction. The sheriff would form a posse. But somebody would get killed. His father might get killed.

Johnny thought it out. He might sneak in and get their guns without waking them up. But when they did wake up they'd know. They might have more guns in that car they'd locked up so carefully before they came in.

He might take the cartridges out and throw them away. But when they awoke they might look at their guns, opening them part way to make sure they were loaded and ready to fire. That was what men who were used to guns would do. And if they did that, they'd find out their guns had been unloaded. They might have more cartridges in their pockets. They probably had more cartridges in the car.

Johnny thought of using lard. But he hunted through the cupboard, moving tins cautiously, until he found a coffee can half full of thin cakes of bullet lubricant. He had watched Grampa make it, rendering down mutton tallow and straining it, putting in bayberry wax and a little cylinder oil, and stirring in finely powdered graphite. Johnny put a cake of the stuff in a clean pan and put the pan on the fire. When the lubricant melted, he set it to one side where it would keep warm.

He opened the kitchen door and listened. They were still snoring. Johnny stole across the sitting room. He located the machine rifle with the flashlight and put the flashlight back in his pocket. He took the rifle in both hands and walked as slowly and as softly as he could back into the kitchen. The gun was very heavy, heavier than Grampa's pet Schuetzen rifle. Johnny had to figure how to open it. But he did it. He made sure there was a cartridge in the chamber.

He stood the butt of the rifle on the floor. It was almost as tall as he was. He put a small funnel in the muzzle. He poured the bullet lube into the muzzle, a little at a time, so it would cool against the cold steel. He poured the barrel almost full. Then he carried the rifle back and set it up where he had found it and got the Springfield.

He took the Springfield to the kitchen and opened the bolt part way and made sure there was a cartridge in the chamber, and then he filled the bore almost to the muzzle with the bullet lubricant.

It was ticklish, getting the two automatics out of their holsters. He had to stand in the dark, within a foot of the tall man's head, and work one gun gently out of its holster and then the other. He found, when he got back to the kitchen with the automatics, that the slides were very stiff. He had to pull and pull against the spring to get those guns open enough to make sure there was a cartridge in the chamber. And he had to be sure. If the chamber was empty, the bullet lubricant would fill it and the man wouldn't be able to get a cartridge in and he would know something was wrong. But if the cartridge was in the chamber, the grease would only fill the space ahead of it. If the man opened the slide a little way to make sure it was ready to fire, he'd see the brass of the case and think everything was all right.

Johnny filled the barrels of the two automatics with bullet lube and got one of them back in its holster. The tall man stirred and turned over. Johnny waited, trying not to breathe, until he snored again. Johnny pressed the flashlight switch to see just where he was and where the holster was. He almost cried out. The tall man was bald. His thick hair had slipped over on the pillow while he slept. It was a wig.

Johnny got the gun into the holster and went back into the kitchen. He had left his shoes in the loft. He'd have to get them. He couldn't walk twelve miles over a rough and frozen road in his stocking feet. He climbed the ladder and crept over to his bed and got his shoes. He tied the laces together and hung the shoes over his neck so he'd have both hands free, crawling back to the ladder and climbing down.

It was two in the morning by the alarm clock on the kitchen shelf. He'd have to hurry. He turned the wick of the bracket lamp low. He had his hand on the knob of the kitchen door when he heard one of the men stir. Johnny waited. The man suddenly came staggering out of bed and toward the kitchen. Johnny hadn't time to do anything. It was the tall man.

The tall man picked up a tumbler and looked about for water and saw Johnny.

He didn't say a word. He got his glass of water and drank it thirstily. He looked at Johnny.

"Where you going, bub?" he asked.

"Out," Johnny said.

The tall man grabbed Johnny by the collar and shoved him into the sitting room and over to the ladder. "Up," he said.

Johnny climbed the ladder. The tall man followed him part way and pulled the trapdoor shut. Johnny could hear him fumbling with the big wooden button that fastened the trapdoor shut. He tried the door to make sure it was fastened. Johnny heard him going back to bed.

The window at the end of the loft was too small to climb through. He couldn't get out. He was trapped.

Johnny lay in bed, shaking with fear. He lay there for hours until he heard the two men getting up. They were starting up the kitchen fire. The tall man came into the sitting room and yelled up at Johnny.

"Where's the coffee, bub?" he demanded.

"I don't know," Johnny said. "But I could find it."

The tall man opened the trap. "Come on down," he said.

Johnny put on his shoes and climbed down and hunted in the kitchen cupboard. He had shifted things around the night before, hunting for the bullet grease.

The tall man had found the coffee can of bullet lubricant, but he didn't know what it was. He only knew it wasn't coffee.

Johnny sat in a corner while they ate their breakfast. It was nearly seven o'clock. Johnny listened for the sound of the car. He had to hear the car before they did. It was his only chance for warning his father and his mother and Grampa.

"I'd better put some wood in the chunk stove," Johnny said.

"All right," the tall man said.

Johnny went into the sitting room. He paused and listened and dropped a chunk in the stove. He listened again and dropped another chunk.

"Come on back here," the tall man said.

"I'm coming," Johnny said. He listened again. He heard the car. He waited for the right moment.

Johnny ran for the kitchen door. He got outdoors before they could stop him. The car was almost at Grampa's shop. Johnny waved his hands and yelled. The car stopped alongside Grampa's shop just as the tall man got Johnny by the collar.

The short man came running out of the house with the machine rifle. Johnny saw Grampa motion his father and mother to get behind the car. Grampa went into the shop.

"Hold it," the tall man said. "Hold it until you can see a head."

The short man rested the barrel of the machine rifle on the hood of his car and trained it on the other car.

"Here comes the old man," the tall man said.

Grampa came out of his shop. He had the hunting gun. He walked toward Johnny and the tall man. He was keeping a tree between himself and the man with the machine rifle as he walked. He reached the tree. There was no more cover. Grampa had to expose himself to shoot.

"Now," the tall man said, and as he spoke he threw both arms around Johnny and held him up as a shield.

Johnny could feel the man's chin pressing into the back of his head.

The machine rifle went off with a sound much louder and duller than a .30-06 usually makes. The short man stood there with a piece of the stock in his hands and blood running down his face. The rifle had blown apart in his hands.

Johnny saw Grampa raise his rifle and point it straight at him. The tall man held Johnny tightly. Grampa hadn't much to shoot at above Johnny's head. But Johnny knew he had enough. Grampa could pull one plumb when he had to.

Grampa's rifle cracked and the arms around Johnny went suddenly limp and the man who held him slumped. Johnny ran toward his Grampa. As he ran he heard an explosion behind him. The short man had fired his automatic pistol. The short man was standing up still, but he reeled as he stood. His pistol was no longer a pistol. It was a twisted piece of steel.

"It's all right, Grampa," Johnny said, "I fixed their guns."

And then Johnny was in his mother's arms and she was calling him, "My baby! My poor baby!" and Johnny's father was saying how lucky it was that the short man's gun had blown up.

Grampa snorted. "Lucky," he said. "Lucky!?" He turned to Johnny. "What did you do?"

"I used some of your bullet lube," Johnny said. "I melted it and poured it into the barrels while they were asleep."

His father and mother didn't know what he was talking about. But Grampa knew.

"Now they'll have to let you have a gun," he said. "Now they'll believe you know about rifles."

CENTER SHOT TO WIN

J.M. Pyne was busy at the bench in his shop in the North Woods, just as he had been busy at a bench every morning for 50 years when he wasn't at a rifle match.

He was old and tired. He wore two pairs of spectacles and used a magnifying glass besides when he wanted to read the micrometer to a ten-thousandth. But he could still do it. He was slower than he had been, and a year or two farther behind with his orders from the rifle cranks who wouldn't let him alone until they got a Pyne barrel. But he could still make a better rifle barrel than anybody else.

He was embittered by the failure of his eyes. He cursed his body, which was small and no longer tireless. He still had that curious knot of muscle and sinew, the swelling as big as his fist, where his neck joined his shoulder. It looked as if his collar bone had been broken and badly set. His collar bone hadn't been broken. The swelling of muscle had come from shooting a heavy rifle off-hand for a hundred and 200 and 300 shots in a day. He had still the knowledge gained in 40 years of competitive shooting. He had still the indomitable heart that had carried him on to win so many long matches against the best shots in the world. But his left wrist was weak from an injury. He could no longer hold a heavy rifle for more than a few shots. And what good is a light rifle for fine work?

J.M. Pyne would never shoot another hundred-shot match. But he had a kind of peace here in the North Woods that he hadn't known before, not even in the old Hartford shop when he had given up his profession of mechanical engineer to work 15 and 16 hours a day making rifles, and had never taken a day off except to shoot. He was living alone now. He felt secure from interruption. He had no telephone. The nearest telephone was

119

at Johnson's, 12 miles away. He had no rural free delivery. Johnson brought the mail and the groceries up every Saturday night. And now that summer was gone, even the most determined customers were unlikely to drive so far into the woods to ask, "Where is that barrel?"

Mr. Pyne felt free to take his time. He could do things in his own way. He had fought the Ordnance officers with fierce glee when he made the barrels for the International Rifle Team, refusing flatly to cut them the way that the armory cut them. But now he could do whatever he liked, without stopping to argue.

He bent close over the chambering reamer he was stoning. A chambering reamer had to be just so. He reached for the micrometer, and as he did so he heard a car outside. He paused to listen. It was a big car - a city car. Mr. Pyne sighed. He wouldn't be truly secure until the snow came and made the road impassable to cars. He heard a knock on the door and called out.

Two young men came in and picked their way around packing cases and the rifling machine and a rack of barrel stock toward the bench. One was tall, with sideburns and a pale face. The other was short and plump. Mr. Pyne guessed that they were foreigners, even before they spoke.

"Mr. Pyne," the plump young man said, "my name is Jimenez, and this is my friend, Juan Moreno."

Mr. Pyne shook hands with them both. Jimenez spoke a precise English, with only a trace of a tendency to say "wiz" for "with". Moreno spoke Spanish.

"We have come to ask a great favor of you, Mr. Pyne," Jimenez said. "We wish to know if you would take a brief trip with us in your professional capacity to" - he paused and looked Mr. Pyne in the eye - "to look at some machine guns and tell us if they are good."

Mr. Pyne shook his head. "I don't know much about machine guns," he said. He was surprised. He had taken on many an odd task in the interests of experiment and research, but no one had ever sought him out as a machine-gun expert before. "Machine guns are out of my line," he continued. "And I can't take the time. I'm three years behind with the work I've got in here now."

Jimenez had a winning smile. "We know we are asking a great

120

deal, Mr. Pyne," he said. "But it will take a few days only. You may, of course, charge what you think it is worth. I can assure you that to us it would be worth a large sum."

"I can't do it," Mr. Pyne said. "But there are plenty of men who could do it better than I could. Why did you come to me?"

Jimenez took a letter out of his pocket. "I have a note of introduction from a old friend of yours, Mr. Herrick, who now resides in my country."

"Not Joe Herrick!" Mr. Pyne said. He had supposed Joe Herrick was dead. He hadn't seen him or heard of him since the last Zettler Club championship, when the war was on. He read:

Dear John:

This is to introduce two young friends of mine - Pablo Jimenez and Juan Moreno. They are all right. If you were down here you would be on the same side of the fence. I would appreciate it if you would tell them what they want to know.

I have told them about you and your rifles and your shooting. While you are about it, show them a Pyne muzzleloader. The .32-40 you made for me is back home in Springfield. I tried it, muzzle and elbow rest, before I put it away, just to be sure it was all right. It was late of one of those Indian-summer afternoons when the light is soft - you know the kind. I got a group of ten shots at 200 yards that was just covered by a silver dollar. Will anything made by man shoot like a Pyne muzzleloader up to 200 yards? I don't think so.

I saw Will Harwood eleven or twelve years ago in Miami. He said your beard had got as white as your hair, but that you were still good enough to win the Election Day match that year - it must have been 1922. You must be 75 now - I'm 73. I know you never answer letters, but if you should answer this one, tell me whether they still shoot the Election Day match and whether, if they do, they are still in a class with us old-timers when it comes to shooting an off-hand gun.

Yours,

J.H. Herrick.

Mr. Pyne wiped his spectacles. The letter stirred old memories. Few men nowadays knew what a Pyne muzzleloader was or about the kind of matches in which Pyne muzzleloaders had been supreme for more than 30 years. He made .22 match barrels nowadays, and .30 caliber long-range guns.

"Where," he said to Jimenez - "where are these machine guns you're interested in?"

Jimenez shrugged his shoulders and smiled that engaging smile of his.

"They have not told us exactly where they have stored the guns. Naturally. It is a secret, for the reason that your Government would frown upon the transaction. We are to meet them in Boston tomorrow. They have some sort of yacht. They will take us to the place."

Mr. Pyne stroked his beard.

"Our government," Jimenez continued, "would be so annoyed wiz us if they caught us that they would shoot us, without waiting for the sun to rise."

"What about the people who are selling the guns?"

"In my opinion," Jimenez said, "they are very bad boys. That is why we came to you. We might be fooled. You cannot be fooled."

"It would be better to deal with people you have confidence in," Mr. Pyne said.

"There are two reasons for dealing with these people," Jimenez said. "In the first place, they are offering us a bargain. They will sell us machine guns that cost $700 apiece for $300 apiece, because they are not brand new. We have a lot of money in a New York bank, but it is clear we can buy twice as many of these guns as of new ones. Secondhand guns will serve our purpose if they are in good working order. In the second place, these guns are stored at some lonely spot on the seashore, from which it is easy to ship them without making explanations to anybody."

Mr. Pyne reflected that it was a long time since he had taken a vacation. He sat down on the cot in the corner and kicked off his shop slippers and fished around for his street shoes.

"You're going with us!" Jimenez exclaimed.

"If Joe Herrick says you're all right," Mr. Pyne said, "you are all right."

Jimenez thanked him with feeling and explained in quick Spanish to his friend Moreno.

Mr. Pyne got his shoes on and opened his shooting bag. He hadn't used the bag for several years. He never went anywhere without a few fine files and several screwdrivers especially shaped and tempered for gun work. He would want his micrometer and his magnifying glass and some 00 buck shot in order to slug the machine-gun barrels and find out what they were like inside. It would be sensible to take a revolver also. But the only revolver in the shop was one a customer had sent in to be fitted with a Pyne target barrel.

"Mr. Pyne," Jimenez said, "we are, of course, in a great hurry. It is a long drive to Boston. But would you take a few moments to show us one of your muzzle-loading rifles?"

Mr. Pyne picked up the stock and action of his off-hand gun. "I took it apart the other day," he said. "I use the action to test new barrels. But I can show you the barrel."

"It looks exactly like a single-shot, breech-loading rifle," Jimenez said.

"It is both a breechloader and a muzzleloader," Mr. Pyne said. He got the barrel and the false muzzle and the bullet starter. "You can shoot it exactly as you would any other rifle, with fixed ammunition such as you buy in a store. Or you can put the bullet in at the breech and push the charged shell in behind it. Or you can seat the bullet through the muzzle with the bullet starter and push it down with the rod, and put the loaded shell in the breech."

He showed them just how it was done.

"Most people suppose that a rifle that is perfectly aimed will put one bullet on top of another at 200 yards. It won't. With fixed ammunition, this rifle will spread 10 successive shots over five or six inches at 200 yards; with the bullet seated in the breech ahead of the shell it will shoot in three to four inches; with the bullet loaded through the muzzle, it will usually shoot in two inches, and often in less."

He showed them his prize group - a bit of paper in which all 10 shots broke into one hole. He laid a dime on the group.

"There," he said, "you will see that every one of those bullets would have hit the dime. That was shot with a Pyne muzzleloader at 200 yards with a telescope sight and a rest. But don't take it too seriously - so far as I know, it never happened but once."

"I wish you would show us how it shoots," Jimenez said. "Why don't you bring the rifle with you?"

"Well --," Mr. Pyne said. He loved to shoot that gun. "It weighs 13 pounds with the telescope sight."

"Put the stock and action in your bag," Jimenez said. "The barrel will go in my portmanteau."

"That barrel is 32 inches long," Mr. Pyne said.

"It will go in," Jimenez said.

Mr. Pyne put the telescope sight in his bag, and the powder flask, and a box of lubricated bullets, and empty shells, and primers, and the re- and de-capper. He felt like a small boy playing hooky from school. But he wanted to play hooky. He locked the shop and stopped at the house for his overcoat and a spare shirt or two, and got into the car with Jimenez and Moreno.

They arrived late the following afternoon at the back room of a saloon in South Boston. Mr. Pyne studied with interest the three men they met there - an enormous man whose name was Katz, and a slim, sleek, dark chap in a closely fitted double-breasted jacket and freshly creased trousers who was called Frankie, and a thug with notably outstanding ears who was called Dutch.

Katz jerked a thumb at Mr. Pyne, but addressed Jimenez. "Where," Katz asked, "did you pick up Santa Claus?"

"My friend's name is Pyne - J.M. Pyne," Jimenez said coldly. "He knows about guns. For that reason we asked him to come with us. He has very kindly consented."

"Is he all right?" Katz demanded.

"I vouch for him," Jimenez said.

"Maybe we can find a bunk for him," Katz said.

They drove to a place on the Connecticut River that night and boarded a good-sized schooner with auxiliary power. Mr. Pyne found himself in a tiny cabin. He heard the men on deck casting off; he felt the throb of the propeller; he went to sleep. When he awoke several hours later, he heard the seas pounding on the schooner's starboard bow. He guessed they were well offshore. He went to sleep again.

He went out on deck the next morning. There was a stiff breeze abeam, but the schooner was still trudging along under power, with no sail set. Either she was short-handed or the crew weren't sailors. She couldn't be making more than six knots. He looked up. The sky was dull, but it was easy enough to tell where the sun was. He guessed that the schooner was heading a little north of east. She was going outside Cape Cod.

It was bright and warm for the season as the schooner ran in toward shore late in the afternoon of the third day. Mr. Pyne stood on deck forward. The cliff ran right down to the beach, leaving only a narrow strip of sand at high tide.

He saw a rough pier and beyond, on shore, a rambling cottage of logs and unpainted boards. The house stood in a grassy plain, 20 or 30 acres in extent, rimmed with high rocky walls.

Jimenez came down the deck and stood at Mr. Pyne's elbow. They hadn't had a chance to exchange a private word since they had joined Katz and Frankie and Dutch.

"The longer I know our host," Jimenez said in Mr. Pyne's ear, "the happier I am that there is a big .45 in the holster under my arm."

Mr. Pyne nodded grimly. He pointed to the shore. Three men were coming down the pier to greet the schooner.

"That makes," Jimenez said, "a total of nine, counting the crew of this schooner. It is three to one."

"Katz is coming," Mr. Pyne said quietly.

Jimenez turned to Katz.

"Gentlemen," Katz said, pointing shoreward, "how is that for a lovely spot?"

"It is charming," Jimenez said.

"A big shot in Wall Street built it before he went broke," Katz said. "He wanted no neighbors. He certainly got it. There ain't another house in 20 miles. Which suits us."

They went ashore. There was an open fire in the living room and a hearty supper waiting. Katz showed them around afterward by the light of a lantern. He led the way into a good-sized building beyond the kitchen. It was piled high with boxes of machine guns, leaving merely an aisle down the middle.

Katz opened the door at the end of the aisle and swung the lantern.

"That's a workshop," he said.

Mr. Pyne caught a glimpse of a bench with a vise and a grinder and two or three belts. They must have some kind of power - a gasoline engine probably.

Katz showed them bedrooms on the second floor and sent Dutch and another man to get their luggage off the schooner. Mr. Pyne got a chance to tell Jimenez to take the barrel of his rifle out of his portmanteau and stand it in a corner where he could find it easily. Mr. Pyne went to bed and turned the oil lamp low and propped himself up with his pillow and smoked one cigarette after another and listened.

Katz and his men were having a good time below. They hadn't done much drinking on the schooner. They were making up for their abstinence now. Mr. Pyne waited for hours. When it was quiet, he got a small electric flashlight out of his shooting bag and crept on his hands and knees down the corridor and into the room where Jimenez and Moreno slept. He got the barrel of his rifle and crept back into his own room. He took the stock and action out of his shooting bag. He put the barrel in the action and turned it up as much as he could with his hands. It wasn't a take-down rifle. He had to have a vise to set the barrel up to the mark.

He went down the stairs. He couldn't crawl with the long heavy rifle in his hand. He had to walk upright, with one hand on the rail, and slowly shift his weight from one foot to the other. His old joints ached with the effort. He went through the kitchen, through the shed full of machine guns, into the workshop.

He laid the flashlight on the bench so it gave some light on the vise. He had no clamps with which to protect the barrel from the vise jaws. He had to mar it. But it didn't matter much. The vise jaws wouldn't hurt the inside of the barrel, and it was the inside that mattered.

Mr. Pyne got slowly and painfully back up the stairs. He went to the window and looked out. It was getting lighter. He got a screwdriver out of his shooting bag and took out the lever pin and fitted the extractor back in the action. The rifle was ready to go, except for the telescope sight. He decided to put the scope on. He couldn't see iron sights any more.

He put the rifle under the mattress on the far side of his bed. He was all in. But he might have no other chance to explore the ground. He got into his clothes and went downstairs and outdoors. He walked north. The cliff came clear down to the sea on the north. He turned back, following the bottom of the cliff, looking for a path up. There must be a way to the high ground above. But he saw no way out that did not require hard climbing, except along the beach to the south and west. The beach curved deeply. It curved so deeply that a man would have to run a mile and a half, perhaps farther, before he got more than a thousand yards away.

J.M. Pyne got back to his room at half-past six. It was broad daylight, but the house was still silent. He was so tired he slumped on the bed. But he had one more thing to do before he went to sleep.

He got the powder flask out of the shooting bag. It had to be fastened upright, so the powder would flow out through a tube at the bottom into a shell as he worked the lever. He'd made a cast-iron fixture with a wood screw on the back by which he could hang up the powder flask. He was glad he had formed the habit of dropping the fixture into the flask so he wouldn't forget it. He got the fixture now, and pushing with trembling hands, he got the screw deep enough in the window casing to hold.

He found the small square bottle of post-card wads and the primers. He had only six shells. He ordinarily used but one shell in shooting the muzzleloader, recapping and recharging it after each shot. But six were little enough for what he felt was coming. He primed the six shells and held them under the powder measure one by one and pushed the lever back and forth and filled them, each with its measured charge. He pressed the wads tightly down on the powder with a lead pencil.

He put the primed and charged shells and a little pasteboard box of lubricated bullets in one side pocket of his coat. He wrapped the false muzzle and starter in a handkerchief and put them in the other side pocket. Then he hung his coat on a chair and slept. He slept until he felt a hand on his shoulder.

"It is late," Jimenez said. "I have been awake for hours. It is nearly noon."

Mr. Pyne climbed laboriously out of bed. He stretched one arm cautiously and then one leg. He was full of aches. He always felt 20 years older when he woke up in the morning than when he went to bed the night before. He always felt as if he would never walk again.

"Today," Jimenez said, "we test machine guns."

"If I were you," Mr. Pyne said, "I'd let them shoot the guns. And if a gun jams when it's shot, I'd step back fast."

"Quite so," Jimenez said. "I will tell Moreno."

They had breakfast with Katz and Dutch and Frankie and the three men who had been at the camp when they arrived. The crew of the schooner had arrived. The crew of the schooner had slept aboard her.

"Now," Katz said, "we will show you how well these guns shoot."

They carried a gun out in three parts and put it together. It was a fairly heavy gun. Dutch got a belt of ammunition. He seemed to know his business. Mr. Pyne guessed that he had trained in some army. He sat the spade into the ground and made sure the barrel was clear. He started the belt in the feed box and threw the cocking lever back and squatted down behind the gun. He looked over his shoulder at the little group behind him - at Katz and Frankie and Jimenez and Moreno and Mr. Pyne.

"Let's go," Dutch said.

The gun suddenly burst forth with a series of sharp, tearing explosions. Dutch stopped it, gave the butt a tap with the heel of his hand, and fired another burst, while the cliffs echoed and re-echoed.

"It's a noisy little toy," Katz said.

Mr. Pyne went up and looked at the gun, peering at the breech mechanism through his two pairs of spectacles.

128

"Well, Santa Claus," Mr. Katz said, "does it shoot? Or couldn't you hear it?"

"I heard it," Mr. Pyne said.

"Are you satisfied?" Katz demanded.

"Yes," Mr. Pyne said, "I'm satisfied."

"We'll get out another one," Katz said.

Mr. Pyne followed them back to the shed. They took down a box and ripped it open. It came open so easily that Mr. Pyne guessed it had been open before. He lingered behind as the three men carried the gun out of the shed. He got another box open and lifted the barrel out and put it in the workshop vise and studied the breech of the barrel and the receiver with his magnifying glass. He nodded grimly. He took a file and tested the metal lightly in several places.

"What are you doing, Santa Claus?" Katz yelled in the doorway.

"Just looking," Mr. Pyne said.

"Come on out," Katz said.

Mr. Pyne went obediently outdoors and joined Jimenez and Moreno. Mr. Pyne saw that Jimenez was trying to catch his eye. Mr. Pyne looked away. He didn't want to tell Jimenez anything just then. He thought Jimenez would run less risk if he didn't know the truth until later.

Dutch fired the second gun in a succession of short bursts.

"Well, Santa Claus," Katz said, "is it a gun or isn't it?"

"It's a gun," Mr. Pyne said mildly.

"Are you satisfied, Mr. Jimenez?" Katz asked.

"I am delighted," Jimenez said.

"Let's all have a drink," Katz said.

Mr. Pyne guessed they would test no more machine guns that day, and he was glad. It gave him time. He watched and waited. He watched and waited until after dinner that night before he got a chance to speak a few words in Jimenez's ear.

"Does Katz know that you and Moreno can sign a check on your New York funds?"

Jimenez nodded.

"Go to bed early then," Mr. Pyne said. "I'll wake you up before dawn. We're getting out of here as soon as it's light enough to see our way."

"But I thought........," Jimenez began.

"Don't argue," Mr. Pyne said. "I know what I'm talking about."

J.M. Pyne went up to his room. He opened his shooting bag. He knew just how he had left the things in it. Somebody had been through it since. But his rifle was still under the mattress. They hadn't known he had it. They hadn't looked hard enough to find it.

He laid his watch out on the floor beside his bed with the electric flashlight beside it. The battery was feeble. But it would give enough light to see the time by. He composed himself for sleep. He knew he could wake up almost on the minute.

He was wide awake at five o'clock. He got his shoes and his coat and hat. He took the rifle out from under the mattress and dropped a bullet in the breech and pushed a charged shell home after it and slowly closed the action, so it would not snap loudly.

He went down the corridor in his stocking feet and into the bedroom where Jimenez and Moreno slept. He pulled gently at the covers until they awoke. He led the way downstairs and outdoors. When they were well clear of the house they sat down and put on their shoes.

"What's happened?" Jimenez asked.

"Shush!" Mr. Pyne said.

When they reached the point where the beach began to curve away, Mr. Pyne thrust a stick in the sand. From then on, he took longer strides and counted the strides. He had almost reached the big pine he'd noted the day before, lying across the beach with its top in the water, when he heard a yell somewhere behind him. He looked back, but he couldn't see much at that distance.

"They're coming out of the house," Jimenez said. "I can see them running."

"Hurry on, then," Mr. Pyne said. "I'm staying here. I can't keep up with you. I'll lie down behind this log. I've got a gun. I can stop them."

"We've got guns too," Jimenez said. He jerked out his big automatic.

"You can't hit anything much with it beyond 50 or 75 yards," Mr. Pyne said. "Even if it's loaded."

Jimenez pulled the magazine out. It was empty. He spoke excitedly to Moreno. The magazine of Moreno's pistol was empty also.

"Now will you go?" Mr. Pyne said. "Run."

"They've got a machine gun," Jimenez said. "They're carrying it out of the shed."

"I've got a rifle that shoots where it's held," Mr. Pyne said. "Run!"

He said it so fiercely that they went.

Mr. Pyne knelt behind the tree trunk. It was a trifle farther than he'd guessed. It was almost exactly 200 yards. The scope sight was set for 200. There wasn't a trace of wind. He calculated once again just how much higher the gun shot when you rested the barrel on something firm, like a tree trunk, instead of on your left hand. He made the correction and looked through the scope at the men with the machine gun. He could see every movement they made. There was scarcely more than half daylight. But the scope gathered light.

Three men had the gun. Dutch was jamming the spade down in the sand. A fourth man was running back for something. It must be for the ammunition belt. Dutch was training the machine gun on Jimenez and Moreno up the beach. Mr. Pyne guessed that Dutch couldn't see much over the open sights of the machine gun in this light. But he knew his business. He'd fire a burst that he knew was short and see where it threw up the water. Then he'd fire another burst. He'd get them in three or four bursts, sights or no sights, unless they found a place where they could climb the cliff.

Mr. Pyne set the rear trigger. He disliked the first shot through a clean, oiled barrel. It often went off center. He wanted a fouled barrel. And a shot over their heads would distract them for a moment. He touched the set trigger.

131

He picked up the false muzzle as the gun boomed out. He started a bullet and rammed it home. He put a fresh shell in the breech. He rested the barrel on the tree trunk again and looked through the scope. Dutch had the belt of ammunition now. The others were staring in the direction from which Mr. Pyne's shot had come. Dutch had the end of the belt in place.

Mr. Pyne held the crosshairs on the feed box of the machine gun. It wasn't much more than an inch high and three inches wide. The crosshairs divided the space neatly. He felt the way he had often felt when firing his last shot in a hundred-shot off-hand match. You couldn't try to pull every shot plumb center when you were shooting a long match off-hand. It couldn't be done and you only tired yourself out trying. You mostly had to take what you could get. But when it came to the end, you could try for plumb center. He'd had to have a center shot the last time up to win the Election Day match ten years ago that Will Harwood had told Joe Herrick about. He'd had to have a center shot to win, then, and he'd got it. Now he needed a center shot to win. It wouldn't do to shoot Dutch. Some other man would take over the gun. He had to wreck the gun.

Mr. Pyne touched the set trigger gently. The gun boomed and set back against his arm and cheek with the old familiar push. He looked through the scope. He smiled grimly. Dutch was jerking at the belt. He wasn't firing the machine gun. Mr. Pyne's bullet had gone into the feed box and cut the belt and smashed up the two cartridges lying on the flat lower side of the box and jammed the gun.

Mr. Pyne reloaded his rifle deliberately. An Army machine-gun crew would have a spare feed box and tools at hand. But Dutch had neither a spare nor tools. He was trying desperately to clear the feed box with his bare hands. He couldn't do it.

Mr. Pyne looked up the beach. He squinted through the telescope. Jimenez and Moreno were climbing the cliff. They'd found a place where they could get up. In another minute they'd be out of sight.

He looked back at Dutch. He was still fighting with the feed box. The bullet must have jammed up the pawls or the extractor.

Mr. Pyne got up and put his rifle over his shoulder and walked down the beach after Jimenez and Moreno. He walked slowly. He was old and tired and the rifle was heavy. His coat dragged on his shoulders with the weight of the false muzzle and starter and the bullets in his pockets.

Jimenez and Moreno were waiting for him. He told them to go on - to get to a telegraph office as fast as they could. He couldn't keep up with them.

"No," Jimenez said. "We will carry your rifle and your tools. Besides, we must talk. What happened? What was the matter with those guns?"

"There was nothing the matter with the ones they shot for us," Mr. Pyne said. "But the rest were the sort the Government sells for the price of scrap steel. Do you know what they do to them before they sell them? They burn gashes through the receiver and the rear part of the barrel with an oxyacetylene flame. Katz bought those guns for a cent or two a pound. He got some mechanic to solder up the gashes and grind the surplus metal down smooth and paint the solder blue-black like the rest of the gun. They looked all right at first glance, but they'd have blown up at the first shot."

"Why didn't you say so?" Jimenez asked.

Mr. Pyne shook his head. "He would have tried to make you pay for them just the same. He would have tortured you until you paid, or until he had to kill you."

Jimenez shook his head. "Even so, I do not know if I can turn informer."

"I can," Mr. Pyne said. "And I will. He won't sell those guns to anybody else. The Government will dump them into the sea."

133

J.M. SHOOTS TWICE

J.M. Pyne saw little flurries of snow outside the shop windows. The leaves were gone, except for those that still clung tightly to the oak trees. The meadow out toward the target butt was brown. It was hunting weather. But he couldn't go deer hunting again. He wasn't up to it. He would have to tell young Ballentyne so. He would have to tell him that he was 75, and no longer able to face the rigors of days afield.

He took a rifle barrel out of the boiling solution in the bluing tank. He held it by a wooden plug in each end of the bore. He had a circular wire brush mounted in the lathe. He pressed the barrel gently against the revolving brush, rolling it and drawing it back and forth to reach every part of the surface. The dull black turned brighter under the brush. It approached the dark-blue color that riflemen admire.

He heard a knock at the door and called out. Young Tim Ballentyne came in with a rifle in a leather case hanging from his shoulder. He waited until J.M. Pyne had finished brushing the barrel and put it back in the tank for another coat of the solution.

"I should have answered your letter," J.M. Pyne said. Young Ballentyne knew that he almost never answered letters.

"But you are going with me?"

J.M. Pyne shook his head. He always shook his head nowadays.

"We won't be gone long. I've just five days away from school."

"I've sold my hunting gun," J.M. Pyne said.

"The one with the twenty-two punch marks for twenty-two deer with twenty-two shots?"

J.M. Pyne nodded. The fellow had said that he wanted to give it to a museum.

"But you've got something in the shop you can shoot," young Ballentyne said.

J.M. Pyne straightened his shoulders painfully. It was only mid-afternoon, but his shoulders ached.

"Let's see your rifle," he said.

Young Ballentyne took the rifle out of the case and handed it over with pride. It was a bolt-action repeating rifle with a stock of fine curly walnut, new and spotless.

J.M. Pyne thought it was clubby. It lacked the grace of the long-barreled, single-shot rifles that he loved. Too much of the weight was in the thick action and too little in the slender muzzle. But he knew it was strong and simple and sound. You could take the action apart without tools.

"You don't really like it," young Ballentyne said.

"It's a fine rifle," J.M. Pyne said. "I don't know of anything better than a bolt-action rifle for the .30-06 cartridge."

"But you like single-shot rifles better."

"Well," J.M. Pyne said, "I like them better for my own use."

He went to the cupboard in the corner and got out the old long-range .30 caliber rifle he had built for himself thirty years ago on a Sharps-Borchardt action. The Sharps Company had gone when the buffalo went. But their actions were well made. The rifle had a long vernier rear sight on the heel of the stock. It was designed for the old way of shooting at a thousand yards, when you lay on your back and put your left arm behind your head to grasp the butt and rested the barrel on your crossed legs.

"It's awfully long," young Ballentyne said.

"Thirty-four-inch barrel," J.M. Pyne said. "Barrel had to be long for shooting on your back, or else you were likely to shoot yourself in the leg."

He put the rifle in the vise and ran a swab of absorbent cotton through it to take out the oil and the dust. He held the muzzle up to the light and looked through the bore. It had been shot a good deal with heavy charges and jacketed bullets. But the curving knife edges of the narrow lands were only slightly rounded. The rifle would still shoot.

"You could take off that wind gauge in front and put on something else and move the rear sight up on the tang," young Ballentyne said.

J.M. Pyne shook his head. "I don't believe I've got any cartridge cases left. I chambered the rifle for an odd case I swaged down from the old .38-72. You can't buy cartridges for it."

He handed the rifle to young Ballentyne and hunted through piles of cigar boxes. He found the right box and laid it on the bench. There were fifteen or twenty of the old cartridge cases, dark with corrosion and cracked at the neck, and a few of the bullets, with a narrow swaged band at the base.

Young Ballentyne could not restrain his curiosity. He hunted through the box.

"Here!" he said. "Here are two brand new ones, never fired."

J.M. Pyne took them. They hadn't been fired. He picked up a bullet and showed young Ballentyne that it was a push fit.

"I reamed the inside of every case neck in the lathe," he said. "The outside fits the chamber and the inside fits the bullet."

Young Ballentyne hunted eagerly through the box for more cartridge cases. There were no more good ones.

"If you could find just a few more," young Ballentyne said, "you could use the gun. You won't need more than ten cartridges on a deer hunt."

"You're allowed one buck," J.M. Pyne said.

"Exactly," young Ballentyne said.

J.M. Pyne straightened up. "I never in my life took more than two shots to kill a deer. Mostly I took one shot."

Young Ballentyne smiled. "You could even go with just two cartridges - you really could."

J.M. Pyne got out the little miner's assay scale and a can of smokeless powder thirty years old and some primers. He primed one of the good cases and weighed out a charge of powder.

"Put up a target," he said.

He shifted the long vernier sight from the heel to the tang while young Ballentyne was putting up a target at the 100-yard mark. He hunted for the old sight readings. He set the sight for 100 yards. He opened the narrow window over the machine rest that he used for testing rifles, when young Ballentyne came back, and loaded the rifle. He took a couple of deep breaths and put the gun up. It wasn't so bad as he had been afraid it would be. When you have shot for sixty years, you don't forget. The front sight didn't hang on the black as once it had. But when the gun spoke and the butt set back hard against his shoulder, he knew the bullet was in the black even before he heard young Ballentyne's exclamation as he peered through the spotting scope at the target.

J.M. Pyne shut the window and walked slowly back to the bench with the rifle at heel. He had forgotten something. He had forgotten how good it was to get off a clean shot. He had given up shooting because he couldn't hold a rifle for ten shots - to say nothing of 50 or 100. But he could still hold a rifle for one or two shots.

He put the gun in the vise and unscrewed the wind gauge, and picked up a small brass punch and a hammer and began gently to tap the sight base out of the dovetail slot.

"You're going," young Ballentyne said.

J.M. Pyne didn't answer. He got the sight base out and looked in a drawer for the large ivory bead he had always liked for hunting. He would have to do some more shooting to make sure he was sighted in.

"You could weigh out some powder charges and put them in glass vials, and take along primers and bullets and the re- and de-capper," young Ballentyne said.

"No," J.M. Pyne said. "What I can't do in two shots, I won't do at all."

They started north the next morning in young Ballentyne's car. It was a gray, wintry day. They came, late in the afternoon, to a bleak little town with a high stone wall on one side of the street and little shops on the other. The street was full of policemen

and guards with revolvers and sawed-off shotguns. Young Ballentyne stopped the car. A policeman ordered him to keep
going.

"That must be Waubun Prison," J.M. Pyne said. "I haven't been
through here in twenty years, but I remember it."

It was only as they were leaving the town that young Ballentyne
could stop for gas and ask the man at the pump what had happened.

"Riot in the prison this morning," the man said. "They killed
three guards, and some of them got away. I hear they've stopped
it now. But some of them got away."

Young Ballentyne looked so eager and excited that J.M. Pyne
could guess what was on his mind.

"It isn't our business," J.M. Pyne said.

"No," young Ballentyne admitted, and drove on.

It was dark when they came to the place where they were to
meet a man named Higgins with a team and a wagon. Young
Ballentyne put the car in a garage.

They found Higgins in the general store. He said it would be
cold. He was wearing a black-and-red Mackinaw himself, and a
cap with ear flaps, and heavy gray woolen socks that came above
his leather-topped rubbers and over his breeches.

J.M. Pyne was tired. The tote road was so bad the horses had to
walk most of the way. J.M. Pyne wrapped himself in his long
overcoat and turned up the collar and sank his chin. It took
almost four hours to make the twelve miles. J.M. Pyne was so
stiff he had to get young Ballentyne to help him down out of the
wagon. He was glad to see the open fire inside the log cabin,
and the hot food that Mrs. Higgins brought.

There were three other hunters there - men from New York who
had got in that morning. They sat round the fire and talked
hunting. J.M. Pyne saw, when Higgins introduced him, that his
name meant no more to them than it had to Higgins. They were
hunters, and not riflemen. They didn't know what a Pyne barrel
was.

J.M. Pyne sat close to the fire when he had eaten, and warmed
his shins and smoked a cigarette and listened. One of the men

from New York was, he said, an experienced hunter who had killed many deer. His name was Esterbrook. The other two were novices. Esterbrook instructed them.

"The first thing you've got to learn if you want to get a deer," Esterbrook said, "is to empty your rifle. You know what I mean?"

He took his own rifle from the rack against the wall and made sure it was empty, and put it to his shoulder and aimed it at an imaginary deer and pulled the trigger and slammed the bolt hard and pulled the trigger, again and again.

"That's what I mean," he said. "You've got to keep shooting if you expect to get a deer. You've got to learn to fire every shot in the magazine before he gets out of sight." He turned to Higgins. "Isn't that right?" he demanded.

Higgins nodded. "That's why I like a lever-action rifle," he said. "You can pump lead with it faster than you can with that bolt action of yours."

He picked his own rifle, of a pattern that Americans through fifty years have made famous the world around, and showed them how fast he could manipulate it.

"You can shoot a bolt just as fast," Esterbrook said, "if you know how."

Higgins would not admit that. They argued endlessly, as hunters will. J.M. Pyne got up and studied a local map tacked to the wall. Esterbrook interrupted his study, wanting to know what kind of a rifle he was using.

J.M. Pyne got his rifle out of its case and handed it to Esterbrook.

"A single shot," Esterbrook said.

"A Sharps, model of 1878," J.M. Pyne said.

He did not say that he had made the barrel himself. If Esterbrook knew anything about rifles, he would note the name "J.M. Pyne" stamped in small Roman capital letters on the barrel.

"How do you expect to get a deer with that?" Esterbrook demanded. "By the time you've reloaded, the deer will be in the next county."

139

"I don't like to shoot unless I see the sight on a vital spot."

"What special spot on a deer do you usually aim for?" Esterbrook asked.

"The neck," J.M. Pyne said. "About four inches below the hair. A bullet there doesn't spoil much meat." He took a bunch of keys out of his pocket, and held them in front of Esterbrook's face. "When you hit a deer in the neck," he said, "he drops like that." J.M. Pyne dropped the bunch of keys on the floor.

Esterbrook raised his eyebrows and smiled, as younger men do smile at an old man's fancy.

"You can put a bullet through the neck of a deer that's jumping down timber as fast as he can go?"

"I didn't say that," J.M. Pyne said mildly.

"What do you do when a deer jumps and goes bouncing off through the brush so fast that all you see is a glimpse of a white flag?"

"I like to go slow and make as little noise as possible, so as not to scare game."

"You've never seen a buck jump and go on jumping, sideways and in and out, so fast you can't get a bead on him?"

"Yes," J.M. Pyne said. "I've seen that."

"And what do you do then?" Esterbrook demanded.

"I don't shoot," J.M. Pyne said. "I stand still and figure on coming up with him later."

"Didn't you ever take a snap shot?"

"Yes," J.M. Pyne said. "But I don't shoot unless I see what I want to hit over the front sight."

"You're like Daniel Boone," Esterbrook said.

"I imagine Daniel Boone hunted more or less that way," J.M. Pyne said. "He must have. He couldn't afford to waste ammunition - not when he had to carry several months' supply of powder and lead."

"It may have been all right for him," Esterbrook said. "Game was plentiful and not easily frightened. And he was a good shot."

"I've been a good shot ever since I was a young man," J.M. Pyne said.

Esterbrook turned and smiled at the company. He made it clear that he was too kind to say what he might say.

J.M. Pyne took his rifle up to his room with him. It was an old habit with him to keep his rifle close beside him. In the old days, when he had travelled to Milwaukee and St. Louis and San Francisco to shoot in rifle matches, he had carried the gun himself. No Pullman porter or bellboy had ever had a chance to drop the gun and knock the front sight askew.

Young Ballentyne stopped at the door. He stepped inside. "I'd have liked to tell that guy who you are, Mr. Pyne," he said.

J.M. Pyne stood his rifle carefully in a corner, making sure it would not slip, and sat down on the edge of his bed. "He has his way of doing things," he said, "and I have mine."

Higgins got them all out at daylight. Higgins made a great racket with a brass bell. J.M. Pyne hated to get up. It was a laborious process to get up nowadays. He was always stiff and sore. But he made it. He dressed and got downstairs only a few minutes behind the others, and ate bacon and eggs and flapjacks with maple syrup and coffee. He was having a second cup of coffee when the thing happened.

A big man in gray dungarees stood in the doorway with a hatchet in his hand. His head was close-cropped. J.M. Pyne turned toward the other door. Another smaller man in the same kind of gray dungarees had posted himself there. He had a short length of iron bar as a weapon.

"Sit tight," the big man with the hatchet said. "Sit tight and do what you're told, and you won't get hurt."

They all sat motionless, staring at the men in gray dungarees, except Mrs. Higgins. She stood with a pan of flapjacks in one hand and a jug of maple syrup in the other, and very slowly her hands relaxed and the pan went clattering on the floor and the syrup jug landed with a solid thump. She sank into a chair.

141

"You watch 'em, Joe," the big man said, "while I look over the guns."

The big man turned to the living room. J.M. Pyne could see him as he picked a rifle out of the rack. They were all bolt-action rifles except Higgins' gun. The fellow laid Higgins' gun on the table, and young Ballentyne's new rifle. One by one, he picked up the three other rifles and slipped the bolts out. He did it as if he knew about bolt-action rifles, with no fumbling. He found cartridges all laid out on the table. He loaded Higgins' rifle and gave it to his partner with the piece of iron. Then he loaded young Ballentyne's rifle and stood in the doorway. He looked at Esterbrook.

"You're nearer my size," he said to Esterbrook. "Take off your clothes."

"What?" Esterbrook asked. He was wearing a gray flannel shirt and heavy woolen trousers and leather-topped rubbers. He had hung his plaid Mackinaw on the back of his chair.

Esterbrook stood up and took off his flannel shirt. The fellow made him take off his boots and his trousers and his woolen socks. He got out of his dungarees and into Esterbrooks' clothes. They were a tight fit for him. He couldn't button the shirt collar, but he got into them.

"Now," he said, "I'll hold a gun on them while you get some clothes, Joe."

Joe chose to exchange clothes with one of the other men from New York. After that, they got a pack sack out of the shed beyond the kitchen and filled it with bread and bacon and salt and sugar.

"Now, Joe," the big man said, "you hold a gun on them while I take a look around."

J.M. Pyne heard the fellow go upstairs. When he came down he had blankets on one arm and he was dragging J.M. Pyne's rifle. He rolled the blankets up and tied them with a piece of clothesline, so he could sling them over his shoulder. Then he picked up the rifle. He studied it. J.M. Pyne knew, from the way he looked at it, that he was not familiar with it - he saw he couldn't slip the bolt out the way he had slipped the bolts out of the other rifles. He threw the lever down. But he didn't see any easy way of putting the gun out of commission.

"Whose gun is this?" he asked.

"It's mine," J.M. Pyne said.

"How do you take it apart?"

"You have to have a vise and tools," J.M. Pyne said.

The big man looked at the rifle. He looked around the room. He saw something on the windowsill. He picked it up and tried it in the muzzle of the rifle. J.M. Pyne saw that it was a lag screw with a great rough thread, and half rose from his chair.

"Sit still, grandpa," the big man said.

He put the small end of the lag screw in the muzzle of the rifle as far as it would go and picked up the hatchet. He smiled at J.M. Pyne and brought the hammer side of the hatchet down on the end of the lag screw, driving it deep into the muzzle. He dropped the rifle on the floor and picked up the blanket roll.

"Let's go," he said to his partner.

Joe went out of the door. The big man turned as he followed. "You stay where you are," he said. "The man who sticks his head out of this door will get a bullet through it."

J.M. Pyne got up and went to the window. They were going north, toward the river. He picked up his rifle. The lag screw was jammed so tightly in the muzzle that he could not move it. The muzzle of his rifle was ruined.

J.M. Pyne turned to Higgins. "Have you got a vise?" he asked. "And a hacksaw?"

Higgins jerked his thumb at the shed beyond the kitchen. J.M. Pyne walked into the shed. There was a light vise and a few tools. He laid the rifle on the bench and went upstairs and got his bag. He had a little kit of tools in a tin cigarette box of the size that holds a hundred cigarettes. He had carried that kit with him wherever he went for thirty years. It had a magazine screw driver with four blades of different sizes, and two or three files, and a small pair of pliers. He carried the kit down to the bench.

There wasn't anything to do but cut the barrel off. He put the barrel in the vise. If he cut the barrel off he would lose his front sight setting. He would have to file a new sight slot first. The barrel had so little taper that moving the front sight back an inch

143

or two would make only a minute difference. He couldn't start the lag screw with the pliers. He found a monkey wrench and managed to turn it out. It hadn't gone in more than an inch. It had jammed in the muzzle and ruined the lands. But only for an inch.

J.M. Pyne marked out the sight slot and began to file. He was in a hurry. He hadn't time to do a nice job. The only thing to do was to file the dovetail slot oversize and key it into place. He could file a wire nail into a lozenge cross section and key the sight in an oversize slot.

J.M. Pyne was aware, as he filed at the barrel, that young Ballentyne stood beside him.

"They're going out for help," young Ballentyne said.

"It'll take them three or four hours to get out to a telephone," J.M. Pyne said. "And three or four hours more for a posse to get in."

"They can't go far with that load of camp stuff they took," young Ballentyne said.

J.M. Pyne filed steadily. He got the slot deep enough. He had a three-inch rule in his pocket. He laid it on the barrel and with his pocket knife scribed as well as he could the center of the front sight across the slot. Then, with a flattened nail for a drift, he drove the front sight out of its old slot and drove it into the new slot. It couldn't, he decided, be more than a couple of hundredths of an inch out either way.

He found a hacksaw. Half the teeth were gone. But it would still cut. He sawed the barrel off just ahead of the new front sight. He put the rifle vertically in the vise and squared the cut with a file. He had to square it by eye. But his eye was trained by many years of work.

When he thought he had the barrel square he opened his pocket knife. He took a small blade and scraped away the burrs left by the hacksaw and the file. He countersank the muzzle slightly, but enough.

He studied the muzzle with his magnifying glass. It wasn't a shop job. The muzzle couldn't be perfectly square. But it was so nearly so that it couldn't make much difference at ordinary ranges. The rifle had shot in three-quarters of an inch at 100

144

yards. It must be good for an inch and a half as it stood. It was good enough for a hunting rifle.

J.M. Pyne figured that in putting the front sight back from the muzzle he might have raised it two-hundredths of an inch. He studied the vernier scale of the rear sight. It couldn't be two-hundredths. It couldn't be one-hundredth. The vernier split a sixteenth of an inch into eighths, and 1/8th of a sixteenth was 1/128th of an inch. He couldn't have raised the front sight more than that. He decided to raise the rear peep up 1/128th of an inch - one division on the vernier. He couldn't be much out. He took one of his two cartridges out of his coat pocket and loaded the rifle.

"What are you going to do?" young Ballentyne asked.

"I'm going hunting," J.M. Pyne said.

"You might run into those two."

"I might," J.M. Pyne said, "if I've guessed right."

"What do you mean?" young Ballentyne asked.

"I've been thinking what I would do in their place," J.M. Pyne said. "I wouldn't drive a lag screw into the muzzle of a Pyne barrel. No matter what I was up against, I wouldn't do that."

"No," young Ballentyne said, "you wouldn't do that."

"That one fellow knew something about guns. I watched him. He knew that one of those rifles used the sear for a bolt stop, so he held the trigger back to get the bolt out. He knew that Ester-brooks' rifle was a Springfield, with the bolt stop on the side. A fellow like that might have brains. You can see he had brains by what he did to my rifle."

Young Ballentyne nodded.

"If I were in his place I'd know my only chance was to make for the river. There's always a boat to be had along a river. You can travel farther and faster in a boat when you have a lot of duffel to carry. And a boat leaves no trace."

"There are two of them," young Ballentyne said. "They've got repeating rifles. You've got a single shot with just two cartridges."

"I'm as good as ever I was for two shots," J.M. Pyne said. "Do you think any convict out of Waubun can shoot with me? If he could, we'd know who he was. He'd have a reputation as a rifle shot."

"But," young Ballentyne said, "you forget--"

"I'll be careful," J.M. Pyne said. "I haven't hunted deer for nothing. I won't be taken by surprise."

"I'd like to go with you," young Ballentyne said.

"Two men make too much noise in the woods," J.M. Pyne said. "And you haven't anything to shoot."

J.M. Pyne cradled his rifle in his arms. "I'll be back before dark."

J.M. Pyne walked westward into the woods. He paused to listen and to watch his back trail, and turned again toward the river. They had an hour's start and they were young. They would travel as fast with their packs as he could travel with nothing to carry but his rifle. He remembered the map. The falls, with half a mile of rapids, were below him. If they got into a boat above the rapids, they would have to portage.

He walked on. The rifle was heavier than ever a rifle had seemed before. He stumbled often, but he kept on. The sky was cloudy. He could see where the sun was behind the clouds. He guessed it was noon when he reached the river bank below the falls. He sat down on a fallen log with his rifle across his knees to rest. He had made about five miles.

If they were in a boat below the falls, he was too late. He could never catch them. If they were still above him, he had only to wait. He had a quiet confidence that they were upstream. He sat so quietly that a squirrel came within two yards of him and sat up, his head cocked warily on one side to study him. He gradually became accustomed to all the little sounds of the forest, so he heard only the unusual noises.

He saw an eight-point buck come down to the opposite shore of the river, a hundred yards away, and drink. He did not raise his rifle. He let the buck drink his fill and turn and go back up the trail out of sight.

J.M. Pyne waited more than an hour before something made him sit up sharply. He heard something. He did not know what. He waited, his head cocked like that of a wild animal as he listened. He heard a stick crack. Then he saw them. They were carrying a canoe, bottom up. Each of them had a rifle in his right hand while he steadied the canoe over his head with his left hand.

J.M. Pyne stood up. He stood beside a tall hemlock tree. He said, "Hi!" The two men dropped the canoe. They dropped it so hard it bounced. They weren't seventy-five yards away.

"Hands up!" J.M. Pyne said sharply.

They didn't put their hands up. The big fellow half raised his rifle and stared into the woods toward the sound he had heard. J.M. Pyne raised his rifle. The fellow was asking for it.

The ivory bead of the front sight settled on the man's shoulder, swung away, swung back. As it swung back, J.M. Pyne pressed the trigger almost without volition. He heard the rifle crack. He felt the butt set back hard against his shoulder. He saw the man drop his rifle and clasp his hand to his shoulder. J.M. Pyne stepped behind the hemlock tree and peered out, exposing one eye, from the other side.

The other fellow had dropped flat on his stomach behind a log. He had that much sense. But he hadn't the sense not to shoot when he couldn't see anything definite to shoot at. He fired three shots wildly at the shadows around the hemlock tree.

J.M. Pyne opened his rifle and took out the fired case and put his other cartridge in the breech. The fellow was lying so low behind his log that J.M. Pyne could see nothing but the top of his head. He didn't want to blow the top of the man's head off. He didn't want to kill him. It didn't seem necessary. So he waited.

He thought he knew, as he waited, what it was like to fight Indians. It took nerve to wait. You wanted to have it over with. And the longer you waited the more intense was your desire to have it over with.

J.M. Pyne waited. J.M. Pyne remembered to take slightly deeper breaths than usual. He wanted plenty of wind when he had to shoot. He wanted wind enough so he could wait for the sights to swing on exactly right.

J.M. Pyne remembered the oldest trick of them all. He knelt down and got a piece of a broken branch, six or eight inches long. He hung his hat on the broken branch and held it out on the left side of the tree. The fellow shot. He didn't hit the hat, but he shot. J.M. Pyne poked the hat out again and peered around the other side of the tree. The fellow was raising himself up on his elbows to shoot. He was aiming intently at the hat. J.M. Pyne waited. He remembered to take deeper breaths while he waited for the shot.

When the rifle cracked he dropped the twig and stepped out enough to see, and shot the fellow neatly through the shoulder.

It was a long way back. There were moments when J.M. Pyne paused and asked himself if he could make it as he drove those two men in front of him. They didn't know he had no more cartridges. They were completely his prisoners. But they walked too fast.

He ran them into a squad of state police and sat down beside the trail to rest. One of the troopers took his rifle for him. Another cut a stick for him. He trudged on, slower and slower, leaning on the stick. He hadn't walked so far in years. He really wasn't up to hunting anymore, at seventy-five.

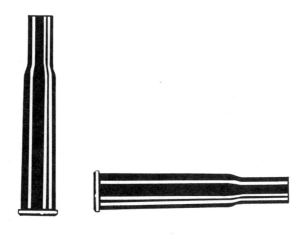

THE SECRET OF THE OLD MASTER

Joe Hill had two target rifles in cases of canvas and leather hanging from his shoulders as he walked down a factory-lined street in Jersey City of a hot Saturday afternoon in August.

He guessed, after half a mile, that he had come to the right corner. There was the little red-brick saloon across the street, and here beside him was the outside stairway sheathed in corrugated iron.

He eased the rifles off his shoulders. They weighed fourteen or fifteen pounds apiece. He sat down on the curbstone and stood the guns upright between his knees. He wanted to rest. But mostly he wanted a minute or two in which to get up his courage. He had sat up all night and all morning in a day coach. He had slept at times, but he had awakened always to the same anxiety. Somehow he had to impress the old man, and by all accounts the old man was not easily impressed.

A hot breeze came down the street between the gray-brown walls of the factory buildings. The cobblestones shimmered in the heat. He knew how bad the mirage would be on a day like this. You would think you were looking at the target through running water. You wouldn't know where the bull really was.

He wiped his face with his handkerchief. He could feel the water running down his chest. He could see where the sweat had turned his blue work shirt a darker blue. He got up presently and hung the rifles on his shoulders and tried the door at the bottom of the stairway. The door was locked. He walked across the street into the saloon. The place was empty, except for the bartender.

"Where is J.M. Pyne's shop?" he asked.

"You mean the old man who fixes the guns?" The bartender pointed through the open door. "Up that stairway. Fourth floor."

"The street door is locked."

"When it's after hours you have to yell for him to come down and open the door for you."

Joe hesitated. It didn't seem right that he should yell to a man as famous as J.M. Pyne to come down three flights of stairs and let him in.

"They all yell for him when they come to see him," the bartender said.

Joe walked out into the middle of the street and looked up at the fourth storey. The window nearest the corner was open at the top.

"Hey, Pyne!" he called out.

There was no answer.

"Hey, Pyne!" he yelled as loud as he could.

The window he was watching went up and an old man with a white beard and a black engineer's cap peered out. He pointed to the stairway.

Joe waited at the door. He heard the old man's slow footsteps. The moment for which he had worked and waited and saved his money was coming.

The door opened and the old man stood there, in a sleeveless undershirt and pants, looking over his spectacles at Joe. The old man had brown eyes. His nose was finely molded. *You'd know,* Joe thought, *that he was somebody, even if you didn't know who he was.*

"Mr. Pyne," he said, "my name is Hill - Joe Hill."

"Come in," the old man said, and held the door wide.

Joe walked up the stairs while the old man climbed wearily after him. The air was hot and dead under the iron roof of the stairway, and the rifles dragged at Joe's shoulders. But he was happy. He was going to see the place he had dreamed of.

The room he went into was fifty feet long and thirty feet wide, and so full of things that only a narrow gangway remained. He walked toward the bench that ran clear across the room and under the bank of windows at the far end, guessing that the long narrow boxes standing on end contained rifles waiting for Pyne barrels, noting a drill press, no longer in use, and what looked like a lathe, but wasn't. He took another look over his shoulder as he passed the machine. It seemed too light and too simple. But it must be the machine from which, for fifty years, those barrels, so smooth inside, so even, so beautifully rifled, had come.

There was so little room in front of the bench that he paused to let the old man pass him. Except for a small clear space around the vise, the bench was piled three feet deep with open cigar boxes and cartons and letters and tools.

"Take off your coat," J.M. Pyne said. "It's warm."

Joe took off his coat and hunted for a place to put it. He laid it across a rack of barrel stock.

"Mr. Pyne," he said, "I've got one of your guns here."

He opened one of his cases and took out a .22 caliber rifle of the sort that is made for off-hand shooting when there are no restrictions as to weight or trigger pull or sights. It had a long barrel as thick as a crowbar and a Ballard action with double-set triggers.

The old man opened the vise and dropped clamps of sole leather inside the iron jaws. Joe put the heavy barrel in the vise. The old man opened the gun and picked up a steel rod that stood against the bench, and a pledget of absorbent cotton.

He put two pledgets through the bore to get the oil out and held the gun up to the light and looked through it. He let the gun down and studied the open breech.

"Who cut it off?" he demanded.

"I did."

"What for?" The old man's eyes were no longer friendly as he looked at Joe.

"The chamber had been rubbed several thousandths out of round at twelve o'clock, so it wouldn't shoot any more."

"They will do that," the old man said. "They won't take the trouble to push a cleaning rod straight, so it doesn't rub."

The old man pushed the lever back and forth, studying the extractor, which was of the kind that travels parallel to the bore in a T-slot. Joe knew that extractor was a nice job. But the old man said nothing. He closed the action. The lever made a distinct snap as it passed dead center and the block came home, the way the lever of a falling-block rifle should.

"The action was in tough shape when I got it," Joe said. "I made new pins for the lever and the link."

The old man took the forearm off the gun and looked at the numbers stamped on the underside of the barrel. Then he got an old notebook out of a drawer under the bench and leafed through it.

"I made that barrel in 1923. I didn't put it on a Ballard action."

"The fellow wanted to keep the action it was on."

"What did you do about the firing pin?"

Joe picked up a screwdriver and took the block out and handed it over.

The old man studied the face of the block with his magnifying glass.

"Where did you get the idea of that circular plate?"

"From one of your guns."

Joe knew his work was good. But he could guess what the old man was thinking. Maybe he was bored.

J.M. Pyne walked down to the other end of the bench and got cigarettes. He offered Joe a cigarette. Joe said he didn't smoke. The old man lit his cigarette deliberately.

"What's your trade?"

"I'm a toolmaker."

"How old are you?"

"Twenty six."

The old man looked at him sharply. "They used to say it took twenty years to make a toolmaker out of a good mechanic."

"I'm still learning."

"So am I," J.M. Pyne said.

He took a cigarette paper and laid it across the breech of the barrel and raised the lever. He had to force it a little, but he closed the gun. He opened it again. The cigarette paper was torn away where the block had met the breech. The block was so closely fitted that it wouldn't quite accept the cigarette paper, yet it worked freely.

The old man picked up his micrometer and measured the thickness of the paper. It came to an even thousandth of an inch.

"Do you know how much your head space is?"

"Forty three thousandths."

J.M. Pyne looked down at the gun. "I don't see anything the matter with it," he said. "How does it shoot?"

"Not as well as a Pyne barrel should. I've tried every kind of match ammunition in it. I haven't found anything that will average better than an inch and three eighths for fifty shots at a hundred yards."

The old man went down to the far corner of his shop and turned on a light and put up a card about five by eight inches in front of a small steel plate. He handed Joe a pair of field glasses.

"If you sit on that stool and rest your elbows on the lathe bed so you can hold the glasses steady, you can see."

He took the gun to the other corner of the room and put it in a machine rest. A little telescope was mounted beside the rest. Joe saw, watching everything J.M. Pyne did, that he had a clean line of fire past the rack of barrel stock, between the legs of the rifling machine, and under a step ladder.

J.M. Pyne began to shoot, firing five shots, and moving the rest a little and firing another five shots. Joe Hill saw that the first group was ragged; the second group closed up, as the gun warmed. But he did not know what to expect of a rifle at such a short distance.

J.M. Pyne paused after twenty-five shots and studied a fired case with his magnifying glass. He handed the case and the glass to Joe.

"Your pin is too big," he said. "It's hitting too far out over the rim."

He took the firing pin out of the breech block and fastened it in the vise.

"Take this stone and the glass," he said. "Reduce it a little at twelve o'clock, but don't make it any shorter."

Joe worked cautiously with the oilstone. When he paused for a moment, the old man took the glass and looked at the rounded end of the pin and nodded to Joe to go on. Joe felt the sweat dripping down his body as he worked. It was hot in the shop. But he would have sweated anyway, doing a job like that with J.M. Pyne watching him.

"All right," the old man said at last. He put the firing pin back and tried a fired case in the gun. He turned the case about under his magnifying glass.

"That may help it," he said. "The area is reduced, so it's hitting deeper, and in the right place."

He put the gun back in the rest and fired five more groups of five shots each. Joe could see that they were closer than the previous groups. J.M. Pyne went down and got the card and brought it back. The groups were only a trifle bigger in diameter than a .22 caliber bullet.

"That gun is all right," J.M. Pyne said.

"Can you really tell - at fifty feet?"

"Yes. You should get some groups under an inch at a hundred yards. I'd guess it will average an inch and an eighth when everything is going right and there's no wind. It won't do it day in and day out, of course. It'll pick up a bit of lead or hard fouling now and then, like any twenty-two, and that'll make it throw wide ones until it shoots out."

Joe knew the moment had come to say what he had come all the way from Indiana to say. How could he say it? Now that he was here he felt how out of line it would sound.

He thought of showing J.M. Pyne the other gun he'd brought along. But it was a Springfield bull gun to which he had fitted a factory-rifled blank. There was nothing about it that would interest the old man.

"I guess...I guess I've taken enough of your time."

J.M. Pyne smiled. "I'm old and I'm tired and I ache all over. My eyes are no good. I can't shoot any more. But I've always had time for anybody who was interested in rifles. What do you want to know?"

"Mr. Pyne.." Joe began, and for a moment the presumption of what he was going to ask overcame him. He knew he was a good workman. But who was he to propose himself as successor to the old master of them all?

"Mr. Pyne," he began again, "couldn't you use a helper?"

The old man shook his head. "I've had two or three helpers in the last thirty years. They got underfoot."

Joe Hill waited.

"Besides," J.M. Pyne said, and Joe could feel that he was softening the blow, "making fine shooting rifles isn't a paying business. I can't afford a helper."

"I wouldn't expect to be paid," Joe said. "I've saved some money."

He had $229 in his pocket. He knew that a man could live four or five months on that if he wanted to.

The old man turned on him then. He eyes blazed as he spoke.

"Why do you want to work for me for nothing?"

Joe could not dodge the question. He had to tell the truth.

"I want to learn the secret of Pyne barrels."

The old man nodded grimly. "I thought so. You...and a lot of others."

"You're the most famous maker of rifle barrels that ever lived. What's wrong with wanting to learn what you know?"

"And setting up in competition with me."

"I wouldn't do that unless you said I could."

J.M. Pyne looked off into the dimming corner of the shop. When he spoke, he seemed to be talking to himself.

"I gave a fellow the run of my shop once. I told him all I knew.

155

And he started out making rifles. I wouldn't have cared, if he'd done a good job. The more fine shooting rifles there are in this country the better. But he didn't make fine shooting rifles. He chambered guns without a pilot on the reamer, so the chamber wasn't concentric with the bore. He botched everything he touched. Time after time men came in here with guns he had made and I had to fix them."

Joe wondered why he'd felt he had to fix the guns his rival had spoiled. He thought he knew. It was part of the old man's passion for fine shooting guns.

"Mr. Pyne.." Joe began. But it really wasn't any use. You couldn't argue with an old master who didn't choose to give you his secret lest you abuse it.

"You come back tomorrow," the old man said. "Come back tomorrow and I'll show you how to fix the triggers on that off-hand gun of yours so the front one won't kick. Leave your guns here tonight."

Joe went back to New York by the Hudson Tube and found his way to the Grand Central where he'd checked his suitcase and his kit of tools. He carried the double load down 42nd Street to Eighth Avenue. He got a room in a small hotel for a dollar. The little room was hot, without a breath of air. He went out and walked back across 42nd Street until he came to Fifth Avenue.

He had never seen Fifth Avenue before. He felt he ought to be thrilled by it. He got on a Fifth Avenue bus and rode down to Washington Square and back. It was almost cool on top of.the bus. And there was something about rolling down Fifth Avenue of a summer night, when the biggest city you'd ever known was Richmond, Indiana. But for Joe Hill the magic was in a cluttered, dusty room, four stories up, in a gray factory building on the other side of the Hudson River, where for so many years J.M. Pyne had done the work no one else in the world could match.

He awoke at dawn the next morning and remembered then that it was Sunday. J.M. Pyne must have forgotten that today would be Sunday, when he'd said to come. But perhaps he hadn't. Joe took his kit of tools. He might need it, and he didn't dare leave it where it might be stolen. He couldn't take a chance on the set of micrometer calipers and a micrometer depth gauge and the chambering reamers and gauges and counterbores and milling cutters he had made for himself through the spare time of several years.

He was sitting on the curbstone close to the locked door of the outside stairway when he saw the old man coming toward him.

"Good morning, Joe," he said. "I'm sorry to be late. I try to sleep on Sunday mornings. I seldom get here before half past eight..."

"The trouble with those factory triggers," J.M. Pyne said, when he had taken off his Sunday clothes, "is they're on small pins. The least bit of wear and they wobble from side to side. They want to be on trunnions. And I put in a kind of recoil block, so the front trigger doesn't kick."

Joe Hill worked for hours under the old man's direction, remaking the triggers of the off-hand gun. Toward three in the afternoon J.M. Pyne remembered that they hadn't eaten. He got out a paper bag of sandwiches and two cans of beer, which he cooled a bit under the tap. They sat opposite each other, eating corned-beef sandwiches and drinking half-warm beer, and the old man grew expansive, and told stories of the days when he had made world records with a rifle. Joe Hill asked himself if it was really he, sitting there in friendly conversation, as if he were an equal, with J.M. Pyne.

They went back to work then. They worked until the light failed and J.M. Pyne turned on the powerful electric bulbs over his lathe and bench. Joe thought the job was done at nine o'clock that night. But the old man, trying the triggers, shook his head.

"They're too light," he said. "Maybe you could shoot them in weather like this. But they would never do in the Election Day match. You can't feel a light trigger when your finger is cold. We'll have to make a new spring."

It was nearly midnight when Joe finished the spring. He drew the temper in a gas flame while the old man watched the color. He put the spring in place. The old man tried the triggers.

He looked up at Joe Hill, smiling. "I could shoot those triggers myself. Let's go home."

Joe picked up his kit of tools.

"What do you want to carry that for?" the old man asked. "Why don't you leave it here?"

"I will," Joe said.

They paused in Exchange Place. The old man was taking a bus and Joe was taking the Hudson Tube.

Joe waited, hoping the old man was going to say he could hang around the shop as long as he wanted to. But J.M. Pyne was looking up at the sky, where the quarter moon gave some light behind the haze.

"Two more weeks of dog days."

Joe Hill was sitting on the curbstone again the next morning when the old man arrived. He hardly spoke. The old man got out a piece of barrel stock and set it up in the lathe. Joe didn't know what to do with himself, so he sat in a corner and watched J.M. Pyne turn the stock to size.

When he had done that he put the barrel in the drilling and rifling machine and got out a drill with a shank longer than the barrel.

"Come over here, Joe."

It was the first time he had spoken in three hours.

"This is my drill," he said. "It's better than any other I ever saw. It takes a smaller chip, so it doesn't choke itself."

Joe studied the odd shape of the cutting surfaces. He could see how well designed it was to drill a deep hole without choking itself. He watched with what care the old man set everything up before he started the machine and the drill began to bite into the rapidly revolving stock.

When everything was going to his satisfaction, the old man asked, "Can you file?"

"Some," Joe said. He knew the things the old-timers could do with files. Few living toolmakers could do them.

J.M. Pyne picked up a malleable-iron casting with a curve to take each finger except the trigger finger.

"That's a blank for a Pyne lever. You ought to have one on your off-hand gun."

There was a lot of stock to take off. Joe filed on that lever for two days and a half, trying all through the last day to make the

158

contours perfect.

That was the pattern of the days that followed. Week after week he went to the shop every morning, seven days a week, and stayed until the old man left, which was sometimes at six o'clock and sometimes at midnight. He saw, several times over, the process by which the old man made a rifle barrel - drilling the blank, reaming it, rifling it, fitting it to the action, chambering it, polishing it with a lead lap cast in the muzzle and pushed out just enough so it could be coated with oil and emery and drawn back, and finally testing it in the machine rest.

But watch as he would, he could not guess the secret. He suspected that the old man put him to work on some simple job when he came to that part.

The money he had saved was almost gone by Christmas. He was lucky enough to sell his Springfield bull gun for 100 dollars. He lived in a tenement where he got a room for four dollars a week. He did not smoke and he had no time for the movies. He got coffee and rolls for ten cents every morning. The big sandwich he ate for lunch cost fifteen cents and his dinner at a cafeteria was forty cents. He figured he could make a hundred dollars last ten weeks.

The old man came down the street one bitter morning in February, and Joe knew he was sick. His long overcoat hung almost to the ground as he bent against the wind and felt for a footing with his stick. It took him a long time to climb the stairs.

"I've got a heck of a cold," he said, when they reached the shop. "I think I'd better lie down for a while."

He spent that day and the next lying on an old couch in a corner. He had a cough that racked him, and when he got up and walked across the shop he staggered like a drunken man.

Joe offered to get a doctor.

"Nonsense," J.M. Pyne said. "I've been my own doctor for forty years."

Joe took his arm when they left that night, and went with him on the bus and saw him safely to his room.

But he didn't stay home. He came staggering down the street the

159

next morning the same as ever.

"I had to come," he said. "I had a letter from Paul French yesterday, saying he'd be in today. His old barrel won't shoot. He wants a new one for the Metropolitan Championship."

The old man lay on the couch, coughing as if he would turn himself inside out, until there was a rap at the door.

"That's Paul," the old man said, and staggered to his feet.

Joe opened the door to a solidly built man of fifty with a rifle in a case over his shoulder.

"How are you, Johnny?" the solid man asked J.M. Pyne.

"I'm sick," the old man said. "But I'll be all right in a couple of days."

The solid man took his rifle out of its case. It was an exceptionally heavy gun on a Ballard action. "The barrel's gone," he said.

"Why wouldn't it be?" J.M. Pyne said. "You've been shooting it ten years."

The solid man said he wanted the barrel in a hurry, the match was only two weeks away. J.M. Pyne said he would get the barrel out.

He went back to his couch again when the solid man had left. He lay there the rest of the day. He let Joe take him home again that night.

"I've got to get that barrel out," he said to Joe. "He's about the best all-round shot there is. He's got to have a new barrel." .

Joe walked up and down the street the next morning in a snowstorm, waiting for the old man. He didn't come at nine o'clock. Joe kept on pacing back and forth, trying to keep warm, for another hour. Then he went back to Exchange Place and took a bus to the old man's house.

J.M.Pyne sat up in bed. "I couldn't make it this morning." A spell of coughing interrupted him. "My keys are in my pants there."

He wouldn't have a doctor. He insisted that all he needed was to rest until he got over the cold. Joe took the keys and went back to the shop. He measured the barrel of Paul French's rifle. It was 32 inches long and slightly bigger than a Number 4. He found a piece of barrel stock long enough and set it up in the lathe and began to turn it to size.

He knew a sixty-fourth of an inch more or less in outside diameter would make no difference that the man who shot the gun would ever know. But he did the job to a thousandth.

When he called on the old man that night he could see that he was feverish and a little out of his head. He thought he'd better not mention the piece of barrel stock he'd turned to size.

Joe went on with the barrel the next day. He set the barrel up and got everything ready. He checked and rechecked the setup. He wanted that hole to come out at the other end within a thousandth of dead center, the way it did when the old man drilled it.

It took all the nerve he had to start the machine. But he did it. He stood there anxiously, watching everything. If the drill struck a hard spot in the stock, it would probably break before he could stop it.

When the hole was drilled he took the barrel out and wiped it clean and looked through it at the light, watching the shadow line. It seemed to him that the hole was straight, and as smooth as a hole drilled by J.M. Pyne.

He got out the six-sided reamers that the old man used, and measured until he found the one that was right. He set the barrel up in the lathe and reamed it, watching it every minute, and putting on the oil with a brush the way J.M. Pyne did.

When the reaming was done, he upset a soft lead slug in the bore and pushed the slug through and measured it. The diameter was right.

That night the old man said he felt better. He said he would be around in the morning. Joe said nothing, feeling that if he urged him not to come, the old man would resent it.

Joe went back to the shop at daylight the next morning and hunted out the rifling head. He knew the cutter had to be stoned just so. Sharpening it was the toughest part of the job. It was hard enough to cut glass. And if the old man came in while he was working on that cutter, he'd be furious. What if he spoiled it?

The old man had said that nowadays he had to have bright sunlight, softened by the dirty window panes of his shop, to make a rifling cutter. It took days to make one, even when the sun shone. And in winter you might not get two hours of sun in a week.

Joe waited until after ten o'clock before he dared take the chance that J.M. Pyne might come in. He worked so cautiously that it took him all day to hone the cutter.

The old man was sure that night that he would be around in the morning. Joe caught himself hoping he wouldn't be.

Joe rifled the barrel the next day, running the rifling head back and forth by hand, the way the old man did, and making a chalk mark on the head of the machine for each pass, and indexing the head for the next cut. It took 40 passes of the rifling head to cut one groove two and a half thousandths deep. There were eight grooves to cut, three hundred and twenty passes. He finished the job toward six o'clock and took the barrel out and wiped it clean inside.

He took a soft lead slug out of the drawer and upset it in the bore and pushed it through. He thought it felt pretty even, without any loose places where the slug jumped ahead, or any tight places either. But his hands were trembling so that he couldn't be sure it was as good as he hoped it was.

Then he held the barrel up to the light. He could see minute tool marks. But then, of course, you always could - even when J.M. Pyne had rifled a barrel. The tool marks came out when you polished with the lead lap.

Joe finished the barrel the next day and fitted it to the action. But he wasn't ready to test what he had done. The old Ballard action was loose. The lever didn't snap up. It took a whole day to get that right.

The old man looked a lot better that night. He would be there in the morning. Joe would have liked to stay away. But he couldn't - he had the key to the shop.

He got there at half past seven the next morning. He took the gun out of the vise and looked through it against the light. It looked good to him. But what did looks amount to? He had made it just the way the old man made his barrels - except for one thing: he didn't know the ultimate secret of a Pyne barrel. The old man had never said a word about that since the first time Joe had talked to him when he had said he didn't want a helper. Joe put the gun back in the vise. He guessed that was the best way to tell the old man what he had done - to let him see it.

J.M. Pyne knocked on the door at nine o'clock. Joe let him in. The old man walked down the narrow gangway and paused at the vise. He looked hard at the gun in the vise, and went on to the corner where he hung his overcoat.

Joe sat down on the couch in the corner. The old man got into his working clothes and went back to the vise. He took the gun out of the vise and looked through it. He put it back and took a lead slug out of the drawer and pushed it through and caught it in his cap. He picked up his micrometer and measured the slug.

Without a word, he took the gun and put it in the machine rest. Joe got up and found the field glasses with which he had so often sat watching the old man shoot.

"Joe," J.M. Pyne said, "what did you do about those triggers you were going to fix on that .32-40?"

"Why," Joe said, "I haven't done anything." He'd forgotten all about them.

"You'd better get to work," J.M. Pyne said.

Joe got out the triggers. The old man began to shoot from the machine rest. Joe's back was to the target as he worked. He guessed that was what J.M. Pyne intended.

The old man shot the gun all morning, firing five five-shot groups on a card and putting up a new card, while Joe worked on the triggers in an agony of curiosity. He guessed that the old man had fired four hundred shots when he took the gun out of the rest and put it in the vise and cleaned it.

The old man said nothing and Joe didn't dare say anything.

There was a rap on the door.

"That'll be Paul," J.M. Pyne said. "How are those triggers coming?"

"All right," Joe said.

"You'd better do something else for a while, so you'll be out of my way. You go back there and read some of those old copies of

163

Shooting and Fishing. You can learn a lot from those old files of thirty or forty years ago."

Joe went back to the far corner where the pile of *Shooting and Fishing* lay, while the old man went to the door. He heard Paul French say, "Johnny, I just stopped by to see how you were coming with that barrel."

"It isn't done yet," J.M. Pyne said.

They moved down to the vise at the far end of the shop and Joe couldn't hear the rest of their talk. He could only sit there and open one old copy of *Shooting and Fishing* and look through it and take up another. When he couldn't stand it any longer, he sat up and looked over the boxes between him and the old man and Paul French.

J.M. Pyne had a sheaf of targets in his hand. He was always showing targets to customers. They might be targets he'd shot ten or 20 or 30 years ago. But as he watched, the old man laid the targets down. The gun was in the vise. And now the old man was hunting in the drawer under the bench. Joe saw that he had some small tool in his left hand. He was picking up a hammer with his other hand. And now he was holding the small tool on top of the barrel.

It couldn't be anything but the stamp that cut "J.M. Pyne" in small Roman capitals on a barrel.

Joe leaned forward, staring, and the old man struck with the hammer.

Paul French was turning to go. J.M. Pyne walked down the gangway with him. He paused at the door.

"It'll take a few days to brown that barrel."

"I know," French said. "I'll be in Saturday to get it."

The old man shut the door and walked wearily back to the vise. Joe got up and went down there. It was true. Cut in the polished steel was the mark of J.M. Pyne.

The old man got a cigarette and lit it with unnecessary deliberation. Then he picked up the sheaf of targets he had been showing Paul French. He leafed through them until he found the one he wanted. He took that one out, and laid the others down and picked up a .22 cartridge. He let the bullet gently into the round hole of the first group.

"You see," he said, "it sticks." He tried the others. The bullet stuck in all of them.

J.M. Pyne looked up at Joe. "So," he said, "I put my name on it."

"But the secret..... I don't know the secret of a Pyne barrel."

The old man shook his head. "There is no secret." He looked at Joe Hill over his spectacles and his eyes were friendly. "Except that you have to know what nice work is, and you have to be willing to take the pains to do it. You knew that when you came here - else I wouldn't have bothered with you."

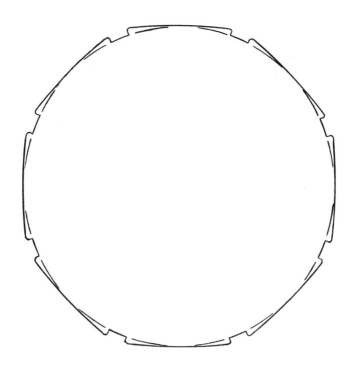

NO CHOICE

Joe Hill was alone in the old man's shop that Friday afternoon. He had a barrel in the rifling machine and he was running the carriage back and forth by hand and marking the passes of the rifle cutter with chalk on the head of the machine.

He felt good. He always felt good these days. J.M. Pyne had okayed the first barrel he had ever made.

"I guess," J.M. Pyne had said, "I guess I'll have to teach you all I know."

Joe realized suddenly that somebody down in the street below was yelling, "Hey, Pyne!" He went to the window and opened it. The winter day was gone. It was nearly dark. But he could see the shape of a man at the door to the outside stairway, and an upturned face. He waved his hand and went downstairs to let the fellow in.

The stranger was a big man, in a big overcoat, with the collar turned up. He said, "Thanks a lot," in a hearty voice, and followed Joe up the three flights of stairs and into the warm shop.

"Where's Pyne?" he asked.

"He's gone over to New York."

"Back soon?"

"Not tonight."

The big man took off his overcoat, as if he intended to stay. Joe hated to be interrupted. So many men came to the shop because they were rifle cranks and wanted to talk or because they wanted to be able to say, the next time they got into an argument about rifles, "As Johnny Pyne was saying to me the other day....." But this man might be an old friend of Pyne's.

"Is there anything I can do for you?" Joe asked.

"I'll just sit down and get warm," the stranger said. "You go ahead with what you're doing and don't mind me."

Joe went happily back to the rifling machine. The cutter was running smooth as silk. He could tell by the feel that everything was all right. The barrel was going to be good. He worked steadily for more than an hour, and then, too soon, for he loved what he was doing, he was through. He took the barrel out of the machine and took it over to the bench and looked through it against the white inside of the shade over the electric bulb. The cutter had left eight beautiful curving knife edges - the narrow lands of a Pyne barrel.

"That's the first time I ever saw a barrel rifled," the big man said.

Joe said nothing. The man was plainly a nice guy, a man of fifty or so, with gray hair and a big bent nose and an easy smile. He had come over to have a look once in a while, but he had kept still all the time Joe was keeping track of the passes and the indexing.

"You're Joe Hill," the big man said.

Joe looked at him. He was smiling. "Yes, I am."

"I heard you were working with Pyne."

Joe nodded.

"In fact," the big man said, "I heard you're the only man he ever let work with him."

The man was so friendly that Joe had to say something. "I guess nobody else has worked with him for a good many years."

Joe felt that the big man was studying him.

"You don't look old enough. You're just a kid."

Joe knew that he was young. But he'd gone to work when he was sixteen. He had spent ten years learning to be a toolmaker.

"You know," the big man went on, "I can't help thinking, from the way you talk, that you might be an Indiana boy."

167

"I am," Joe said.

The big man got up and held out his hand. "Put her there, brother."

Joe shook hands with him.

"I'm Alex Brown, of the Brown Engine Company in Terre Haute," he said, and Joe knew, from the way he spoke, that he was somebody successful and important back in Indiana. "We make a line of gas engines. You must have heard of the Brown engine."

"Yes," Joe said, "I have."

"Listen," Alex Brown said. "It's getting on toward seven o'clock. You got to eat sometime. How about knocking off and going to dinner with me? I'd like to get some information out of you."

Joe wasn't hungry. He was never hungry when a new barrel came off the rifling machine. He wanted to upset a soft lead slug in the bore and feel the evenness of it. But Alex Brown just might be a friend of the old man's. Besides, he was the kind of person that is hard to turn down.

"All right," Joe said.

They took the Hudson Tube to New York, and Alex Brown led the way to the kind of restaurant Joe had heard about, but had never been in. He shocked Joe by ordering a steak for two that was listed on the menu at four dollars.

"I'll tell you my trouble," he said. "I've been given one of the Government's educational orders. You've heard about them."

Joe nodded. He had heard that where possible the Government was giving educational orders to Middle Western plants.

"My order is for two thousand .50 caliber machine-gun barrels. I've got a Sharp and Whitney rifling machine and a deep-hole drill and the tools. But I haven't got a man in the shop who ever saw a rifling machine before. I can't find a man anywhere who ever rifled a barrel. That's why I came to see Pyne this afternoon."

Joe shook his head. "I'm afraid Pyne wouldn't be interested in that kind of work."

168

Alex Brown leaned forward and looked Joe in the eye. "I wasn't thinking about him. I was thinking about you."

"I couldn't do it," Joe said.

The waiter came then. He served them with slices cut from a rare thick porterhouse and with French-fried potatoes.

"Let's eat," Alex Brown said. "We can talk later."

Joe knew, as he ate, that the man would come back at him. He guessed that Alex Brown was in a position to force him to go to Terre Haute and make .50 caliber machine-gun barrels. He didn't know just how. But there must be ways for a man with an educational order from the Government to get what he wanted. Joe braced himself to defy Alex Brown and the United States Army.

"After what I saw this evening," Alex Brown said at last, "I know you could run the rifling machine I've got."

"I don't want to run it."

"Wait a minute. I haven't told you the whole story. In the first place, there's good money it - a dollar an hour, with a dollar and a half for overtime. You'll make sixty or seventy dollars a week. What you making now?"

Joe was averaging sixteen or eighteen dollars a week. But there was no reason he should tell Alex Brown that.

"I'm making enough to get by on," he said. "That's all I care about."

"How about some pie?" Alex Brown asked. "I don't go much for restaurant pie, but the pumpkin pie they have here isn't bad."

"Okay," Joe said.

Alex Brown turned to Joe when he had ordered the pie. He had the face and the voice of a man who is on the up and up. "You don't care about money?"

"You don't understand," Joe said. "Pyne is the greatest maker of rifle barrels there ever was in this country, and that means the world. I've got a chance to learn from him."

"You know how to make a rifle barrel."

"Do you think I've learned in a few months what it's taken the best man in the world fifty years to find out?"

Alex Brown grinned. "I see how you feel, Joe. Of course you want to go on working with the old man while you've got a chance."

For a moment Joe thought that was the end of it. But he saw it wasn't.

"I got off on the wrong foot with you," Alex Brown continued, "talking about big money. Besides, it isn't the real argument." He leaned forward again and spoke earnestly. "Did you ever stop to think that in a time like this, fellows like you and me have got no choice? I didn't want that order for machine-gun barrels. I knew it would be a headache when they gave it to me. But they said it was part of the program for national defense. How could I turn it down?"

He waited for Joe to speak. Joe had nothing to say. He looked down at his plate.

"Joe," Alex Brown went on, "we're all in the same boat. As soon as you get this job done, you can come back here and work with Pyne. But right now I need you."

"Any machinist can run one of those big rifling machines," Joe said. "It's practically automatic."

"Keeping the tools in shape isn't automatic."

"You've got toolmakers in your shop."

"We haven't anybody who ever sharpened a rifling cutter."

"It's tough to hone a Pyne .22 caliber cutter. It's so small and it has to be just so. But most any good mechanic can work on a big .50 caliber cutter for machine-gun barrels. That isn't nice work."

"Joe," Alex Brown said, "you ought to know we've tried. And the work just wouldn't pass the inspection."

Joe Hill knew he was licked. But he tried once more: "You get somebody else. There are plenty of men in this country who know how to run a rifling machine."

Alex Brown shook his head. "The ones that know how are doing it. You know that. The big arms companies are running three shifts. The arsenals..."

"All right," Joe cut in. "You win. But don't think I'm going to stay any longer than I'm needed."

"You won't have to," Alex Brown promised. "And when you get ready to leave, you get your fare back here."

He took out his wallet and found an envelope that he tossed on the table.

"There's your ticket for Terre Haute. I expect you'll want to see Pyne before you leave."

Joe asked himself how the old man would take it. But of course the old man would understand.

He felt pretty sunk when he got back to his room in Jersey City. But he couldn't help feeling a little proud too. No one had begged him to stay on in Richmond, Indiana, when he had left his toolmaking job on the chance that he could make good with J.M. Pyne and learn how to make rifles. And now he was somebody that a man came all the way from Terre Haute to get.

He didn't realize until the next morning when he saw the old man coming down the narrow gangway between the tall narrow boxes of rifles waiting for Pyne barrels, how hard it was going to be to tell him.

"Good morning, Joe," J.M. Pyne said. He smiled as he said it. He was always smiling at Joe as if he were happy to have found a young man who could learn what he had to teach.

He took off his coat and got into his working clothes. When he put on the black engineer's cap he always wore in the shop, he lit a cigarette and came down to the bench where Joe had the new barrel in the vise.

"How did it go last night?"

"All right," Joe said.

The old man took a lead slug out of the drawer and upset it in the bore and pushed it through and caught it in his cap. He looked up at Joe over his glasses.

"That's nice," he said. He picked up the micrometer to measure the slug.

171

Joe felt worse and worse. How could he tell the old man that he was leaving?

J.M. Pyne looked up from the micrometer. "It's all right," he said. He smiled at Joe, the smoke from his cigarette curling up out of his beard. "I'll have to start you in on .30 caliber barrels. I've got a special cut for bullets with hard jackets."

"Mr. Pyne.." Joe began. Everybody else called the old man "Johnny," but Joe had always had too much respect for him to do that. "Mr. Pyne.. " Joe began again and stopped. He couldn't say the words.

"Well, Joe," the old man said, "what is it?"

"I've got to quit. I've got to go out to Terre Haute."

"What for?"

Joe told him about Alex Brown, of the Brown Engine Company, and the machine-gun barrels.

"You fell for that," the old man said when he had finished.

"He's right," Joe said. "I've got no choice."

The old man looked hard at Joe. "Don't you know he can get plenty of men to run a big machine like that? He doesn't need a man who can do nice work. How much is he paying?"

"A dollar an hour, a dollar and a half for overtime."

"So that's it."

"No, Mr. Pyne," Joe said, "it isn't. You know me well enough to know it isn't."

"What is it, then?"

"Well..." Joe said, hunting for words. Now that he knew how J.M. Pyne felt, he began to wonder if Alex Brown had been kidding him along because he didn't want to bother with finding somebody else. "Well, the way things are, it's important."

"And what you can learn here" - the old man made a sweep with his arm that included the whole shop, the rifling machine, the rack of drills, so much better than any other rifling drills, the drawers full of special tools - "isn't important?"

"You know it's important to me," Joe said, "but --"

"I might have known this would happen. I told you in the beginning that I was afraid you wouldn't stay long enough to learn what you need to know and you'd go to making Pyne barrels before you were ready."

"I'm not going to make Pyne barrels," Joe said. "I'm going to make machine-gun barrels for the Government."

"You've never done Government work. I have. I worked 17 hours a day for months in the wartime drilling nine-inch holes in some stock they furnished. At fifty cents a hole. They told me the tolerance was nothing minus and half a thousandth plus. Their stock was awful stuff to drill - stuff I wouldn't have in the shop for my own use - and so full of hard spots I had to grind my drills twice in nine inches! I didn't make two dollars a day. And do you know what they did when I'd lost my shirt and was almost through? They changed the tolerance to fifteen thousandths - fifteen whole thousandths when they'd been holding me to half a thousandth for no reason on this green earth."

Joe sympathized with the old man's bitterness. Drilling a hole to within fifteen thousandths of exact diameter was quick and easy. Drilling a hole to within half a thousandth of an inch of exact diameter took time and pains and skill. One meant making good wages and the other meant not making enough to live on.

"No reason," Joe said, "except that some damned fool in Washington didn't know the difference between half a thousandth and fifteen thousandths."

"Exactly," the old man said. "It's always been that way - either they don't know their business or they're so wound up in red tape they can't do it. I don't suppose anybody in the Government would think it important for you to learn what you can learn in this shop. But I had a notion you knew better."

"Mr. Pyne," Joe said, "all I want to do is to go on learning from you. But right now I can't do that. Right now I've got to go to Terre Haute. But I'll be back as soon as the job there is over."

The old man shook his head. "You're a fool," he said. "You needn't come back."

"Mr. Pyne ..." Joe began. But he knew it was no use. The old man could be ever so patient. But he could be stubborn too. He

173

thought Joe was a fool. He had said so. That was the end of it. Joe might as well pack up his tools. He had to catch a train before noon.

Alex Brown was plainly glad to see him when he arrived at the office of the Brown Engine Company. But his smile died as he looked at Joe.

"What's the matter?" he asked. "Are you sick?"

"Where's the machine?" Joe asked.

Alex Brown led him from one building to another and into a newly painted room.

"There you are," he said.

Joe looked at the big machine, so long and so heavy J.M. Pyne's rifling machine would have looked like a toy beside it.

"You'd think," Joe said, "they made it to rifle guns for battle-ships."

"It's a good machine," Alex Brown said. "It's supposed to be the best there is."

"Where are the rifling heads?" Joe asked.

Alex Brown showed him. "You can start figuring the whole thing out in the morning," he said.

Joe opened his bag and took out his overalls and a set of micrometer calipers.

"It's nearly five o'clock," Alex Brown said. "The morning's time enough."

Joe got into his overalls. "How long can I have power and light?"

"As long as you want it."

"Okay," Joe Hill said. "Leave me alone."

Alex Brown turned to go, and then he paused. "You're sore," he said.

"That's right," Joe said.

174

"There's no use being sore."

Joe walked over to the rifling machine. He saw it had a carriage that could be traversed by hand. He began to traverse it, watching how it worked. He heard Alex Brown's retreating footsteps.

Four hours later he had checked a rifling head and got the big machine going. It didn't take long to rifle a barrel with a big power tool. But the Brown Engine Company had closed down for the night. He couldn't find anything with which to slug the barrel and find out how good the machine was. He might as well hunt a place to sleep.

Alex Brown came in at eight o'clock the next morning and stood there watching the rifling machine at work.

"You get it going?" Alex Brown said.

Joe didn't bother to answer. The man could see the machine was running.

"I been figuring," Brown said. "I figure we've got to run twenty-four hours a day to fill the contract. You let me know when you're ready to show a man how to run the machine."

"I'm ready now," Joe said. "But if you're going to run three shifts, I'll need three men. The tools will keep me busy."

"You want them all at once?"

"Yeah," Joe said.

"You get them," Alex Brown said.

"Can you give us enough bored and reamed blanks to keep three shifts going?" Joe asked.

"We're way ahead of you. We've been drilling and reaming for weeks."

Joe worked seventeen and eighteen hours a day. It took him two weeks to teach three men how to run the rifling machine. They made too many mistakes. They spoiled a lot of blanks.

Alex Brown called Joe into his office early one morning. "We aren't going to make it," he said.

"You'd better get another rifling machine."

"I can't - I've tried, and I can't."

Joe shrugged his shoulders, but his mind was busy.

"Can't you think of some way to speed it up, Joe?"

"Double cutter rifling heads might do it."

"You mean cut two grooves at once?"

Joe nodded. "It would almost double the output."

"Is that practical?"

"Pyne made some double-cutter heads."

"Could you make them?"

"Maybe."

"Go to it, Joe," Alex Brown said.

Joe knew he was in for it. He hadn't the least idea how to make two opposed cutters exactly alike in height and pitch and contour. They'd have to be alike or they wouldn't track, and one would spoil the cut made by the other. It was the kind of job no man could do by hand. It would have to be done on a machine in some kind of special jig or fixture.

"I'll have to do some figuring. I'll have to make some sketches."

He knew, five hours later, that he was stuck. How could he set up a lathe to shape those two cutters to the same pitch, the same contour, the same height?

He decided, by midnight, that he'd have to do the job on the rifling machine. At least he could get the pitch right on the rifling machine. But how was he going to hold two rifling cutters so they would be planed exactly to the same shape on both sides?

It was a case of improvising tools to make tools. He knew it could be done, because the old man had done it. But how?

Joe made sketches for two days and then he thought perhaps he had the answer. It seemed too simple. But maybe all he needed was confidence in himself - the kind of confidence he would have if he talked his scheme over with J.M. Pyne.

Alex Brown came in to the toolroom while he was turning a

176

piece of stock.

"How are you coming?" he asked.

"I don't know," Joe said. He handed over his last rough sketch.

"You aren't stuck?"

"Maybe I am."

"Why don't you write the old man and ask him how to do it?"

"The old man isn't telling me anything anymore."

Joe had finished his fixture when Alex Brown came back several days later. He had still to make the rifling head that would hold two opposed rifling cutters.

"I saw the old man yesterday in Jersey City," Alex Brown said. "I told him what you were doing."

"Did you tell him how I was doing it?"

"I tried to."

"What did he say?" Joe asked. "Did he think it would work?"

"He didn't say. He just grunted."

"That's the way he is when he doesn't want to talk."

"He's got no good reason to be sore at you."

Joe had learned to like Alex Brown. After all, Alex Brown had told him the truth when he'd said he needed him. But now he couldn't help thrusting his chin out at him.

"You don't understand," he said. "The old man is the best there ever was. Everybody who knows anything about it knows that. He knows it. And he gave me something he never gave anybody else before. He offered to teach me everything he knew. And I quit him. Of course he's sore. Why wouldn't he be sore?"

"You didn't quit because you wanted to," Alex Brown began. "You..."

"Listen," Joe said. "When Pyne locks the door of that shop in Jersey City for the last time, the things he knows are gone forever. He doesn't want them lost. He wants them carried on. And he got so he believed he could teach me to do it. And I quit him.

That's all. I quit."

"Just the same, he's wrong," Alex Brown said. "He ought to.."

"You go to hell," Joe said. "You can't knock J.M. Pyne to me."

Joe got down the next morning at seven o'clock. It looked to him as if the tools he was making ought to work if he got them just right.

He was drilling out his rifling head when he heard Alex Brown's voice behind him. He looked up. Alex Brown was coming down the shop, and beside him walked an old man with a white beard and an aquiline nose and a jacket whose pockets bulged.

"Good morning, Joe," he said.

"Good morning, Mr. Pyne," Joe said.

"Let's see how you're doing it."

Joe handed him the sketch. The old man took off his street glasses and put on the reading ones and studied the sketch.

Joe couldn't wait for him to speak. "Do you think that might do it?" he asked.

The old man took something wrapped in a handkerchief out of his pocket and slowly unwrapped it and laid it on the bench. "That's what I used to make my double-cutter head," he said.

Alex Brown leaned over to look closely at the tool. "It's the same idea that Joe's got," he said.

J.M. Pyne looked up at Alex Brown. "Why wouldn't it be the same idea?" he asked. "Don't you know that this boy has got the same kind of brains that I have?"

"I thought he was stuck," Alex Brown said, "I thought he didn't know what he was doing."

"Why don't you let us alone?" J.M. Pyne asked. "Why don't you let the two men you've got that know how to do the job get to work on it?"

"Sure," Alex Brown said.

Joe saw that there was a faint grin on his face as he turned and went away.

"I guess," J.M. Pyne said to Joe - "I guess if the Government really needs these machine-gun barrels we've got to get busy and get them out - even if they do get everything all balled up and change the specifications on you overnight."

J.M. Pyne took the black engineer's cap he always wore in the shop out of his pocket and put it on.

"This fellow Brown came into the shop day before yesterday and told me you were in trouble," the old man went on. "So I took a bus." He looked at Joe over his glasses and his brown eyes had the glint in them they always had when he was feeling good. "I had no choice."

REVENGE IN MODERATION

J.M. Pyne was at the bench, honing a rifling cutter. Joe Hill was at the lathe, turning up the body of a new double-cutter rifling head. Behind them the rifling machines were running sweetly and the men they had taught to run them had almost finished their shift without spoiling more than a couple of blanks apiece.

They'd had plenty of trouble. And they'd hardly got things going right before the Brown Engine Company had succeeded in getting in more rifling machines and taken a second order for .50 caliber machine-gun barrels. They were both busy from seven o'clock in the morning until seven or eight o'clock at night, keeping the tools in shape and seeing that the barrels the Government wanted so badly were coming off the machines in a steady procession, twenty-four hours a day. It looked as if it might be months before they got back to J.M. Pyne's shop in Jersey City, and what they wanted to do.

But they liked big easygoing Alex Brown and they were proud of getting out the barrels. Joe felt that J.M. Pyne was as well satisfied as he ever would be doing any other work than the kind that had made him famous.

They both looked up when Alex came into the shop with a short, plump man of sixty or so in an elegant double-breasted gray suit with a dark red tie. He was wearing a pair of eyeglasses with a flat gold bow across the top of the lenses and a wide black ribbon hanging from them. He had his shoulders thrown back and his chest thrown out and it was easy to see he was a big shot.

Joe Hill heard J.M. Pyne say something in his beard that sounded like one of the saltier words in his salty vocabulary.

Alex Brown was smiling as he came toward them. The man with him, who looked so completely out of place in a machine shop, was smiling, too, though not as if he meant it.

180

"Mr. Waterhouse tells me you know each other," Alex Brown said to J.M. Pyne.

"Hello, Johnny," Mr. Waterhouse said, trying to sound hearty. Joe could see that he was laying it on thicker because he did not feel it.

"Hello, Fred," J.M. Pyne said.

Watching the old man take the hand that Mr. Waterhouse offered reminded Joe of the way he took a bad piece of work that a bad mechanic held out to him for his approval.

"It's like old times, Johnny," Mr. Waterhouse said, "being in the same plant with you."

"Yes," J.M. Pyne said.

Mr. Waterhouse was fidgety under his important manner. Joe saw that he was afraid of the old man and what he might say next. He turned to Alex Brown, and Joe could feel how hard he was trying to be easy as he spoke. "Johnny Pyne and I were both with the J. Thompson Arms and Tool Company, in Hartford, thirty years ago. I was just out of engineering school and he was the most famous maker of target rifles in this country. I don't think he liked having a younger man for a boss."

"No," J.M. Pyne said, "I didn't."

With an effort that made his smile look tighter than ever, Mr. Waterhouse slapped J.M. Pyne on the back. The old man took it as if it were a blow.

"I'm older than I was then, Johnny," Waterhouse said. "I won't bother you much. I'm going to be pretty busy with some fifteen-ton assemblies for big-gun carriages they're moving into the big shop. I'll just drop in here occasionally to see that everything is going as well as I know it is."

Joe guessed then that Mr. Waterhouse had been put in charge of the whole works. And, of course, the old man guessed it too.

"Everything is going as well as could be expected here," J.M. Pyne said.

"As it would be," Mr. Waterhouse said in a manner that would have been agreeable in anybody else, "with you in charge."

"I'm not in charge," J.M. Pyne said. "Joe is."

Alex Brown introduced Joe to Mr. Waterhouse. Joe felt he ought to wipe the oil off his hand before he shook the hand of Mr. Waterhouse, but he didn't have time. He saw that the man was looking at him keenly through those swanky eyeglasses.

"You must be one of the world's best mechanics if Johnny Pyne is willing to work under you," he said.

Joe wanted to explain it wasn't like that - to tell Mr. Waterhouse that the old man had come all the way out to Terre Haute to help him when he thought he was stuck. But Mr. Waterhouse gave him no chance.

"So you've still got a boy for a boss, Johnny," he said.

It didn't sound so good, the way he said it.

"Joe is a good workman," J.M. Pyne said. "He hasn't shown any sign of being bossy."

Alex Brown took Mr. Waterhouse away then. Joe saw the old man staring after them, after Alex Brown's broad back, with its easy roll as he walked, and Mr. Waterhouse's back, with its stiff rightness.

"You don't like that guy," Joe Hill said.

The old man didn't answer. He lifted his chest a little wearily and turned back to the bench and picked up the stone he had been using on the rifling cutter and made several precise strokes. Then he studied the edge of the cutter with his magnifying glass.

Joe felt that something bad had happened. The smell of lard oil was no longer as sweet as it had been. Behind him he heard a faint, ominous sound from the No. 2 rifling machine. He yelled at the man on the machine to stop it and hurried over to see what was wrong. It proved to be nothing worse than another spoiled blank. He went back to the lathe. The old man straightened up and looked at Joe over his spectacles.

"We stand pretty well with Brown, don't we?"

"Of course we do."

"We can keep any hours we choose as long as we get the work out?"

"Sure."

"Then we'd better keep different hours."

"Why?" Joe asked.

182

"Because that..." J.M. Pyne paused to select the right names for Waterhouse, and Joe listened with astonishment at what came from the old man's mouth - "will drive us crazy if we're around here when he is."

"How did Alex Brown ever come to hire a stuffed shirt like that?"

The old man shook his head. "He's a good engineer on paper. He writes pieces for the technical journals. But he couldn't run - why, that fellow couldn't run a drill press! And if there's any way to get a shop in a jam, he'll find it."

"Is that why you've got it in for him?"

"I'll tell you about that sometime." Joe knew it wouldn't do any good to ask more questions just then.

"I've been thinking," J.M. Pyne went on. "If we came in about half past three in the afternoon we would have half an hour to see how the day shift had been doing. We could stay through the second shift and till three or four o'clock in the morning, when the last shift is halfway through. That way the work would go just as well and we'd hardly ever see Frederic Mortimer Waterhouse."

Joe felt that J.M. Pyne made the man's name sound worse than any of the other things he had called him. "Okay," Joe said, "that's what we'll do."

The old man talked at supper that night about the experiments with rifles he had wanted to make for so many years, trying out things that no one knew the answer to. He had never had the time or the money. He had worked on, year after year, trying to keep up with the demand for his match barrels, and never getting ahead because he couldn't charge a good shot what a Pyne barrel was worth and he saw no use in making barrels for men who had money and couldn't shoot, and hoping that someday he could quit work and go back to the New England country he came from, and have a shop where he could make experimental barrels, with a range outside the window for his testing.

"There are a lot of things I'd like to try," he finished, "but I never will."

Joe Hill thought it probably was too late. He felt it was a crime that J.M. Pyne, who knew more about rifles than anybody else, had never had the chance to learn all that he could learn.

"What is it you've got against Waterhouse?"

"That's a long story," J.M. Pyne said.

"I wish you'd tell me."

"It was a long time ago. It was thirty years ago. It doesn't matter now."

"But it does," Joe said. "He did something to you."

"Yes," J.M. Pyne said, "he did."

"I think I ought to know."

"It was when I was at Thompson's. I had a five-year contract to make my barrels in their shop. They sold them as Thompson-Pyne barrels. Waterhouse married Thompson's daughter. That's how he got the job of superintendent when he didn't know the difference between the bore and groove diameter. He was hell to have around, always wanting me to do things his way instead of my way, when all they'd hired me for was to find out my way. There aren't many bosses like Alex Brown with sense enough to let a man alone."

The old man paused, and when he spoke again it was of something else. Joe Hill waited patiently, and presently J.M. Pyne came back to his story.

"I had to tell Waterhouse to get out of my shop and stay out. He did. I made my barrels the way I wanted to and none of them went out of Thompson's that wouldn't shoot - not with my name on them. But Waterhouse was bound to get even with me. And he did.

"I had been at Thompson's about two years when old Colonel Maynard, of Smith and Maynard, sent for me. He said he was going to spend some money on experiment. He asked me if I'd do the work. I told him what he wanted might take five years. He said he figured it would. I told him it might cost a hundred thousand dollars. He said, "That's all right, the Company isn't paying for it - I am."

J.M. Pyne sighed and shook his head. "The Colonel was really interested in what rifles could be made to do, and he had the money. Can you see me hurrying back to Hartford to tell Waterhouse I was quitting?"

"Yes," Joe said, "I can. It was your big chance."

"Only it wasn't. Waterhouse said my contract had three years to run and he'd hold me to it."

"But he couldn't do that," Joe said, his fists clenching at the thought of anybody's doing a thing like that to J.M. Pyne.

"I had to tell Colonel Maynard I couldn't do his work. He came over to Hartford to see me. He said he'd buy my contract. He said he would put a codicil in his will, so if he died before the work was done it could go on just the same. I put that up to Waterhouse. Do you know what he did? He actually asked that Colonel Maynard pay double what my contract was worth."

The old man paused so long that Joe was afraid he wasn't going to tell him the rest of it. "What happened?" he demanded.

"The Colonel never knew about that. He had a heart attack. When he was safely buried, Waterhouse fired me."

"You had a contract."

"I made them pay. But that didn't bring back my chance to do experimental work."

"How could he do it?" Joe asked.

"Waterhouse was an engineer - he thought I was just a mechanic."

"You were famous for the things you made with your hands. He wasn't."

"I don't suppose he ever knew that I graduated from M.I.T. 15 years before he did."

"He wouldn't."

The old man grinned at Joe. "I'd like to give him his comeuppance," he said.

"I'd like to kill him," Joe said.

They took to coming in at half past three in the afternoon after that, and quitting toward four o'clock in the morning, if everything was going all right. They'd stop at an all-night dog wagon on the way home for coffee and a sandwich. They never talked long before the old man fished an envelope out of his pocket and made a sketch on the back of it to show what he meant.

He showed Joe priceless things - the Pyne fly, for instance, let in to the working part of the forward trigger in a pair of set triggers, which locks when you press the trigger in shooting and goes free

185

afterward, so the trigger lies dead on your finger, the way a trigger should, without movement and without kick; and the Pyne compounded extraction for a single-shot rifle, which, the old man said, would move the hinges of Hell.

They'd walk home in the dawn, J.M. Pyne feeling his way with his stick and Joe Hill thinking how lucky he was to have the confidence of the best - the best there'd ever been.

They managed to avoid Frederic Mortimer Waterhouse for more than a week.

But one afternoon they found Alex Brown waiting for them. "What are you two birds up to?" he asked.

He was smiling and Joe thought that he had proved to be what he had seemed the first time Joe had ever seen him - a nice guy.

"We figured," Joe said, "that we'd do better if we worked nights. So that's what we've been doing."

"It makes no matter to me," Alex Brown said, "when two men get out the work the way you two get it out. Only," - and he turned to J.M. Pyne - "I like to know what's going on. Is that the whole story?"

"No," the old man said, "I wouldn't say that's the whole story."

Alex Brown's face went grave. "You don't care much for my engineer."

"He hasn't bothered us so far," J.M. Pyne said.

"I noticed you didn't like him the day I brought him in here. And maybe he isn't the kind I would have picked if I'd had my choice. But Washington wanted me to take him. And, after all, if I take what Washington asks me to and there's trouble, I have an out."

J.M. Pyne said nothing.

"I have an idea," Alex Brown went on, "that Waterhouse is good on the theoretical side."

Still J.M. Pyne said nothing.

"Johnny," Alex Brown said, "you don't have to tell me what you think of Waterhouse if you don't want to. But I need your help. I just grew up in this business. I'm no mechanic and no engineer. You're both. Let's go and see Waterhouse. He's designed a new gadget. It's going to tie up the toolroom to make it. You have a

186

look at the drawings, will you?"

J.M. Pyne nodded. "Come on, Joe," he said.

They followed Alex Brown into the big shop. Down the middle stood a row of great steel assemblies. Alex Brown turned into a passage off the big shop and paused. "If you can say something nice about it, Johnny...."

J.M. Pyne nodded.

Alex Brown knocked at a door that was lettered in gold: FREDERIC MORTIMER WATERHOUSE, M.E. It was the only lettered door that Joe had ever seen in the Brown Engine Company's plant.

"Mr. Waterhouse," Alex Brown said as the plump man with the fancy eyeglasses stood in the doorway of his office, "I've brought J.M. Pyne and Joe Hill around to see your drawings. I've told them they're the finest I have ever seen."

Mr. Waterhouse swelled out his chest. "They must see the assemblies first," he announced.

They followed Waterhouse back into the shop. He led them to one of the big assemblies. "You see that keyway slot," he said. "How would you finish it?"

"Scrape it and fit it," J.M. Pyne said.

"That," Mr. Waterhouse said, "would be the ordinary way. In fact that is what the Army expects. But I've designed a tool that will save all that hand work. Now come back to my office."

Waterhouse hurried them back, threw open the door, and pointed in triumph to the drafting table.

Joe Hill saw, looking over J.M. Pyne's shoulder, the drawings, beautifully made, of an enormous broach. He knew little more about broaches than the way they worked. Most cutting tools revolved, or else the work revolved. A broach was different. You pulled or pushed a broach against the work.

Waterhouse hovered over them. He couldn't keep still any longer. "Those teeth," he said, pointing to the drawing, "have a shear angle of five degrees. The rest is conventional broach practice."

"Except for the size," J.M. Pyne said.

187

"Except for the size," Waterhouse agreed proudly. "I doubt if a broach as big as that was ever made before."

"How are you going to raise it as it cuts?"

"That's the pretty part of it," Waterhouse said. "That edge opposite the cutting edge will be ground to a taper of two thousandths to the inch." He unrolled another big drawing and laid it over the first. "And here's my wedge. It will be made of bronze, with the same taper as the body of the broach. See how it is notched every half inch? Keys in those notches will give me an adjustment of one thousandth per inch."

Joe wondered how long it would take the tool room to make a thing so big to such close dimensions. It would be a lot of work. But of course it could be used to finish one key slot after another.

"It looks like a good tool to me," J.M. Pyne said.

"It's a beautiful tool," Waterhouse said. "Wait till the Army hears about how we're finishing those key slots. They'll wonder why they didn't think of it."

J.M. Pyne nodded gravely. "No one thinks of everything," he said, and got away as soon as he could.

Alex Brown walked with J.M. Pyne and Joe Hill back through the big room.

Somebody yelled, "Watch it!" and they all ducked in time to miss a fifteen ton steel assembly that the travelling crane overhead was bringing down the shop.

They went on back to where the rifling machines were.

"Is it really all right, Johnny?" Alex Brown asked.

"It's a good tool," J.M. Pyne said.

Joe felt that the old man spoke without enthusiasm. He knew it wasn't easy for him to praise anything that Waterhouse had done. But there was something more - something he wasn't saying.

"All right," Alex Brown said. "The tool room gets the job of making that fancy gadget for you."

Joe Hill and J.M. Pyne heard things about what went on in the tool room during the next three or four weeks. Mr. Waterhouse ran the tool room ragged. The tool room spoiled two broaches and one wedge before they got anywhere. But one evening when the second shift was on the rifling machines and everybody else in the plant had gone home, Alex Brown came in to tell them that the broach and the wedge were finished.

"I wish," he said to J.M. Pyne, "that you two would come in and have a look. Waterhouse is like a mother with a new baby, and somebody has got to tell him how much it looks like its father. We really ought to have a party in honor of what he's done."

"Why," J.M. Pyne said, "I'd like to see it."

Joe was surprised at the eagerness with which the old man replied to Alex Brown, as if he wanted to go in and admire the work of Frederic Mortimer Waterhouse.

The broach and the wedge were laid out on sawhorses in the tool room. Waterhouse, his hands behind his back, his chest swelling, was walking round and round the tool, as if he couldn't take his eyes off it. "Look," he said, when he saw J.M. Pyne.

J.M. Pyne stood staring at the shining steel and bronze. Then he, too, walked around the broach, as if he were studying every detail of it. Joe felt it was something to look at more than any picture.

"I haven't measured it, of course," J.M. Pyne said at last, "but..."

"I have," Waterhouse interrupted, "and it's right to two ten thousandths. It took a lot of doing to get a job as nice as that out of the tool room."

"So I heard," J.M. Pyne said.

Waterhouse swelled a bit more. "You have to stand over them to get good work out of them. You have to let them know exactly what you want, and that you are going to get it if it takes all summer."

"It did take nearly a month," Alex Brown said.

"How," J.M. Pyne said, and paused as if to make sure that they were all listening, "how are you going to use it?"

"What do you mean?" Waterhouse asked.

Joe knew then what the catch was. He should have thought of it before. He was a fool not to have thought of it before.

"I mean how are you going to move your broach?"

"Move it?" Waterhouse repeated.

"Why, yes," J.M. Pyne said. "You pull a broach against the work, don't you? How are you going to do that?"

"Why," Waterhouse said, "you use a press, of course."

Joe could see that Waterhouse had got it now. There wasn't in all the world a press big enough to take those fifteen-ton assemblies in the shop outside. Waterhouse had been so fascinated with his beautiful tool that he had never thought how he would use it. And now that J.M. Pyne had made him think, all the air had gone out of his inflated chest and his face was white and little drops of sweat were coming out on his forehead.

"You remind me of Robinson Crusoe," J.M. Pyne said. "Crusoe built a boat so big he couldn't move it to the water."

Joe felt sick, seeing what J.M. Pyne had done. The old man must have thought this out the day he had seen the drawings. He must have known all the time there was no way to use the broach. And yet he had told Alex Brown it was a good tool. How could J.M. Pyne do a thing like that? Waterhouse had it coming to him. But you couldn't hang up a Government job for a month to pay off a private grudge.

"Johnny," Alex Brown said, "you knew this all the time."

J.M. Pyne raised his eyebrows. "I wondered how he figured to move his broach."

"But you didn't tell me."

Alex Brown stood there looking at J.M. Pyne, as if he couldn't believe it. "Johnny," he said, "I didn't think you'd do this to me. I thought you were honest."

"He is honest!" Joe burst out. He didn't know what he was going to say, but the words came hot and fast. "Don't talk to J.M. Pyne like that. He knows how to use that broach or else he would never have told you it was a good tool."

J.M. Pyne turned and looked at Joe over his glasses, and Joe saw the glint in his eyes, the glint they always had when things were going the way he liked to have them go.

"Why, Joe, what makes you think I know?"

"I know you," Joe said. He turned on Waterhouse. "You'd better ask a real engineer what to do with your broach. You'd better beg him to tell you. You know you had this coming to you. You..."

J.M. Pyne stopped him by putting his hand on his arm. "I've got all I ever wanted, Joe," he said.

Waterhouse looked at the old man and his eyes were pleading. "Is it true, Johnny?" he asked. "Do you know?"

"If it was my job, Fred," J.M. Pyne said, "I'd get a drawbar and a rope sling. I'd put one end of the sling through the eye of the drawbar and I'd put the other end over the hook of that travelling crane you've got out there in the big shop and I'd pull that broach through the key slots of those assemblies."

"Would that work?" Alex Brown demanded.

"Yes," Waterhouse said. "Yes, it will work. I should have thought of it myself."

J.M. Pyne turned to go. Joe followed him. They walked across the big room toward their own shop. Joe felt shaken still. There had been a moment when he had thought the worst of J.M. Pyne.

Alex Brown caught up with them. "I guess you birds don't need to work nights any more," he said. "I don't think anybody will ever bother you."

191

HARMLESS OLD MAN

Ellen Gray was busy until ten o'clock that summer morning helping Mrs. Bowman get ready for Mr. Pyne's visit. The old lady, plump, pink-cheeked and white-haired, was dusting pieces of frying chicken in corn meal when she saw what time it was.

"I guess you better hitch up Belle," she said. "After that you'll just about have time to change your dress before you have to start."

Ellen had never known anything about hitching up a horse until she'd come to live with Mrs. Bowman the previous September and teach the Dover's Corner school, but she was expert by now.

She led Belle out to the stone hitching post near the side door, tied her and ran into the house to change. She put on a crisp blue-and-white-striped cotton dress that she had made and laundered herself, and used her lipstick sparingly.

Mrs. Bowman was sitting at the kitchen table shucking peas.

"You look right nice," Mrs. Bowman said. "If you ain't the prettiest girl in Howard County, I'd like to know. You want to ask Bill to supper tonight?"

"I'd like to, if I see him."

"'Tain't likely you won't see him," Mrs. Bowman said. "I've noticed when two young people like each other they generally manage to find each other in a town no bigger'n Winchester is. You tell Bill I'd like him to come. He can talk guns to J.M. Pyne. The way I remember him when he come up here to visit Tom thirty years ago, he didn't talk about much else."

Ellen got into the buggy. She knew it would take a good hour to cover the seven miles over the hills to Winchester. But she was too happy to care. Bill knew she was meeting the 11:45 train, and even if he was on patrol he'd be around somehow or other.

She was in the main street of Winchester when she heard the sound of a motorcycle behind her. Bill came alongside and waved her to the curb.

"Madam," he said, "I'll have to give you a ticket. You were going more than forty miles a week."

Ellen smiled at him as he took off his goggles. He had blue eyes under black eyebrows and he was smiling back at her.

"Like all state policemen, you are young, tall, handsome and stuck on yourself."

"Listen," Bill said, "I've only got a minute."

"How about supper tonight?"

"What time?"

"Half past six."

"I can make it."

"Come on over to the station with me," Ellen said. "We can talk until the train comes in."

Bill shook his head. "I can't. I'm on my way to the barracks now to report. We're busy today. Traffic's heavy - heaviest Saturday we've had so far this summer. And a couple of murderers got away from a sheriff up near Cornwall Falls last night."

"Murderers!" Ellen said.

Bill nodded grimly. "Killed a poor old farmer and his wife for a few hundred bucks. We figure they took to the hills. But they can't hide out long. They'll steal a car and try to get away. We've been stopping cars since nine o'clock last night."

"Oh, Bill," Ellen said. "Be careful! I hate to think of you hunting men like that. If you found them they might kill you."

"I'd give my shirt to catch those guys," Bill said. "What do you think a cop is for?" He waved his hand as he roared off.

Ellen stood at Belle's head while the train came in, though it wasn't necessary.

She saw a smallish man with a white beard at the top of the car steps and knew he was J.M. Pyne. He had a bag in one hand and in the other, a stick that looked as if he'd cut it in the woods. The stick had a fork at the top. Before the old man started down the steps he hung his stick in the buttonhole of his coat lapel so his right hand would be free to grasp the rail. Ellen went quickly to meet him.

"Mr. Pyne," she said. "I'm Ellen - Ellen Gray."

The old man looked at her over the top of his glasses and she saw that he had fine brown eyes and a bold handsome nose. There was something quietly impressive in his manner as he took off his hat and held out his hand, something dauntless. He put his bag and his stick in the buggy. He had his troubles climbing in. "I'm not feeble," he said, "but my joints are bad. I've always thought there ought to be some way to refit the bearings when a man gets to be my age, but apparently there isn't."

Ellen clucked to the mare. Mr. Pyne sighed as they left the village and turned into a dirt road.

"It's like being a young man again," he said. "It must be thirty years since I've ridden behind a horse."

"It seems awfully slow nowadays."

Mr. Pyne smiled at her. "I'm seventy five. I'm not in a hurry any more." He was silent for so long that Ellen felt she ought to say something.

"I hear," she said, "you're the most famous maker of rifle barrels in the world."

"Yes," he said.

Ellen decided he wasn't boastful. He merely had no false modesty about accepting a fact simply because it was complimentary to him. "Bill says you were a marvelous shot. He says you made world's records."

"Who's Bill?"

Ellen told him about Bill and Bill's ambition to own a Pyne rifle.

"He's coming to supper tonight," she finished.

"I don't make many rifles any more," Mr. Pyne said. "I'm way behind with my orders. But maybe I can do something for Bill, if he's really interested."

"Oh, but he is," Ellen said. "Bill knows a lot about guns."

Mr. Pyne changed the subject. He told Ellen how sorry he was to hear of Tom Bowman's death more than a year after the fact.

"It's got nowadays so I don't dare write to any of my old friends. So many of them are gone. Time was when I used to hear from Tom often. Years ago I came up here to visit him when the hay was cut and you could see a woodchuck far enough away to make it interesting."

"The hay doesn't get cut around us any more," Ellen said. "They say it doesn't pay. The old meadows are growing up to brush. And the deer are getting so thick you can hardly raise a garden."

"Martha Bowman doesn't farm the place?"

"She keeps a cow and chickens. She puts up corn and peas and tomatoes and strawberry jam and raspberry preserves and pears. Winters, she hires a man to cut the ice on the pond and fill the icehouse and get in wood."

"That's the way I'd like to live," Mr. Pyne said. "I like the old ways best."

Ellen could have told him how lonely it was all fall and winter, with no neighbor within two miles and no telephone. It wasn't lonely any more, because of Bill. She thought of Bill swooping down the cement road on his motorcycle and stopping a car and hoping he'd find those two killers. What if he stopped them and they shot first? But then she remembered they'd got away from a sheriff after they'd been arrested. They wouldn't have guns unless they'd stolen them since.

Mr. Pyne pointed as they came to the top of the last hill and saw the house a little way down - a white, square, New England house, built around a central chimney, with an L at the back, and a side porch and a long line of sheds all the way out to the barn.

"Looks just the way it did thirty years ago," he said. "Except the orchard. That was newly planted then."

Ellen turned in beside the house and Mrs. Bowman came briskly out to meet them.

"Hello, John," she said.

The old man got stiffly down from the buggy and took her hand.

"It's good to see you again, Martha," he said.

"You know you didn't come up here to see me," Mrs. Bowman said. "You know that you wouldn't be here at all if it weren't for that rifle you want to look at. Come right in. Dinner's ready ... Ellen, you hurry up and get Belle in the barn while I show John

195

his room."

"John," Mrs. Bowman said, as they sat down, "I hope you haven't lost your appetite for country vittles."

"A man doesn't lose his taste for the best food in the world," Mr. Pyne said.

"I will say that practically everything on this table came off the place," Mrs. Bowman boasted. "Everything except the sugar and the coffee and the flour I made the bread out of."

J.M. Pyne complimented her cooking in word and deed, eating two helpings of fried chicken, and the first new potatoes of the season, and peas, and finishing up with a quarter of a green-apple pie.

"And now," Mrs. Bowman said, "I take it you'd like to see that rifle you wrote about."

"Yes, Martha," Mr. Pyne said. "I would."

Mrs. Bowman went into the parlor and came back with a long heavy rifle. "Bill says this is the one you meant. All Tom's guns are packed away in the attic. Bill read your letter and picked out this one."

J.M. Pyne took the rifle. "Bill's right," he said.

"What's so extra special about it?" Mrs. Bowman asked.

"It's the only seven-millimeter rifle I ever made," Mr. Pyne said. "After I made this one for Tom I lent my tools to Charles Newton. He died and I never got them back. And Tom never wrote me what the gun did. I've always wanted to know how good it was."

"Seven millimeter," Mrs. Bowman said. "What's that? Some kind of foreign thing?"

"In a way," Mr. Pyne said. "It's about twenty-eight caliber."

He took the bolt out of the rifle and laid it on his handkerchief and pointed the muzzle at the window, so he could look through the barrel from the breech.

"It's got oil in it," he said. "I'll need a cleaning rod."

"You go out in the shop and find what you want," Mrs. Bowman said. "You remember, it's beyond the woodshed."

Mr. Pyne laid the rifle across the arms of a chair and went out. Presently he came back with a long, slim steel rod and some absorbent cotton. He pushed several pledgets of cotton through the bore of the gun. Then he pointed the muzzle at the window again and studied the inside of the barrel, craning his neck to get the light just right. Then he reversed the rifle and looked through the muzzle.

"Martha," he said, "I don't believe Tom ever shot this rifle more than a few times. The lands don't show any wear, even at the throat. It's just as clean and sharp inside as it was the day I finished rifling it."

"I wouldn't wonder," Mrs. Bowman said. "I don't know much about guns and I never paid much attention to what Tom was doing with them."

Ellen got up to clear the table. Mrs. Bowman helped her. Mr. Pyne followed them out into the kitchen.

"Martha," he asked, "you got any idea where the loading tools and the ammunition are? I'd like to shoot this gun from a rest and see what it's like."

"Look in the chest of drawers in the dining room," Mrs. Bowman said. "It's full of Tom's gun stuff. If what you want ain't there, it must be in the shop. You look where you've a mind to."

J.M. Pyne went into the dining room. Mrs. Bowman made a suds in the dishpan and began to wash the dishes while Ellen wiped.

"I didn't want to tell him," Mrs. Bowman said, "but Tom always figured that rifle was a mistake. He said John Pyne made it a sight heavier'n he'd expected. It was too heavy to carry deer hunting. Tom always killed a fat buck every fall and dressed him and froze him. Sometimes two. If it's rightly hung and rightly cooked, venison is as good meat as there is. It was the only fresh meat we had all winter."

Mr. Pyne came out to the kitchen with the rifle as they were finishing the dishes.

"There isn't any seven-millimeter stuff in there," he said. "I'll have a look in the shop."

"You make yourself to home, John," Mrs. Bowman said.

When the old man had gone, Ellen looked at Mrs. Bowman. "Do you suppose he'd like my devil's-food cake?"

Mrs. Bowman snorted. "I s'pose you mean," she said, "you want to bake the kind of cake Bill likes best."

"Well---" Ellen said.

"Go ahead," Mrs. Bowman said. "I was young once myself."

Ellen put wood on the fire in the range and opened the drafts to get the oven hot, and went to work to mix the cake. Mrs. Bowman sat at the kitchen table, keeping her company. It was hot in the kitchen. Ellen felt sweat on her forehead as she stirred the rich mixture. But there was something satisfying in making a cake for Bill.

When the cake was in the oven she looked at the clock on the shelf. It was twenty minutes past five. The cake would be done by six o'clock.

She had taken the cake out of the oven and was spreading the chocolate frosting over it when two men, hatless, in overalls and work shirts that did not fit them, came to the side door. Mrs. Bowman went to see what they wanted.

"Could we have a drink of water?" one of them asked.

"The pump's right there," Mrs. Bowman said.

The two men moved toward the pump. Mrs. Bowman turned to Ellen and raised her eyebrows. Ellen knew she was asking who they could be. No stranger had ever stopped at that door, on a road impassable to motorcars. The two men pumped water for each other into the tumbler that stood under the spout. One of them was a tall, heavy man, nearly bald. The other was smaller, darker, with thick black hair. When they had drunk, they came back to the screen door.

"Where's the boss?" the big man asked.

"I'm the boss," Mrs. Bowman said.

"Where's your car?"

"We don't have one - all we have is a horse and buggy."

The big man looked at his companion. The smaller man shook his head. "We're hungry," the big man said, and swung the screen door open.

They looked as if they had been out all night. But it was more than that. Cornwall Falls wasn't more than fifteen miles away across country. Ellen tried to still her fear by telling herself they couldn't be the men who had got away from the sheriff. But she knew they were.

"Sit right down," Mrs. Bowman said ... "Ellen, set the table."

Ellen knew from her voice that Mrs. Bowman was trying not to show that she was scared. Ellen went to the cupboard to get plates. She couldn't stop her hands from trembling. It wouldn't do any good to give these men food and hope they'd go away. There wasn't time. Bill would be along in a few minutes. These men would hear him coming. You could hear a Harley Davidson police motorcycle half a mile away. They'd guess he was a cop. They'd be ready for him. They'd jump on him before he knew they were there, before he had a chance to get his gun out of its holster.

Mrs. Bowman put the cold veal loaf they'd intended for supper on the table. Ellen got bread and butter. The two men buttered bread and made themselves sandwiches and ate hungrily.

Ellen thought that if Mr. Pyne had found the ammunition for the rifle he could do something. She started toward the woodshed.

The big man jumped up. "Where you goin', sister?"

He put his hands on her shoulders and pushed her down into a chair. The other man grinned at her. His eyes were bloodshot. Ellen shrank back from his wolfish grin. He reached across the table and pulled the cake Ellen had baked toward him. He cut it with the knife he'd buttered bread with and stuffed a hunk of it in his mouth. Mrs. Bowman got a pitcher of milk and two tumblers.

Ellen heard the creak of a door opening beyond the woodshed and then J.M. Pyne's slow steps coming toward them. Her heart leaped. She pictured him, an old man, but dauntless. He'd have the rifle in his hands. These men would have no chance against him.

"Who's that?" the big man asked.

"Only the old man," Mrs. Bowman said.

J.M. Pyne came slowly through the doorway, leaning on his stick. He had the rifle in his other hand. But he wasn't holding it ready to shoot. The gun hung from his hand, the butt almost touching the floor, as if it were too heavy for him. He stood peering at the two strangers over the top of his glasses.

"Good evening," he said.

He wasn't what Ellen had hoped he'd be. He was merely an old man, looking a little foolish.

"Let's see the gun, grandpaw," the big man said.

Ellen knew that the big man saw what she saw - a harmless old man.

J.M. Pyne handed him the rifle. The big man took it, looking at it as if he wasn't sure how it worked.

"It isn't loaded," Mr. Pyne said.

The big man turned up the bolt knob and opened the rifle. "Where's the shells?"

The old man reached into the side pocket of his coat and brought out a handful of cartridges.

Ellen gripped the seat of her chair with both hands. The old fool must think these men were neighbors. He was going to give them the gun and the ammunition to kill Bill with. Didn't he remember what she'd said at dinner about the two murderers? Couldn't he see that these men weren't friendly? Couldn't he feel the tightness in that room?

The big man took a cartridge and looked at his companion. "Dumdum bullets," he said.

"They're more reliable than the original dumdum," Mr. Pyne said. "They're what we call soft point bullets. They mushroom when they strike flesh, and they tear a big hole where they come out."

Ellen had to know what time it was, but she didn't dare look at the clock and see how few minutes were left before Bill would ride in on his motorcycle. She forced herself to turn her head. It was twenty minutes past six.

The big man was putting a cartridge in the gun.

"I wouldn't do that if I were you," Mr. Pyne said. "The first thing to do before you load a strange gun is to look through the barrel and see that it's clear."

Ellen saw that the old man took a childish pleasure in telling the man how to handle a rifle. As long as he had an audience for his gun talk, he forgot everything else in the world.

Mr. Pyne took the bolt out of the gun. The big man looked through the barrel. "It's all right," he said.

Mr. Pyne put the bolt back in the gun and shoved it home. "It's cocked and ready to fire, but it isn't loaded. Try the trigger pull."

Ellen heard the sharp "snap!" of the falling striker.

Mr. Pyne pointed out the safety and showed the man how it worked.

"Now load the gun."

He helped the man put a cartridge in the chamber and press other cartridges down into the magazine until it was full. Ellen looked at Mrs. Bowman. Her cheeks were still pink from the heat in the kitchen, but her face was drawn. She knew that Bill was coming any minute.

The big man aimed the rifle through the screen door. He seemed satisfied. He turned to Mrs. Bowman.

"Get a lunch for us to take with us," he said. He sat down with the rifle across his knees, facing the doorway.

Ellen got up to help Mrs. Bowman. The big man told her to sit down. Mr. Pyne took a packet of cigarettes out of his pocket and lit one.

"Give us all the cigarettes you got, grandpaw," the big man said.

Mr. Pyne rummaged in his pockets. He found two packets of cigarettes and handed them over. Even then he didn't seem to realize these men weren't friendly. He sat looking over his spectacles at them and smiling like a person who is anxious to be agreeable, but doesn't know what it's all about.

Ellen, straining to hear every sound, heard, far off and faintly, the staccato explosions of a motorcycle. She knew as well as if she could see him that Bill was coming across the flat on the other side of the hill at sixty miles an hour. She heard the sound of the motor change as he started up the hill and had to slow down.

The big man must have heard the motorcycle. He got up suddenly and went to the open window and listened. After a moment he turned and jerked his thumb at Ellen and Mrs. Bowman and Mr. Pyne, and said to his companion, "Watch them."

The smaller man stood up. The big man pushed the screen out of the window. It clattered on the porch floor outside.

Ellen knew by the sound of the motorcycle that Bill had got off. He was working the machine around one of those rock ledges that stuck up so high a car couldn't clear them. She heard him race the motor. He was coming on again, the thunder of the big V-twin engine loud and clear.

He shut the gas almost off and she knew he'd topped the hill. He had only a couple of hundred yards more before he'd come coasting into the yard. The big man was kneeling on the floor, the rifle barrel resting on the window sill. Ellen took a deep breath, getting ready to do the only thing she could do.

She screamed in warning as hard as she could scream. She caught a glimpse of Bill's blue uniform and the bright nickel of his machine through the doorway as a hard hand struck her across the mouth and the gun roared at the window.

Somehow she held onto her chair and didn't go over with the blow. She saw that the big man at the window was holding a hand over his right eye as if he were hurt. A splinter stuck out of his cheek as if it were an arrow. The other man started forward. Mr. Pyne's stick came down hard behind his ear. The man fell against the table as he went down, knocking the pitcher of milk and the dishes onto the floor.

Bill was in the doorway. He wasn't dead. He had his revolver out and he was yelling, "Put 'em up!" The man who had the rifle was still on his knees, holding his eye. Bill knocked him over.

"Where's a rope?" he asked.

Ellen ran to get the clothesline.

J.M. Pyne held Bill's revolver on the men while Bill tied them up.

Bill held her tightly in his arms and the relief was so great that she sobbed on his shoulder.

"You're sure you're all right, Bill?"

"Yes," he said. "I wasn't more than twenty feet away when he fired, but he missed me."

Mrs. Bowman had a broom and a dustpan, though she wasn't using them with her usual deftness.

"Never saw such a mess in my life," she said, as she swept broken

202

glass and dishes and devil's-food cake into the dustpan. "Ellen, get a mop."

"You sit down," Bill said to Ellen. "You sit down until you stop trembling."

"No," she said, "I'd rather help."

She got the mop and started on the spilled milk.

Bill went over to the window and picked up the rifle the big man had dropped.

"It's that seven-millimeter rifle of yours I go out of the attic last week," he said to J.M. Pyne. "How did they get it?"

"I gave it to them," the old man said.

"You gave it to them?"

"It was the only thing I could do," Mr. Pyne said.

Ellen could see that Mr. Pyne was feeling pretty good, as if he'd accomplished something, instead of getting Bill shot at.

Bill was looking at the gun. "It blew back," he said. "The stock's splintered. And that's why that fellow's eye is burned. The gas got him."

"Yes," Mr. Pyne said.

Ellen saw Bill look at the old man and she knew Bill couldn't understand why he was so pleased with himself.

Bill opened the gun and took out the empty cartridge case. "The primer blew..." And then Ellen heard the surprise in his voice as he added, "It isn't the right cartridge! It's got a rim - it's a thirty-thirty case."

Bill looked into the breech, turning the gun so the light would shine in. "So," he said, "that guy didn't miss me. He never had a chance. The bullet's stuck right there in the throat. It never came out of the gun."

"That was the idea," Mr. Pyne said.

Ellen couldn't follow what they were saying. But she knew it was important to them. "What are you talking about?" she asked.

"Just a minute, Ellen," Bill said. "I want to get this straight."

"I couldn't come in here with the gun and corner those men when

I heard the way they were talking," J.M. Pyne said. "I couldn't find any of the right cartridges for the gun. But there was a lot of .30-30 stuff. So I gave the fellow some of it and let him do the shooting."

"Is the .30-30 case so much shorter than the seven-millimeter that it'll go in the chamber even if the bullet is too big for the barrel?" Bill asked.

"That rifle isn't chambered for the foreign seven-millimeter case. It's chambered for our .30/06 case, necked down to 7mm. The .30-30 goes in and doesn't go so far it won't fire. But when it does fire, the bullet won't go through the barrel."

"Then," Ellen said, "it wasn't an accident that saved Bill's life?"

Bill put his arm around her. "No, darling," he said, "it was brains."

J.M. Pyne bent thoughtfully over the gun. "I believe it's all right," he said. "The stock's busted, but the action held. And the barrel isn't damaged."

Mrs. Bowman had put away the broom and dustpan. Now she turned on them.

"Are you two men going to talk guns all evening?" she demanded. "Bill, you go telephone the barracks to get those men out of here... John, I'm tired of hearing about your seven-millimeter rifle... Ellen, you see what's left in this house for supper after those men ate up all the veal loaf and spilled your devil's food cake on the floor."

"Mr. Pyne," Ellen said, "I hope you'll forgive me for what I thought about you when you were showing that man how to load the rifle." J.M. Pyne looked at her over his glasses, and she saw that he was smiling. "Because," she said, "I think you're wonderful."

LET THE GUN TALK

Joe Hill backed his battered roadster up to the store-room and asked for a case of Government .30 caliber ammunition.

"Okay, Mr. Hill," the boy said.

Joe noticed the "Mr". He had been a mechanic ever since he was big enough to say he was 16. He had become a toolmaker, trusted with nice work. He had made good with J.M. Pyne. But he had never been a boss until he came to Gaylord Arms. He wasn't used to being mistered.

The boy would have put the case aboard, but it weighed a hundred pounds and he was a skinny kid. Joe hoisted it easily into the rumble seat and drove across the factory yard to what they called the Water Shop, because in the beginning it had been powered by a waterwheel which took its water from a dam several hundred yards up the river. They hadn't used it since the 1890's, so they had given it to the old man.

The gun was lying on the bench. J.M. Pyne was wearing his Sunday clothes, and his beard had been freshly trimmed. He was rummaging in a case that looked like a doctor's bag. He spread the contents out on the bench - screw drivers, two kinds of pliers, a dozen shapes of needle files, and spare action springs. He had carried that kit to rifle matches for 40 years, because his rivals expected him to stop shooting and fix their rifles when anything went wrong with them, while his own gun got cold and the wind shifted and the light changed. He had made world's records just the same.

The old man looked at Joe over the top of his glasses. "You're feeling pretty good."

Joe knew what he meant. It was his way of saying, "You think you're going to get somewhere with the gun this afternoon."

205

"It's a nice day," Joe said. It was a nice day - clear and bright and warm.

The old man stared out of the iron-barred window at the river rushing by below them. The river was at flood after a week of rain. But now the sun was shining on the dark water.

"Yes," he said, "it's a nice day. I hope you still think it's a nice day when we get back here."

He had been like that about the gun ever since the first time Joe had seen it, two months back. They had been packing up the stuff in the Jersey City shop, getting it ready to ship to Gaylord Arms, when Joe had found the box, with a card tacked on the lid addressing it to an Army officer at Aberdeen Proving Ground, and asked what was in it. The old man had put him off. Joe had bothered him until he had opened the box and pulled out the wadded newspapers, dated July, 1929, and there it was - a semi-automatic military rifle, ugly after its kind, but beautiful in its simplicity.

J.M. Pyne said he had changed his mind about sending it in for trial when he had heard that the Army was working on its own semi-automatic rifle. He had decided it wasn't any use. He didn't much care. He had satisfied himself that he had solved the problem. Why try to convince men who knew less about it than he did? He'd had enough of trying to tell the Army something about small arms.

J.M. Pyne bent his head over the tools on the bench. "You don't know what you're getting into, Joe," he said.

"The gun is good."

"What's that got to do with it?"

"I'd like to put it over."

The old man growled something about having been young once himself.

"It's a quarter of two," Joe said. "You ready?"

"In ten minutes."

Joe picked up the gun. The old man turned his head. He glared at the gun in Joe's hands as he spoke. "I don't like semi-automatic rifles. They won't shoot."

He knew how the old man felt. J.M. Pyne had given his whole

life to making rifles that were more accurate than any others. He was famous for his knowledge and for his precise workmanship. He couldn't get the results he demanded from a semi-automatic rifle. The tolerances had to be bigger. Besides, being a military arm, it couldn't weigh more than 10 pounds. He couldn't put enough weight in the barrel for fine shooting.

"You can't compare it with one of your 300 magnum bull guns," Joe said. "Of course it isn't as good as they are."

"What's the use of it, then?!"

Joe wanted to remind him that his semi-automatic rifle had shot as well as other military rifles. But he knew it was better not to argue. He put the gun in the car. He guessed he had time to walk through the barrel shop and make sure that everything was going all right. He had 200 men under him. He would soon have 400 - maybe a thousand. Gaylord Arms had been dying for 20 years. Now it was alive again. Joe, though he still didn't quite believe it, was superintendent of the works. He was 28 years old.

He looked into the reception room as he was passing the door. The girl at the information desk was known to have ignored - with a cool, contemptuous stare - all attempts to kid her along. But she had a way of giving Joe a long, slow, sidewise look, as if they shared a secret. It was a year since he'd had a date with a girl. Betty had made it plain, without a word, that he had only to ask. But she wasn't there at the moment.

A girl with gorgeous red hair, slim and smart in a blue-gray dress, was standing at the information desk. Joe paused, without thinking what he was doing, to get a better look at her, and she turned and caught him staring at her. He could have walked on down the hall toward the barrel shop as if their eyes had never met.

"Is there anything I can do for you?" he asked.

"Yes," she said, "I came to see Mr. Pyne."

Her voice was the kind he liked, low-pitched, and her smile was pretty swell. But Joe felt that her manner took it for granted that if she wanted to see the old man, somebody would go running to fetch him.

"Mr. Pyne is busy right now," he said. "Is it a personal matter?"

"Yes," she said. "I mean it always is with him, isn't it? I want him to make me one of his target rifles."

Joe shook his head and smiled at the absurdity of it. She was, of course, the daughter of some rich man, and so spoiled that she thought she could have anything that struck her fancy, whether she had any use for it or not. She needed to learn that there were some things she couldn't have just because she was nice to look at.

"Do you have to be so rude?" She said it without raising her voice, so it irritated him more than if she'd got mad.

"You don't understand. J.M. Pyne doesn't make rifles for everybody. He hasn't time. He only makes them for men who are good enough shots to need them."

"How interesting." She looked straight into his eyes. "Is it true?"

Joe hesitated. It wasn't strictly true. The old man would do anything for a friend, even if he couldn't shoot.

"It doesn't matter," she said. "I'm a good shot."

Joe smiled again. Half the people he met said that about themselves, and believed it. Rifle shooting was neither fashionable nor spectacular, so most people never saw any good shooting. They picked up a boy's rifle in the country and hit tin cans at 50 feet and thought they knew how to shoot. Their choice of so big a target proved they didn't know what rifles were for.

He had to get rid of the girl. He had been trying to get J.M. Pyne to make more models of his semi-automatic rifle. He'd stayed up nights milling out two new receivers, which housed the working parts of the gun, from solid blocks of tough alloy steel, to save the old man as much work as he could. If this crazy girl barged in on him she might persuade him to make a rifle for her, and that would mean another delay of a week or a month.

"I'm sure you are a good shot," Joe said, trying to be diplomatic.

"You mean you're sure I'm not."

"That's right," he said, letting her have it straight.

If she was surprised, she didn't show it. "Last weekend," she said, "I broke five pop bottles in succession."

She thrust her chin out at him as if daring him to say that wasn't good shooting.

He didn't laugh. But she guessed what he thought.

"You aren't impressed."

"No," Joe said.

"What would you call good shooting?"

"Nowadays, the .22 rimfire shooters use a target at 100 yards that has a 10-ring two inches in diameter. The top men in a prone match will have all their shots in the 10-ring. They call that a 'possible' - a clean score."

"Then who wins?"

"They had to put a one-inch ring inside the 10 ring to decide that. They call it the X-ring. The man who has a clean score and the most X's wins."

"That makes pop bottles just funny, doesn't it?" She dropped her eyelashes in confusion. He saw how soft her skin was, with freckles faintly showing on either side of her slightly turned-up nose. Her cheeks were delicately flushed. "And," she added, "they weren't a hundred yards away - they weren't anything like that."

Joe thought it was sweet of her to admit that she was wrong. It would be easy enough now to persuade her not to bother the old man about the barrel. His irritation left him. He wanted to be kind and helpful.

"Anyway," she said, looking up at him, "it was fun."

"Of course it was."

"But you think I don't rate a Pyne rifle."

"You don't need it. You'd find it much too heavy. You can buy a perfectly good light rifle for $10 in a hardware store."

"Thank you ever so much," the red-headed girl said. "You've been so - so educational. I mustn't take any more of your time. But may I ask one question?"

"Yes, of course."

It was only then that he saw how scornful she was.

"Can you speak for Mr. J.M. Pyne?" she asked.

"No one speaks for J.M. Pyne."

"That's what I thought."

Betty came in and sat down behind the information desk. The redheaded girl asked her for a sheet of paper.

"Take my chair," Betty said.

The girl wrote rapidly. Joe stood staring at her bent head. Her hair was a marvelous red, and so thick and soft and curly it made you want to run your hand through it. She folded the note and held it out to him.

"Will you be so good as to give that to Mr. Pyne?"

"If you insist," Joe said, trying not to show how angry he was.

The old man was trying the door of his shop to make sure it was locked. He had two bandoleers of ammunition over his shoulder.

"What have you got there?"

"Some 1938 National Match stuff."

Joe remembered that lot. They had shot several hundred rounds of it, testing the semi-automatic rifle. It was loaded with the boat-tail bullet that had so greatly increased the range of the service rifle. The old man must have some pride in his gun, no matter what he said, or else he wouldn't have taken the trouble to bring along the more powerful ammunition the Army had given up when they adopted the Garand rifle. He wanted to show that his gun could handle the load that had done so well at long range in the 1903 Springfield.

He smiled as he read the note the redheaded girl had written. "It's from Frieda Guerdner. She's Fritz Guerdner's daughter. I used to shoot with Fritz at the old Schuetzen club here in Waterford. I lost track of him years ago when I moved my shop to Jersey City. I heard he'd gone out West."

"If you want to see the girl," Joe said, "I'll tell her to come back tomorrow."

"What for? I'd like to see her now."

Joe knew it wasn't any use. You couldn't force the old man. You had to get around him. And this girl was doing it. Somebody had told her how to manage J.M. Pyne, or else she just knew, without being told.

"All right," he said. "I'll get her."

She was sitting in the reception room. She looked up, ever so innocent.

"Mr. Pyne will see you," Joe said.

"Oh," she said, "I was sure he would."

Joe was too sore to say anything.

J.M. Pyne took both her hands in his. Joe had noticed before that the old man liked pretty girls. He might be 75, but he was just as susceptible as anybody else. He told Frieda Guerdner that she must go with them to Reuben Gaylord's farm and see the gun shoot.

"I've got my car," she said. "But I could leave it here."

"Joe will put your car in the yard," J.M. Pyne said. "You ride with us."

He handed her into the roadster with an old man's gallantry.

She gave Joe her key. Her car was a convertible coupe, of the same year as his roadster, and looked as if it had taken the same kind of beating.

When he got back, she and J.M. Pyne were old friends. Joe squeezed in behind the wheel. There was so little room that the girl was pressed against him. It didn't seem to bother her, but it bothered him. He stared straight ahead, as if she wasn't there. But he could hear everything that she said, and he could imagine how she was looking at the old man when she told him she had heard about him all her life and longed to meet him and dreamed of someday having a Pyne rifle.

"I'll make you a rifle," J.M. Pyne said.

Joe knew by the tone of his voice that the old man was flattered. He had heard that kind of thing from gun cranks. It only made him crustier than usual. But when a girl with lovely brown eyes said it, he fell for it as if he were a college boy and she'd been telling him that he was so big and strong she was afraid of him.

"I've got a barrel nearly finished," he went on. "I intended it for Joe here. But he can wait. If it shoots when I put it in the machine rest, it's yours."

Joe thought if she had any sense of decency she'd offer to do the waiting. The old man had been promising him that barrel for a year.

211

"Oh," she said, "how nice of you! But it's only fair to tell you that Mr. Hill thinks I'm not a good enough shot to need a Pyne rifle."

"What has Joe got to say about it?" the old man demanded.

Joe wondered where the girl had got her fixed idea. Did she think a Pyne rifle was something to hang on the wall and brag to her friends about? It wouldn't get her much. A Pyne rifle looked like other rifles, except on the inside. And you had to know what to look for to see what was there to see. Not one man in 50,000 could appreciate the perfection with which the grooves were cut. She certainly couldn't. To let her have a Pyne rifle was like letting a baby have a chronometer to play with.

The road bore south, sometimes close to the river, sometimes half a mile from it, through a country of small fields enclosed by stone walls, with wooded hills rising tier on tier in the distance. Joe turned off the concrete highway into a dirt road and then into the long, winding drive, with a row of elm trees on either side, that led to the Gaylord place. The house, half hidden by trees and shrubbery, had once been a plain, rectangular one with four chimneys. The wings on either side were plainly of a later date. It looked big and shabby and comfortable.

J.M. Pyne pointed to a long, low wooden building, with many small-paned windows, off to the right. "That," he said to Frieda Guerdner, "is where the first Reuben Gaylord made carbines for the Union Armies before he built the Water Shop in Waterford. When I started making rifles 50 years ago, I used to buy my barrel steel from the old gentleman, and it was smooth-cutting stuff. Yonder is the big meadow where he had his rifle range."

The meadow sloped gently to the river, where there was a homemade footbridge suspended on wire cables well above the water. On the far side the meadow extended northeast for a good half-mile, until it met a steep wooded ridge that made a natural backstop for bullets.

Joe saw, at the firing point, the things he had asked for - a table and a spotting scope, a tub of water, and a wheelbarrow load of garden dirt with a spade sticking in it. The driveway ahead was full of cars. He had to stop.

The old man got stiffly down and gave his hand to the girl.

"Joe," he said, "don't claim too much. Let the gun talk."

II

They had to meet a lot of people on the east terrace. Some of them were friends of the Gaylords - country-club people in sports clothes who didn't matter. Joe guessed that most of the others were the sort of chiselers, disguised as businessmen, who swarmed whenever arms or ammunition could be made, in the hope of running a shoestring into a bankroll while no one was looking.

He saw one man he couldn't place - a tall man with graying hair and a proud unsmiling face who carried himself as if he had been a soldier or an athlete. He had a scar across his cheek, almost from his mouth to his ear, that might have been a saber cut. What made Joe look again was the dog that stood at the man's heel, obedient, but trembling with eagerness. The dog was big, with the short black coat and tan markings of a Doberman pinscher, only taller at the shoulder and more powerful.

Joe started back to the car to get the gun, and guessed he'd better check first with the Gaylords. Reuben Gaylord, looking more like a nice college boy than a man in his middle 30's should, was busy at the table where the whisky had been set out. Mrs. Gaylord was talking to a little group of chiselers.

He waited for her, admiring the way she did it. She knew what they were as well as he did. She was being a good hostess. He did not like the kind of make-up she chose - dark tan, with the lips and fingernails a purplish red. But he knew her artificiality was only color deep.

"Do you see anybody who counts?" he asked when she got away.

She shook her head, "Reuben did the best he could. It seems all the purchasing commissions are at New Haven looking over the new submachine gun. There isn't a single person here who rates anything. But the newspapers've all sent reporters and photographers. And" - she made a face - "Winthrop Harris said he'd be here."

He did not feel free to ask Mrs. Gaylord what Winthrop Harris rated at Gaylord Arms. The story around the plant was that Harris represented new money in the Company, but that Reuben Gaylord was still president in fact as well as on the letterhead.

"And," Connie Gaylord went on, "Harris is bringing an Army officer - a major or a major general or something."

213

Joe smiled. She understood as well as he did how it was with Army officers. The Army had adopted the Garand rifle in 1936. The choice had been so strongly criticized that the Army was touchy on the subject.

"Who," Joe asked, "is the fierce man with the big dog?"

"Oh," she said, "you mean Winkler. I suppose Reuben asked him because he has money. But he's only interested in his dogs. He breeds them and trains them to capture criminals."

Joe found J.M. Pyne beside the roadster with the rifle in his hands.

"Let's get started," he said.

"Mrs. Gaylord says there isn't anybody in the whole crowd who knows anything about guns."

"Mrs. Gaylord is mistaken," the old man retorted, and went off toward the firing point with the rifle.

Joe followed, lugging the case of ammunition. The old man sent two boys off to the two-hundred-yard butts with a sheaf of targets, and orders to stay in the pit until they had pulled the targets down and raised a red flag as a signal to cease firing.

"What did you mean?" Joe asked. The old man did not answer.

"You said she was mistaken."

The old man grumbled something. Joe saw that the boys had to wade to reach the footbridge. The river was over its banks. He turned toward the terrace. Reuben Gaylord had started his guests toward the firing point. Joe braced himself. The hardest thing he had to do was to speak his piece about the gun. He wondered if he ought to begin by saying, "Ladies and gentlemen." He guessed that would sound too stiff.

"We should have had Reuben string a rope to keep them away," the old man said. He sat down on the camp stool behind the spotting scope, within reach of the field telephone on the table that connected with the target pit. The crowd stood in a semicircle, two or three deep. Joe picked up the rifle and faced them.

"Ladies and gentlemen," he said, "the rifle I have here was made, lock, stock and barrel, by J.M. Pyne. You all know who he is. The gun is a recoil-operated semi-automatic rifle. In other words, it fires each time you press the trigger."

214

He saw Winthrop Harris coming across the grass with the Army officer. He couldn't think of what to say next. He stood there sweating. Winthrop Harris and the officer joined the semi-circle. It was getting unbearable, when he remembered a sentence from the speech he had started to write that morning.

"The gun has certain advantages over any other semi-automatic rifle. It is loaded from standard Army clips. It takes two 5-shot clips at a time, so it is good for 10 shots without recharging - in fact, for 11 shots if you put one cartridge in the chamber. Thanks to its design, the gun does not heat up as fast in rapid fire as others. It is more accurate than other semi-automatic rifles. In our tests on this range it has proved as accurate as the Springfield service rifle with the same ammunition."

"Just a minute, Joe," J.M. Pyne interrupted. "The gun shot as well as the two service Springfields we had. We are not certain those two were up to standard." Joe saw several people smiling at the old man's insistence on the precise truth.

"I stand corrected," he said. "But all these are minor points, compared with the fundamental superiority of the gun. You all understand that modern mass production can go into high gear only when the product is designed to be built by mass production methods. The Pyne rifle is the only semi-automatic rifle ever designed to take full advantage of such methods.

"It will not take 18 months or a year, or even 6 months, to tool up to make it. At most, it will be a 90-day job. And when you have tooled up for it you can make it three times as fast as you can make any other gun with its speed of fire. It overcomes the only serious objections to supplying every private in an army with a semi-automatic rifle - slowness of manufacture and high cost. You may have wondered why the armies now fighting in Europe and Asia are not armed with semi-automatic rifles. The answer is simply that no country in the world, except the United States, can afford to wait for, or to pay for, the kind of semi-automatic rifles now being made."

Joe found himself out of words. He took a quick look over his shoulder. The targets were up. He saw Reuben Gaylord handing out cotton.

"Before I shoot the gun," he went on, "and while Mr. Gaylord makes sure you all have cotton to put in your ears, I want to tell you that the targets down there at two hundred yards are Army targets with a 10-inch bull. It is no trick to stay in the bull from

215

the prone position when you take your time. I am going to see how many I can keep in there while shooting rapid fire. The Army says the ordinary soldier can fire 40 aimed shots in 60 seconds with the Garand. I'm going to shoot here at that speed... Reuben, will you hold a stop watch on me?"

He stripped two clips of cartridges into the gun, put a dozen more clips on the grass and lay down in the military prone position. He felt the sling go tight as the weight of his head and shoulders went into it, felt the wood of the stock warm and friendly against his cheek, felt the earth solid under his belly and his legs, saw the bull sitting on top of the sight, and all his nervousness was gone. He was home again. He was no talker. But this gun could talk.

"Fire," Reuben Gaylord said.

Joe broke the shot dead on, without conscious effort, and the front sight leaped up across the bull at twelve o'clock the way it should, and he had the good feeling with which the gun sat back against his shoulder and he heard the sharp clean blast from the muzzle ringing in his ears as he pulled the front sight down to 6 o'clock and again the gun sat back. He was in the groove, getting them off fast and clean, when the gun mis-fired.

He reached out for the bolt handle. He yanked the bolt back. But no cartridge came flying out. The gun had failed to feed. It had never happened before. It couldn't happen. But it had happened. The next cartridge just hadn't come out of the magazine to be picked up by the bolt as it went forward.

The old man leaned toward him. "Put in another clip."

Joe stripped a fresh clip into the magazine and the gun worked perfectly for 5 shots. He had to go on that way, putting in a fresh clip every 5 shots on top of the 5 cartridges that refused to come out of the magazine until he had fired his 40 shots.

"They're pretty well bunched," J.M. Pyne said, studying the target through the spotting scope.

"The time," Reuben Gaylord said, "was one minute and fifty-eight seconds."

Joe got off the ground. He saw the grin on the Army officer's face. He felt he had to say something, to admit that the gun had failed to do what the Garand would do.

"That was twice as long as I intended," he said.

216

The gun was pretty hot to handle, but he got the magazine out, meaning to see what was the matter with it.

"Let it alone," J.M. Pyne said. "You can't fix it now."

Joe put the magazine back. There wasn't anything else to do. He turned to the crowd again.

"We'll have that target up here in a few minutes," he said. "While we're waiting, I'll give the gun a mud test."

He spread out the pile of garden dirt, making a hollow, and dumped the tub of water into it. He puddled the mud and laid the gun in it. When he figured it was cool he picked it up and wiped it off on the grass.

"Before I shoot the gun again," he said, "I'm going to take one precaution that would be difficult with any other semi-automatic rifle. I'm going to look through the barrel to make sure that there isn't enough mud inside it so that the first shot will blow the muzzle off."

He took the barrel out, saw that it was clear, and put it back again. The gun fired 5 shots in spite of the mud in the action when he worked the bolt by hand, but quit on the 6th shot as it had before.

The boy had come back with his 40-shot target. Joe saw that he had all but three of his shots in the black and gave the target to Reuben Gaylord to pass around.

He did most of the things he had planned to do. He took the gun completely apart with no tools but a loaded cartridge, and put it together again. He fired two successive 10-shot groups, taking his time, to show what the gun would do at 200 yards, and both times he kept the spread of the shots under 5 inches.

But he knew the show was a flop. The gun had talked. And nothing else mattered.

He asked if anyone would care to shoot the gun. Two news photographers came forward.

"We want a picture of a girl shooting the gun," one of them said. "How about that redheaded one?"

"It's up to her," Joe said.

They brought Frieda Guerdner over. Joe loaded the gun with the National Match ammo. It would kick more. He hoped she'd feel it.

"I'll need the sling shortened," she said.

Joe was afraid then that she knew what she was doing. She was taller than most girls and wider in the shoulders. But she would need the sling a good deal shorter than he did. He took up three holes.

She got down into the prone position. He could see that she was used to it. She had the loop of the sling high on her left arm, her left elbow under the gun, her left arm stretched far out, her right thumb around the grip, her legs at the proper angle to her body and spread wide apart as she hugged the ground.

"Lend me your hat, will you?" she said to J.M. Pyne. "The sun is in my eyes."

The old man gave her his hat and she jammed it down over her eyes. Joe wondered if she was nervous. The sun couldn't possibly bother her.

"I want one sighter," she said as she settled again into the sling. "Will you tell me where this one goes?"

Joe knew that was what he would have asked in her place. A rifle sighted in for one person was right for another only if their eyes and their ways of aiming and holding were the same.

He watched her finger on the trigger. He could see her taking up on the pull. She did not flinch as she got the shot off, and he could see no sign that the recoil surprised her.

"You're in the black between one and two o'clock," the old man said. "About four inches from center each way."

"That was a good hold," she said. "I'll take a chance on it." She reached for the rear sight. "How much do I give it?"

"They're half-minute clicks," Joe said, hoping she didn't know what a half-minute of angle meant.

She knew. She gave the elevation screw four clicks down and the windage screw four clicks over.

He watched her as she shot. The recoil lifted that red hair of hers each time, but it did not disturb her rhythm. She got her first 5 shots off at regular intervals. He knelt down and loaded another clip into the gun.

218

When she had fired her 10 shots, J.M. Pyne turned to Joe. "I thought you said she couldn't shoot. Take a look."

Joe looked through the spotting scope. Her sight correction hadn't been quite enough. You really couldn't correct a sight on the strength of one shot. But her group was better than either of his 10-shot groups. He guessed it wasn't over four inches.

He knew how to take being beaten in a match with other men. But to be beaten by this girl was maddening. How had she learned to shoot like that? And what for? Why should a girl want to shoot? This one had deliberately deceived him with her story about hitting pop bottles, knowing that it would convince him she didn't know anything about shooting.

"I was wrong," Joe said to the old man.

The photographers asked Frieda Guerdner to pose for them standing up. They said the pictures of her they had got would be nothing to look at. The hat had hidden most of her face and the prone position was not graceful.

"I'm sorry," she said, "but I won't pose."

Joe looked at her. He would have guessed that she would like to see her picture in the papers. But it was plain she meant what she said. The photographers were astonished and indignant. They argued and cajoled. But it didn't do them any good.

III

Connie Gaylord asked Frieda Guerdner and J.M. Pyne and Joe to come in when the crowd had gone. Joe let the others go into the house ahead of him. He wanted to check that magazine.

The Gaylords were in the gun room. One wall was lined with cases displaying examples of all the rifles Gaylord Arms had made, beginning with the Civil War carbines and continuing through a series of buffalo rifles and long-range match rifles, and ending with the current model, a well-made single shot that had no sale to a public that demanded repeating rifles.

Over the fireplace was a large portrait of Reuben Gaylord the first, looking a good deal like U.S. Grant. On a stand at one side of the room was the first Gaylord power plant - a little 5-horse steam engine, all polished brass and steel, that the founder had built himself.

The room was, Joe felt, a museum that told the story of the rise and fall of Gaylord Arms. He looked at Reuben Gaylord, glass in hand, leaning carelessly against the mantel under the portrait of his grandfather, and the contrast saddened him. Everybody liked Reuben Gaylord, but no one took him seriously. He had inherited Gaylord Arms. It hadn't paid a dividend since.

"Joe," Reuben said, "what was the matter with the gun?"

"Somebody tampered with it."

"What?" Reuben said.

Joe saw that they were all leaning forward, startled and curious - all of them except J.M. Pyne.

"The magazine spring is a flat ribbon of steel," Joe said. "It is shaped like three V's in succession. Somebody cut off one whole V. That made the spring too short. It was only long enough to feed the first five cartridges."

"Who would do a thing like that?" Reuben asked.

"Who had a chance to do it?"

"I did," J.M. Pyne said.

"But what for?" Reuben Gaylord demanded.

"I saw too many strangers when I got here this afternoon."

They all looked at the old man as if they thought he was a little cracked.

"I decided it was better," he added, "if the gun didn't do too well. The word will go out now that the gun is no good, and no one will bother about it."

"You mean," Reuben said, "that no one will buy it?"

"No one would buy it anyway," the old man retorted. "It's too different from the others. And the Army isn't interested, or the Marine Corps. They've adopted the Garand. They won't look at any other gun. But I'd just as soon no one stole the idea."

Reuben started to say something, and thought better of it. No one said anything. It was not easy to tell J.M Pyne he had taken care against an imaginary danger. Joe felt sore and puzzled. He remembered bitterly the moment when the gun had talked for the first time. It wouldn't have been so bad if he hadn't said he was going to shoot 40 shots in 60 seconds. He could still see the self-satisfied grin on that Army officer's face. The old man had let him down. It wasn't like him. It wasn't like him to be so fearful either.

But Joe saw now that it hadn't done any good to demonstrate the gun to a crowd, and that it wouldn't have done any good, no matter who had been there or how well the gun had performed. He had taken it for granted that when you had a good thing, all you needed to do was to show it. Pyne target rifles had never needed any selling. His friends shot them and found out how good they were and talked about them, and other men wanted them. The old man had never been able to keep up with the demand.

But a semi-automatic rifle was different. It wasn't something hand made to suit an expert. It was a mass-production job. The superiority of Pyne's design was of a kind that only a man who was both a mechanic and an engineer could appreciate. And if he was a mechanic and an engineer who had grown up in an old-fashioned factory - and all firearms factories were old-fashioned - he probably wouldn't see it. You'd have to prove to him that the Pyne gun was faster to produce by producing it faster.

"Pyne is right," Joe said. "There's no chance to sell the gun to the Army, and as long as it's just an idea there isn't any chance to sell it to anybody else either. The market is full of buyers, but they aren't buying ideas. They want rifles. Springfield Armory and the big arms companies are making all they can for the Government. They will be for years to come. The purchasing commissions from the Dutch East Indies and the South American countries don't know where to turn. The State Department is glad to license sales to them. The Government wants them to have rifles. But where are they going to buy?"

"I know," Reuben Gaylord said. "But what can we do about it?"

"There's the whole West Shop," Joe said. "It's full of lathes, milling machines and drill presses. They're old, but they're good. All they need is jigs and fixtures. We could have the forgings delivered by the time we were tooled up."

"It would take $100,000 to start," Reuben said.

"What's $100,000?" Joe asked.

"A lot of money," Reuben Gaylord said.

"Not in times like these. Not when you're tooling up to make millions of dollars worth of stuff. You'd get your money back

221

with one million-dollar order and make a profit besides."

"Maybe," Reuben Gaylord said. "Maybe you would. But somebody's got to stick his neck out first. Somebody's got to put up the $100,000, maybe $200,000."

"So what? I'm not talking arms factory production. I'm talking about the way the automobile people do things. Suppose we brought a man down here from Detroit - like that fellow Bostwick you went to M.I.T. with. He'd make an engineering study and lay out the West Shop for real mass production. It would be a small unit by Detroit standards. But we'd show what could be done by using modern methods to make a gun like Pyne's. We'd produce guns three or four times as fast as they've ever been produced before. We'd get all the orders we could fill. And the time is coming when the Army is going to take anything it can get. The Army will give us orders if we're in production. And that's the only way we'll ever have a chance to prove that Pyne's gun is better than the Garand."

Reuben Gaylord smiled at Joe. "Have you any idea what George Bostwick gets for making engineering studies? His fee would be at least $5,000."

"I'm not surprised."

"It's too bad you're talking to me, Joe," Reuben Gaylord said, "instead of to my grandfather." He looked up at the portrait of Reuben Gaylord the first. "You might get somewhere with him. If you could sell him on your proposition, he would go out and get the money even if he had to hock everything he owned."

He poured himself another drink. Joe thought he'd had enough.

"The trouble is, Joe," he went on, "I'm a grandson. Did it ever occur to you that there's the whole trouble with New England? The grandsons have got all the fine old factories and all the fine old names. And they're a timid lot. Their only ambition is to hang on to what they have.

"You can see how it is with me. I own this old house and the 700 acres that used to be a good farm. I own almost half the stock in Gaylord Arms, and if it goes to pot, as it will as soon as this little boom is over, I'll still have enough money to live here. Maybe I could raise $100,000. But why should I risk it? Why should I let myself in for all the grief that sort of thing means? I'm just not that kind of guy, Joe." He looked down at the tall glass in his hand. "I don't really care."

Joe felt there wasn't anything to say. He looked at J.M Pyne to see if he was ready to go. The old man was sitting with his hands clasped around one knee and staring up at the portrait of Reuben's grandfather. Frieda Guerdner was sitting on the sofa beside him with her chin in her hand. She hadn't said a word, but Joe could see how interested she was.

Connie Gaylord stood up and started to leave the room. "I want to talk to Joe," she said.

He followed her out into the hall. She walked into the dining room and kicked the door shut.

"I like men who have no illusions about themselves, don't you? Who never let you down because they never promise anything. Who haven't got much on the ball and admit it. Who haven't any ambition and don't pretend to have."

"Yes," Joe said, because that seemed to be the thing to say.

"So," she said, "you really are dumb. You believe anything you hear, and never think."

Joe waited.

"Don't you know that's only his alibi?" she went on. "He says he doesn't care, and he cares so much he can't go to sleep at night. All his pride is in Gaylord Arms. Do you think he wants Winthrop Harris to take it away from him? Do you?"

"No," Joe said, "I don't suppose he does."

"Why do you think he went out to Jersey City to get you and J.M. Pyne? Because he doesn't care?"

"No," Joe said. "But he didn't seem much interested in tooling up to make the gun."

"He thought you were just talking, and maybe you were."

"No," Joe said, "I wasn't just talking. And he knew it."

She looked up at him, and he saw that her eyes were full of tears.

"I've got to save him," she said. "Don't you see I've got to save him? You can help. You can break through that pose of his. You go to work on him."

"All right," Joe said, "I will."

"If it was anybody else, I'd think you were yes'ing me. But there's

223

something convincing about you, Joe."

She started for the door of the dining room. Joe took her arm and pulled her back.

"Listen," he said. "The first thing to do is to get George Bostwick."

"Consider it done," Connie Gaylord said. "What next?"

"Ask those South Americans up here and make them believe we are going to build the Pyne gun, and high pressure them into giving us a letter of intention, so we can get a clearance from the State Department."

"I can do something about that too," she said. "You'd be surprised. But you understand, don't you? Please understand. Nothing matters except Reuben. He's sunk now, but if this thing goes through, he won't be."

"I understand," Joe said. "All I care about is the gun. We've got to make the gun."

The traffic was bad, driving back to Waterford at the hour when the day shifts from the big airplane factory and the machine-tool plants were coming out and the night shifts were going in.

Joe found a kind of relief in the difficulty of getting into town. He did not hear what Frieda Guerdner and the old man were saying. He was busy with his own thoughts.

He had come a long way since the day, a year ago, when he had appeared at Pyne's shop in Jersey City, hoping to persuade the old man to teach him how to make fine shooting rifles. Until then, his only tough problems had been those of a toolmaker. You didn't solve those with your hands alone. You had to think. But you worked with things you had learned how to control. You might have to make something to a tolerance of nothing minus and a half a thousandth plus. When you did, you knew where you were. You could prove it with a micrometer caliper.

But if he was going to put the gun over, he would have to work with people. You couldn't change them to suit your purpose - heating them to cherry red, quenching in oil, and drawing to the right color. You had to take them as they came, even if they were as crotchety as the old man, or as badly licked as Reuben Gaylord, or as hard to take as this redheaded girl beside him.

IV

They went to a place called Brick's for dinner - a large square room with a bar across one end that looked as if it had not changed in 50 years. Frieda noticed that Joe Hill carried the gun in with him and laid it on a chair beside him, and the waiter showed no surprise.

"I used to come here with your father," J.M. Pyne said to Frieda, "before you were born. The steaks are just as good now as they were in those days."

Frieda said she hadn't had any lunch, so steak appealed to her. The old man ordered steaks for three.

She looked across the table at Joe Hill and wished she had resisted the temptation to take him for a ride when he had told her that J.M. Pyne only made rifles for men who shot well enough to need them. Her impression of him at the moment had been that he was a big dumb young man who needed to be taken down, and she was the girl who knew how to do it. Now that she had seen him in action, she knew she had made a bad mistake. He wasn't dumb. He was merely not given to bright chatter, after the manner of the young men she knew in New York. And if he was arrogant, he had some right to be. He wasn't handsome - unless you counted his long, lean, hard build - but he was increasingly impressive. She wanted to make him talk. She had always found it too easy to get men to talk about themselves. But she was afraid she had alienated this one so completely that he would never tell her anything. The calm with which he ignored her was apparently final.

She saw that he had a cartridge he was turning back and forth in his fingers.

The cartridge wasn't the usual color. It was nickeled or tinned.

"Why the color?" she asked.

"It's a blue pill," he said. He rolled the cartridge across the tablecloth to her.

"I don't know what that means," she said.

"It's loaded to much higher than normal pressure for use as a proof load. The color is to prevent it being mixed with regular cartridges. I meant to fire that one this afternoon to show that the Pyne gun would stand it."

225

"The gun would take it," J.M. Pyne said. "But I don't hold with firing blue pills from the shoulder. You run too big a chance of getting your head blown off. At Springfield Armory they put the gun in a rest with steel plates around it, so if anything lets go no one gets hurt. Joe, you put that where you won't pick it up by mistake."

Joe Hill obediently put the blue pill in the watch pocket of his trousers.

That was that, so Frieda tried again to make Joe Hill talk.

"I feel guilty," she said, "taking a barrel that J. M. Pyne intended for you."

The old man chuckled. "You needn't. If Joe wants a barrel, he can make it himself as well as I can."

"It wouldn't be a Pyne barrel," Frieda said.

"No one could tell the difference if he used my tools," the old man said. "At least I couldn't."

The steaks came then. The old man grew reminiscent as they ate, telling them about the days when he had shot off-hand at 200 yards against men like Fred Ross and Michael Dorrler and Doctor Hudson. But over his coffee he remembered the semi-automatic rifle.

"I'm sorry about this afternoon, Joe," J.M. Pyne said. "Maybe I should've told you that I had cut off that spring."

"I wish you had. I wouldn't have made such a fool of myself in front of that Army officer."

"I know that came hard, Joe. But I thought it would look better if you were surprised when the gun balked. And I had to do something when I saw Winkler there."

"Why?" Joe Hill asked. "What about Winkler?"

"You saw him, didn't you, Frieda?" the old man said. "The man with the big dog and the scar across his face."

"Yes, I did," Frieda Guerdner said, remembering how the man had stared at her.

"He's made a hobby all his life of rifle actions, and he's the most successful thief of rifle actions in the world."

"Connie Gaylord told me he had no interest in guns," Joe said.

226

"I wouldn't know any more about him than she does if it hadn't been for a German gunsmith I went to New Haven with 10 years ago," J.M. Pyne said. "My friend saw Winkler on the street and pointed him out to me. He told me some things about Winkler. I told him that when I was working on the Bennett semi-automatic pistol in 1917, one pistol disappeared. In the '20's a copy of that pistol was patented all over Europe. They even sold it here. Bennett was dead by that time and his heirs didn't have any money to fight with. My friend said he had no doubt Winkler had the pistol stolen and sent it over."

"You think he's working for somebody over there?" Frieda said.

The old man shrugged his shoulders. "From what I've heard, he's working for Winkler. That's why he's rich."

"What good did it do to cut off the spring?" Frieda asked. "He'll try to steal your gun just the same, won't he?"

"In the long run, there's no way to stop the theft of military arms. The moment a thing goes into production it can be stolen, and it is. I don't doubt that Winkler has a Garand of the latest model."

"But what if he stole your gun now?"

J.M. Pyne smiled. "He won't - not after what he saw today. He thinks it's got a bug in it, and he'll wait until we get the bug out. They always like to wait until a gun is perfected before they take it. That's why I say Winkler probably has the latest Garand. He wouldn't want one of the first 40,000, before they changed it so it would shoot decently."

"You speak of it as if it were all a matter of course," Frieda said.

"In my experience," J.M. Pyne said, "stealing is a matter of course. There's nothing romantic or exciting about it. You can bet Winkler never takes any chances. He hires somebody for a few dollars to steal something he expects to make thousands out of. Perhaps sometimes it's just a case of adding to his collection. I understand he takes great pride in having the best collection of modern military small arms. But mostly he's out to make money."

"Why can't something be done about him?" Frieda asked.

"What?" J.M. Pyne asked.

"I thought there was a law forbidding individuals to possess machine guns unless they were registered."

"Including sawed-off shotguns and .22 caliber pistols with shoul-

227

der stocks," J.M. Pyne said. "But like most laws about guns, it's only obeyed by honest men. If you wanted to get out a search warrant against Winkler, you'd have to get evidence. He's got money and he's got position. He's probably a director of the First National Bank, if not of Waterford Aircraft, so it would have to be good evidence. And if you did get a warrant, you wouldn't find anything."

The old man talked of other things after that. When he said he was tired, they walked with him around the corner to the place where he and Joe Hill had found rooms over a second hand store.

"Frieda," the old man said, "I'll be seeing you at the shop in the morning."

"You truly don't mind my watching you work?"

"I'll be glad to have you," he said. He turned to Joe. "I'd put the gun in the safe."

Frieda walked with Joe Hill to his roadster. He was driving her back to Gaylord Arms to get her car.

"You're sore," she said, as they started off.

"You could have told me you knew how to shoot."

"I did."

"No, you didn't. You told me that pop-bottle story because you knew it would make me think you didn't know what rifle shooting was about."

"You had it coming. You were so superior when I said I wanted a Pyne rifle. You might as well have laughed out loud."

"I didn't mean to high-hat you," he said. "I was trying to keep you away from the old man."

"You're bound to make him do what you want," she said, hoping to sting him out of his matter-of-factness. "You don't care what he wants."

"He should be making another model of his gun," Joe Hill said. "So far, he hasn't even got up working drawings. He made this one by cut and try."

"I'm sure you can make him do whatever you want him to."

"He'll go to work on the gun just as soon as you get out of here,"

228

Joe Hill said.

"At least he'll have a few days of doing what he loves to do before he has to work on something that doesn't interest him."

"I'm not so sure as you are that the semi-automatic rifle doesn't interest him. You don't know how important it is. He does. He knows he's got something the whole world has been trying for ever since 1918. Longer than that, of course. But especially since then."

Frieda did not try again to get under his skin until the watchman in the shanty at the gate to Gaylord Arms had let them in and Joe Hill had stopped alongside her car.

"I think it's stupid of you to worry about what J.M. Pyne does," she said when she had got out. "What you need to worry about is how you're going to make the gun."

He was opening up the rear deck of his car. He paused and looked her up and down as if he were appraising a rifle he had to make up his mind about.

"Maybe," he said - "Maybe you aren't the dumb little rich girl I picked you for."

For a moment she wanted to yell at him that she was not dumb, not little and not rich - especially not rich. But she recovered herself in time.

"I earn my own living," she said.

"As a model?"

"No!" She realized she had spoken hotly when there was no reason to. She had modelled clothes for photographers in New York. She could do it then because she hadn't had enough to eat while she was at the art school in Chicago. She was still slim by ordinary standards, but she no longer had the paperdoll flatness of a model. "I'm a commercial artist," she said.

V

She spent 10 hours a day with J.M. Pyne, watching the painstaking way in which he did things and listening to his talk of rifles and riflemen, and marvelling at the passion for his chosen work that still burned in him. She knew, from what he said, that Joe Hill came into the shop after they left and worked until two

229

o'clock in the morning on some kind of gadget to be used in making the Pyne gun, but she did not see him until toward the end of the third day.

J.M. Pyne had her new rifle in the vise. He was turning in the last of the screws that held the telescope blocks.

Joe Hill stood watching. He must have noticed that the old man had chosen a Gaylord action with fine English scroll engraving and found a stock made from a beautiful piece of crotch walnut, with a full feather figure running the length of it.

"I thought," he said, "that you didn't care how the outside of a rifle looked."

J.M. Pyne acted as if he'd been caught in something he didn't want to admit.

"I don't usually," he said. He glanced at Joe Hill over the top of his glasses. "Why not go to dinner with us, and come back here afterward and see how this gun shoots?"

Joe Hill said he would have to leave early, because he had a date.

At dinner, he told the old man how hopeful he was about the semi-automatic rifle. Reuben Gaylord had actually wired Bostwick, who would be in from Detroit in time for lunch the next day, which was Saturday; and he had a promise from the South American crowd that they would be in Waterford on Monday.

"One other thing," Joe Hill said as he was leaving. "I've asked Reuben to have the Water Shop wired for the watchmen's clocks. The electricians start tomorrow, and thereafter a watchman will go through every hour, seven days a week, just as he goes through the rest of the plant."

Frieda saw that J.M. Pyne was eager to get back to the rifle. They followed Joe Hill out. She saw his car ahead. He stopped beside the curb and a girl got in. J.M. Pyne didn't notice, so she said nothing. But presently she remembered where she had seen the girl before. It was at the information desk in the offices of Gaylord Arms.

She remembered the narrow, slanting Slavic eyes that gave the girl a slightly exotic look, and the rounded feminine figure, positively luscious, and, finally, the red hair. It wasn't exceptional red hair, Frieda thought. It didn't approach her own. But perhaps a man like Joe Hill couldn't see the difference.

"There's going to be a thunderstorm," J.M. Pyne said. "Have you got a raincoat?"

She knew better than to argue with him. She stopped at the hotel and got her raincoat.

The old man put the rifle in the machine rest and gave her a little telescope with which to watch the target, and began to shoot. When he had fired 10 shots, she saw that he was smiling. When he had fired 50 shots, she saw that he was happy at the way the gun was shooting.

He went on and on for hours, while the storm broke outside the shop, the thunder rolled, and the lightning flashed and the rain drove against the window-panes, trying one make of match ammunition after another. It was 11 o'clock when he took the gun out of the rest and cleaned it.

"Tell me," Frieda said, "how do you feel about the semi-automatic rifle? Do you care whether they make it?"

He did not answer in words. He went to the big old-fashioned safe against the wall and turned the combination. He came back to the bench with the breech action and stock of the semi-automatic rifle in one hand and the barrel in the other. He put the gun together and held it in the pool of bright light from the big bulb over the bench.

Then he took it apart, stripping it down quickly, until all the parts lay on the bench.

"I hope I'll be remembered as a maker of fine shooting rifles," he said. "But -" he made a gesture with his hand at the parts on the benchtop - "that took more brains than anything else I ever did. Of course I want it made."

He picked up the barrel as if he were going to fit it back in place, and then he looked at Frieda over his glasses.

"It's good," he said. "It's as good as Joe thinks it is."

She was looking straight at him, thinking what a fine old man he was, so patient and so knowing and so gentle, when a harsh voice spoke out of the darkness behind him. "Be quiet and you won't get hurt."

The old man whirled, the rifle barrel in his hands, and struck hard and low. The intruder groaned as the iron bar hit his shin, and he went down. The next instant J.M. Pyne slumped to the floor as someone struck him from behind, and Frieda saw that there was a second man behind the first - a short and heavy man, with little eyes peering out from folds of flesh above the handkerchief he as wearing as a mask.

VI

"Madam," he said to Frieda, "I am Henry." For a moment she could only stare at him in panic, and then the meaning of his words came to her. He was addressing her with a deference that could only mean he regarded her as his superior, and friendly to his purpose.

He took off the handkerchief he was wearing as a mask, revealing as ugly a face as Frieda had ever seen, with thick, protruding lips and a nose that looked as if it had been smashed flat, except for the big nostrils. He was short, for a man, no taller than she was, but wide, thick and powerful. She felt that a gorilla, wishing to make friends with her, would smile as he was smiling now.

She knew it would do no good to scream. She couldn't possibly be heard outside the Water Shop, and the watchman was either in his shanty at the factory gate a hundred yards away, or making his rounds of other buildings. He never came into this place.

She did the thing she had to do. She knelt down beside J.M. Pyne and put her hand over his heart. His body seemed quite lifeless. A bruise on the side of his head was swelling fast. But his heart was beating.

Her mind leaped ahead. She told herself that this thug who had knocked out the man from behind with a blow so quick and cruel, and then said to her "I am Henry," thought she was somebody else. He had addressed her as "madam". He didn't know the name of the woman he supposed she was, or he would have used it. His manner said that she was his superior, and that he wanted to please her, and that they were both there on the same errand. Until he found out how mistaken he was, she had power over him. And if she was guessing right, the bolder she was the better. She took one quick breath and assumed the role he so innocently suggested.

"At least," she said as she stood up, "you were not clumsy enough to kill him."

"I have been taught how to hit with this." He held out in his hand what looked like a long leather pouch containing something heavy. "They go to sleep for a time. That is all that happens. I know how to do it."

"You know nothing," Frieda said. "You are stupid and careless." She pointed to the tall man who still sat on the floor holding his shin with both hands. The handkerchief had slipped down and she saw that he was a boy of nineteen or twenty, with a nice face. He had blue eyes and close cropped blond hair, and his mouth was drawn with pain. "Look at him!"

"Please," Henry said, and his tone was abject, "how could we know that a man so old would do such a thing?"

She was secretly delighted. He was a tough criminal, probably a murderer, but he was no more proof against a woman's words than gentler men.

"Why didn't you wait until I had gone?" Frieda demanded. "How do you think I can get away now?"

"Please do not be angry," Henry begged, and she saw that he was fearful of her anger, and she guessed he was afraid that she might make a bad report of him to somebody higher up. "We will take you with us."

The idea, which he seemed to take as a matter of course, was so startling to her that she had to have time to think about it.

"If you had waited, everything would have been so simple."

"But, madam, you had him open the safe. I thought you meant us to come in while the gun was out. What if he had put the gun back while we waited?"

"You do not know how to open an old safe like that?"

"I know how, yes. I have the tools. But it takes time. It makes a noise. It is late. We have a long way to go."

She looked straight at him. He dropped his eyes before hers and she made her decision. He was afraid of her, and because he was afraid she might somehow save the Pyne gun.

"Very well," she said, shrugging her shoulders to let him know how impatient she was with his excuses. "I will go with you because you have made it impossible for me to do anything else. Do your job."

Henry stood behind the boy and put one hand under each of his arms and lifted him to his feet.

"How bad is it, Louis?" he asked.

"It feels as if it were broken," the boy said, holding one foot off the floor.

"Here, rest against the bench."

The boy supported his weight on the bench while Henry leaned down and felt the injured shin. The boy shut his teeth.

"No," Henry said, "it is not broken."

He took a long, narrow bag, like a sail bag, from his belt. He picked up the rifle barrel with which J.M. Pyne had struck the boy and stuffed it in the bag, then the stock and the other parts lying on the bench. He tied the drawstring and hung the loop around his neck so the bag hung down his back, and took a flashlight out of his pocket.

"Come, Louis," he said, "rest one hand on my shoulder... Gracious lady, will you be so kind as to follow us?"

Frieda picked up her raincoat and her purse and followed them into the next room. She saw a pistol butt sticking out of Henry's back pocket and knew it for a Luger. She noticed for the first time that both men had taken off their shoes and were wearing heavy knitted socks. Henry opened the door into the next room, which was dark. His flashlight showed that it was half full of empty packing cases. Frieda guessed that they had waited there, perhaps for hours. The partition was of rough wood, with cracks between the boards, so they could have heard everything in J.M. Pyne's shop and probably have seen everything too.

Henry opened another door. She felt a draft, damp and cool, as if a window were open on the river. Then, as he swung his flashlight, she saw the window. There was a long, light ladder on the floor. Louis sat on a packing case and Henry turned off his flash. She heard the ladder scraping across the floor.

Then he turned the flashlight on and laid it on the floor so the light did not shine out of the window.

He found two pairs of heavy workman's shoes against the wall. He gave one pair to Louis and put on the other pair.

"I will go down first," Henry said, turning off the light, "and lash the ladder."

She heard him climbing over the sill. She stood in the dark, unable to see anything and hearing nothing but the rain outside and the boy's breathing close beside her, for what seemed a long time. Then she heard Henry climbing back through the window. His feet struck the floor heavily.

He turned the flashlight on, keeping it low, until he found a heavy canvas bag with a light line fastened to the leather handles. She guessed that the bag held the tools he had brought in case he had to break open the safe. His flash went out as he lowered the bag out of the window.

"Madam," he said, "I will go first because I will have to help Louis. When I get him down, you come. You will have to do it by feel. But do not be afraid. I will be below you on the ladder, ready to catch you. It is only 12 feet to the boat. If you are careful there will be no danger. You are not afraid?"

"Of course not," Frieda said, and put her hand hard against her mouth, so he could not hear her teeth chattering.

The boy groaned once as he climbed through the window. Frieda could hear Henry's words of encouragement. She walked to the window and put her hand on the sill and found the ladder. The ladder creaked with the weight of the two men down there in the dark. She could hear the river rushing by, and the rain.

"Come now," Henry called to her.

Frieda took hold of the ladder. She had only to give it a quick hard push outward and run back into the shop and on into the factory yard. They could not follow her. But J.M. Pyne's gun would be gone. If she went with these men, she would have a chance to do something. Henry had said they had a long way to go. They must have a car parked across the river. Once they were in the car, she could tell them to stop at a gas station while she telephoned. She could telephone the police.

She buttoned her raincoat and swung one leg over the window sill, feeling with her foot in the dark for a rung of the ladder. Her foot found a rung. She could feel, as she let her weight rest on the rung, that the ladder was not solid. She remembered that it stood in a boat. Of course it wasn't solid.

Her breath came short. She told herself not to be frightened. What was there to be afraid of? Henry was afraid of her. And then she heard him speak.

"Take it easy," he said.

She swung the other foot over the window sill, holding tightly to the ladder. She reached down into the dark for another rung. Then she felt Henry's weight on the ladder below her. She took another step down. His big hand grasped her ankle and guided her foot down to the next rung. She went on down quickly and he helped her to find the broad seat in the stern of the boat.

His flashlight went on, and she saw how neatly the ladder was lashed to the thwart in the middle. Louis was up forward. Henry had a knife in his hand as he turned off his flash. Frieda heard him cutting the lashings of the ladder and then the big splash as he tossed the ladder overboard.

"Here, Louis," he said, "cut the bow line."

Henry leaned so close his shoulder touched hers as he cast off another line. She heard an oar scrape against the stone foundation of the building. He dropped the oars in the locks and she felt the boat jump ahead as he pulled. He swung the bow downstream. Frieda felt the current take hold of the boat.

The rain lashed her face, forcing her to keep her eyes almost closed. There was water in the bottom of the boat; she could feel it soaking through her light pumps.

"Gracious lady," Henry said, "would you be so kind as to hold the gun? It is in my way and I cannot put it on the bottom of the boat because of the water."

She took the gun in its cloth bag and laid it across her lap. Henry picked up his oars again, rowing with quick short strokes.

Frieda did not dare ask any questions, for fear she would ask something to which she was supposed to know the answer. She could only wait for whatever might happen. She felt her hair. It was so wet she could squeeze water out of it. A trickle of water ran down behind one ear and on down her neck.

"I am sorry it is so wet," Henry said. "But if it were not raining, it would be moonlight. The rain is better for us."

"I don't mind getting wet," Frieda said.

She asked herself how long it would be before someone would find J.M. Pyne. It was close to one o'clock by now. No one would go into the Water Shop except Joe Hill. When he got home and found that the old man hadn't come in, he would be worried about him. He'd drive to Gaylord Arms to look for him. But Joe Hill had gone places with the girl from the information desk. It might be daylight before he got home.

The boat suddenly struck hard aground, so hard that she was thrown forward on her knees. She heard Louis groan. Henry turned on his flash, and she saw that they were on a narrow sand bar around which the current swept. Henry stepped overboard into shallow water and shoved the boat off, and climbed in again.

"If you would be so kind, please take the light," he said to Frieda. "Turn it on every once in a while, and if I am going ashore tell me."

Frieda stole a glance at her watch the first time she used the flash. It was five minutes past one. She was aware of a strange roaring sound in the distance.

"What is that?" she asked.

"A dam," Henry said. "Keep the light on. I want to go as close as I can, but it would be bad if we went over."

He ran the boat aground a few yards above the dam, and got overboard and helped Louis ashore.

"You sit here," he said to Louis, "and I will come back after you." He turned to Frieda. "If you will hold the light, I will drag the boat around."

He dragged the boat 10 or 15 feet before he stopped to rest and asked her to turn off the flash. She could hear his heavy breathing.

"It is hard," he said. "But it is better this way. They will send out an alarm over I do not know how many states to look for us. They will be stopping cars on all the roads from New York to Canada, but we will not be in a car. We will be safe in our little house by the pond."

He hauled the boat 50 or 60 yards before he got it close to the water below the dam. "I made a mistake," he said, as he straightened up. "I should have killed the old man."

"Do you really think so?" she asked, trying to sound as matter of fact as she felt he would expect her to be.

"The old man knows too much. It would have been better. But it is too late now. If you will sit here in the boat, I will go back for Louis."

VII

Frieda watched the spot of light from the flashlight flickering ahead of him. The news he had so casually given her about the house by the pond meant the end of her hopes. She couldn't say she had to telephone. She couldn't scream at a passing policeman. She could only go with these men down the river in the dark. When they found out who she was, they would certainly feel that she knew too much.

She tried pushing the boat. If she could get it into the water before Henry came back, she could go on with the gun. She tried again, lifting until she thought her heart would burst. But it was no use.

She sat down on the gunwale of the boat. The gun was lying on the thwart. She could throw it into the boil of water just below the dam and run. Only she couldn't run in the black dark. She couldn't help making tracks in the mud and Henry could travel a lot faster with a light than she could without one. He would find her with the light, and he would shoot.

She looked back. Henry was coming with Louis. It couldn't be long before she was exposed. These men had a boss. They thought she was a friend of his. Her pose was good only until the moment when he saw her.

She loosened the drawstrings of the bag that held the gun and reached in. She felt the barrel and stock. She reached down to the bottom of the bag and found the bolt. But if she took the bolt it would be noticed the minute they got the gun out of the bag. She wanted something special, something that would not be noticed at once, and that would not be easy to replace. She felt the trigger guard. But it was like a Springfield trigger guard. She found the hammer. She knew that was something special. Most bolt-action guns had no hammer, but the Pyne gun had one. Its design was something of which J.M. Pyne was proud.

She took the hammer and put it in the pocket of her raincoat, an oddly shaped piece of steel, thicker than a silver dollar, but not so big around, and no heavier. She pulled the strings of the bag tight again and calculated her chances. They wouldn't discover that the hammer was missing until they tried to put the gun together; they wouldn't discover it then unless they knew about it. But without it you couldn't fire the gun. She wondered if a gunsmith who had never seen the hammer could figure out the shape of the missing part.

238

Henry and Louis were within a few yards now. If she tossed it into the river they would never know. She would run no risk. But if something happened so that Pyne got his gun back he would want the hammer. Joe Hill had said he had no working drawings. He would have to cut and try to replace the hammer. It might take him a week.

Henry picked up the bow of the boat, which she had been unable to lift, and pulled it forward. Then he got behind the stern, his legs bent. With a heave and a grunt, he shoved the boat into the water. He helped Louis into the bow. Frieda sat down in the stern.

Henry rowed steadily for an hour. "I think," he said, "we have come almost far enough. Now I will have to keep close to the bank to find the place."

He swung the boat over to the right bank and let it drift with the current. They drifted along close to the bank for half an hour, until they came to a rocky cliff that rose almost straight up from the water, higher than the light of the flash would reach.

"Soon we will be there," Henry said.

After a few minutes Frieda saw a break in the cliff. Henry swung the boat toward it. She had a glimpse of a small brook boiling down over boulders into the river. Henry got overboard.

"We walk from here," he said, holding out his hand to her.

Frieda stepped into the water that swirled up over her skirt, pulling at her legs. She started for the shore, hoping that her pumps would stay on until she got there.

"No, no," Henry said. "Do not step on the bank. We must not leave footprints. We must walk in the stream."

Frieda sat on a boulder that stuck out of the water. Henry helped Louis out of the boat and to another boulder. He handed the gun to Frieda and the bag of tools to Louis.

In the light of the flash, the leaves of the trees, washed by the rain, were a strange pale green. Henry picked up stones from the bottom of the brook, some of them as big as he could lift, and dropped them in the boat.

When the stones had sunk the boat so low the gunwales were only a few inches above the water, he reached in and pulled a plug in the bottom of the boat. Then he walked back to the

239

boulder where Louis sat and slung the bag of tools over his shoulder. He took the gun from Frieda and slung it on top of the tools.

"Now," he said to her, "if you will walk ahead holding the light, I will help Louis."

"I can't walk in the water," Frieda said. "My shoes will come off."

"I will fix them," Henry said.

He cut long pieces of the light braided line with which he had lowered the bag of tools from the window of the Water Shop to the boat.

"Please to hold up your foot."

Frieda managed, sitting on a boulder, to hold one foot at a time clear of the water. He tied her pumps on, putting the cord around several times, making sure it was not too tight for comfort, and tying the ends with a knot she had never seen before.

"Now," he said, "we go."

Frieda staggered upstream, holding the flashlight. One foot went down in the crack between two big stones, grinding the ankle bone so hard that tears came to her eyes. She looked back. The boy was tall. He looked a foot taller than Henry. He had one arm around Henry's neck and Henry had one arm around his waist as he hopped forward on one leg.

It seemed impossible for them to travel a hundred yards that way up the boulder-strewn bed of the brook. But they were coming on. Frieda clenched her teeth. Once she stumbled and fell to her knees, but she kept on until she came to a tight barbed-wire fence, stretched between trees on either bank. The water was flush with the lowest strand.

Henry lifted the wire while she ducked under it. He had to lift it higher for Louis. He put one hand on the bottom of the brook, his chin in the water, and shoved the wire high with the other hand. They sat down to rest after that, each on a separate boulder.

"Come," Henry said, "we go."

They came to an old stone dam, five or six feet high, with one end broken out where the brook tumbled down over a pile of rocks. They climbed up the rocks in the rushing water on their hands and knees. For a few yards they walked on a smooth, sandy bottom. And then they were in the boulders again.

"Henry," the boy said, "I can go no more. Leave me here."

"Come, Louis," Henry said, "it is only a little way to the road."

"I can go no more," the boy said. "Let me sleep."

"You can sleep all you want when we get home. You can sleep until Sunday - when he comes," Henry said, dragging the boy relentlessly forward.

So, Frieda thought, *the boss is not coming until Sunday.*

They trusted her. It would be simple to run away as soon as it was light, and find a house and a telephone. It must be nearly daylight now. She'd go as soon as they were asleep.

She guessed that they walked a good quarter of a mile farther up the brook before they came to a bridge of logs with rotting planks on top, a bridge that had sagged so low the flooded brook was running over it inches deep.

"From here it is easy," Henry said. Frieda stepped on a rock and was raising one knee to the bridge when her foot slipped and she went down, turning her ankle. The pain was sickening. She scrambled up again, determined to ignore the ankle, and found she couldn't put any weight on her right foot. It hurt too much.

"What is the matter?" Henry asked.

"I've sprained my ankle." He got down into the water to help her. "It is nothing," she added, wanting to believe it.

He lifted her up and sat her on the bridge. "Wait," he said. "First I will get Louis ashore where it is not so wet, and then I will help you. It is only a little way from here."

Henry got Louis over to the bank and came back with the flash. He lifted her to her feet and put his arm around her.

"It is only a few meters," he said. "Lean on me."

Frieda hopped forward across the bridge onto a woods road which had not been used for years. It was hardly wider than a footpath.

"I've got to rest," she said at last. She managed, with his help, to sit down.

"You had better let me carry you," he said.

"No," she said, "I can go on."

"It is only a little way now," he said.

This time he was telling the truth. After 50 yards the flashlight showed a low cabin with an addition on either side and windows with heavy board shutters.

"We will go around to the front," Henry said.

They passed between the cabin and an open shed, with a half-built boat upside down on wooden horses under it, and beyond, Frieda saw the gleam of water. That must be the pond Henry had mentioned.

She sat down on the step while Henry unlocked the front door and lit a large oil lamp that hung from the cëiling. He came back and helped her across the porch and into a chair.

"This," he said with pride, "is our home."

Frieda saw a small room with a rough stone fireplace, a few chairs, a phonograph, and a portable radio on a shelf against the wall. An alarm clock that hung from a nail above the fireplace said half past four.

"In here," he said, opening a door, "is your room."

Frieda had a glimpse of a small room with a white iron bed on either side and a chest of drawers at the end with a mirror over it.

"Over here," Henry said, opening the opposite door, "is our room." He opened a door to a third room and went in and lighted a lamp hung from the wall on a bracket, with what looked like a round concave mirror behind it. "And this is the kitchen."

She saw a room hardly bigger than a yacht's galley, with an oil stove on one side and a sink with a pump at the end. She heard him pumping water. Then she saw him put a tea-kettle on the stove and light a flame under it.

"I am heating water for your ankle," he said. "It is best to soak it in hot water. Then I will bandage it. I am good at bandages."

He knelt down in front of her and lifted the injured ankle gently. She gave a sigh of relief when he pulled the free end of the knot and took the cord off.

"Go back and get Louis," she said.

"First I will get your ankle into the warm water," Henry said.

"Do what I tell you. The ankle can wait."

He stood up and bowed, with a little jerk of his head. "I am here to do whatever you ask."

Henry went into the kitchen and got a bottle of whisky and glasses and a pitcher of water. He poured whisky.

"Drink," he said. "You are shivering. You were in the water too long."

"It is true," she said, glad that he did not guess why she was shaking.

The fear of what might happen to her had gripped her again, but she managed to raise the glass without spilling any.

"Go and get Louis," she said.

VIII

Frieda heard the screen door shut behind him. She waited a full minute before she stood up. By pushing a chair along and supporting herself with her hand on the back of it, she reached the radio. She turned the switch, and presently a light began to glow, so she knew it was working. She turned it off again.

She was afraid that Henry and Louis would listen to a news broadcast from the Waterford station. There was one at noon every day. The story of the burglary at Gaylord Arms would be on by noon. Henry and Louis would learn that she wasn't the person they thought she was. If she could get inside the box she could loosen the connections.

The back of the box was fastened with screws. She hadn't time to hunt for something that would turn the screws. She did not dare push the box off the shelf and let it fall on the floor. That would be harder to explain than the news.

She went back to the chair at the table where Henry had left her. Then she saw that her clothes were still dripping water on the floor. She had left a trail of water wherever she had gone. But it didn't matter so long as she hadn't knocked the radio off its shelf. She took off her other pump and what was left of her stockings. She felt in the pocket of her raincoat for the gun hammer. It did not seem a safe place for it. She put it in her brassiere.

243

She heard Henry and Louis coming. Henry half carried Louis across the porch and to a chair. The boy's wet face was white and set. Frieda knew by now what it was like to hop along on one foot. She wondered how the boy had lasted through that trip up the brook. She looked down and saw that his shoe was oozing blood.

Henry brought a small galvanized iron tub half full of cold water and put it down in front of her and poured boiling water into it from the tea-kettle while he tested the mixture with his hand.

"Try that, please," he said.

Frieda tried the water. It was very hot, but she managed gradually to get her foot down in it. She looked again at Louis. His teeth were clenched, the muscles of his jaws were standing out with the effort he was making to avoid groaning with pain. He was as tall and broad-shouldered and lean and hard as Joe Hill. But he was a boy and he was hurt. She remembered things she had heard about injuries to a bone and how serious they could be.

"Let us see how bad his leg is," she said.

Henry pulled Louis' chair under the overhead lamp and raised the injured leg up on the seat of another chair and took off the shoe and the blood soaked sock. He was about to roll up the leg of the boy's heavy denim trousers when Frieda stopped him.

"Use your knife," she said.

Henry obediently took out his knife and cut away the heavy cloth, and shook his head at what he saw. Frieda knew that if infection set in, the boy might lose his leg.

"Get some warm water," she said. "Have you any absorbent cotton?"

Henry shook his head.

"Clean towels, then."

He went into the kitchen and brought a tin wash basin half full of water, and several towels. Frieda picked out the oldest and softest towel and dipped it in the basin.

"I will do it," Henry said.

"No," she said, "pull my chair around so I can reach."

She bathed the wound as gently as she could and washed away the blood that covered the leg and the ankle below it. Then she poured whisky over the whole surface and began to make bandages by tearing a towel in strips.

"I can do that," Henry said. "I know how."

Frieda gave him the strips, and he bound up the wound with the same skill he had shown in tying on her pumps.

"The bandage must be kept wet," she said. "And he must not put his weight on that foot. I know that much."

Henry picked the boy up in his arms and carried him into the bedroom. He came back and got the whisky and a glass.

"I will now give him a big drink so he can go to sleep," he said.

Frieda could hear them talking about their night's work.

"You are badly hurt, Louis," Henry said. "But at least we have done a good job. We have the gun."

"Do you think he will be angry because of his girl?" Louis asked.

So that was what they thought - that she was the boss's girl. But why did they think that?

Henry came back into the room to ask her if she would like food. "I have rye bread and Swiss cheese and sausage."

Frieda shook her head. He went into the kitchen. Presently he came back with two enormous sandwiches, made of thick slices of bread with cheese and liver sausage between, and bottles of beer.

"I am hungry," he said, "and so is Louis."

With an effort, Frieda spoke in her normal voice, "I am going to bed."

"Let me bandage your ankle first."

"No," she said, "it won't do any good to bandage it. But you can help me."

He put down his sandwiches and beer and got a roll of adhesive tape.

"Please," he said, "this will help. I have done it before."

He took her foot on his knee, passed the adhesive tape under the arch of her foot and, pulling it tight, crossed it over the top of her instep. Frieda had to admit to herself that the ankle felt better.

He got a tin candlestick and lit the candle and put it on the chest of drawers between the two iron beds in the room he had said was hers. Then he got matches and a clean towel and helped her into the room. She sat down on the one chair.

"Louis must have a doctor," she said.

"It is impossible until he comes tomorrow. I cannot leave here to get a doctor until he has come for the gun."

"You mean not until Sunday?"

He nodded. "But do not be afraid. We rented this place a long time ago. We are known to be workmen in the big Waterford machine shop. We drive to work every day except Saturday and Sunday. Our car is parked at the end of the good road half a mile from here. We have no neighbors. As long as no one sees you, nothing can happen."

"What about the gun?"

"That I will hide, so if anyone did come, he would not find it."

"Very well," she said.

He said good night and closed the door behind him as he went out. Frieda saw that the only fastening to the door was a wooden button. She supported herself on the chair, pushed it to the door, and turned the button. Then she looked at the bed. The pillowcase and the sheets were fresh.

She saw herself in the mirror. Her short-sleeved cotton dress, which she had chosen because it was such a lovely green and so becoming to her red hair, hung on her like a wet rag.

She hung her clothes on the chair and tucked the hammer in her purse and dried her hair with the towel. She put the candle on the seat of the chair where she could reach it.

She could hear Henry and Louis talking. She crawled to the door and listened. They sounded as if they were a little drunk and talking louder than they knew.

"Is it really true, Henry," Louis asked, "that redheaded women are warmer in love than others?"

"I have never known but one," Henry said, "and she tried to kill me with an axe. Maybe they are all like that - I don't know. But he likes them. He will have no other kind."

Frieda crawled back to the bed.

IX

When she awoke, the sun was shining on the floor, and from somewhere outside came the sound of a cheerful hammer. It was five minutes of eleven by her wristwatch.

She sat on the edge of the bed and reached for her clothes. They were still damp as she put them on. Her hair was dry and so tightly curled that she could hardly get her pocket comb through it. Her ankle seemed less swollen than it had been the night before, but she still couldn't put her weight on it without cringing. She hung on to the furniture to save it as she got the door open.

"Good morning, gracious lady," Louis called out.

She made her way, with the aid of a chair, to the doorway of his room.

"How is the leg, Louis?" she asked.

"It aches like a tooth," he said. "But it is no worse. Please call Henry. He will get you coffee."

She hobbled to the door and looked out.

Henry was busy at his workbench in the shed beside the half-built boat. When he saw her he took something out of the vise and came toward her.

"Good morning, gracious lady. I have been making crutches for you. But I have to measure them."

He came in, bearing two lengths of peeled sapling. He had inletted a crosspiece at one end of each of them. He placed the crosspieces under her arms, his thick lips pursed in thought.

"Please let your arms hang," he said, taking a pencil from behind his ear, "so I can mark where the handles will go."

He marked the place and went into the kitchen and heated coffee and gave her a hand to a chair at the living room table.

"If you will excuse me," he said, "I will have them done in 10

247

minutes. Then I will make breakfast."

Frieda sat at the table, looking out at the pond shimmering in the sun. She guessed it was a quarter of a mile across and a good deal longer than it was wide. She couldn't see either end of it. On the other side the land rose steeply to a high ridge.

"Madam," Louis called out, "can you play checkers?"

"A little," she answered.

"After breakfast I will beat you," he said. "I am a good checker player."

Frieda wanted to laugh. Louis was so obviously the child who is lonely because he has to stay in bed and wants someone to amuse him. Henry was happily making work for himself on a Saturday, like any good suburban father of a family.

So this is what life with two murderers is really like, she thought.

Henry came in with the crutches for her approval. She told him they were marvelous, because it would have hurt his feelings if she had said anything less.

"First," he said, "I must pad them."

He hunted out a torn pillowcase, thriftily saved for emergency, and tore it into strips, which he wrapped around the crosspieces of the crutches.

"Now," he said.

Frieda took the crutches and propelled herself out across the porch and into the bright summer sunshine.

"Oh," she said, "what a beautiful day to sit in the sun."

"It is a beautiful day," Henry said, "but --"

He looked out at the pond, frowning unhappily.

"But what?" Frieda asked.

"Sometimes men fish on the pond, on Saturday afternoons especially," Henry said. "It is forbidden, but they do it. Someone might see you."

"You don't think anyone would recognize me from the pond, do you, Henry?"

"Hair like yours can be seen a long way. The police have, of course, sent out word to look for a beautiful red haired lady."

"Very well, Henry. I will try to keep out of sight of the pond. But I must sit in the sun."

"First I will make breakfast," he said.

Frieda went into the house and he followed her.

"Ah," he said, "it is nearly 12 o'clock already. Then is the broadcast."

He turned the radio on and went into the kitchen. Frieda could hear him getting out pots and pans. She sat down at the table and tried to brace herself for what was coming. She told herself that if she thought fast enough, she could explain anything the broadcast said about her.

The voice that came out of the machine was so loud that Henry hurried across the room to turn down the volume.

"It is now 12 o'clock, Waterford watch time," the voice said, and went on to give the weather report, which promised fair and warmer after the two inches of rain that had fallen the night before.

"Early this morning," the voice continued, "masked men entered the Water Shop of Gaylord Arms from the river, blackjacked J.M. Pyne, the most famous riflemaker in the country, and stole the model of his semi-automatic rifle. Before he went down, Mr. Pyne, who is a man of 75, struck one of the intruders with an iron bar. Mr. Pyne is under the care of a physician, but his injuries are not believed to be serious. He saw only one of his assailants, who, he said, was a tall man, before he was knocked out. When Mr. Pyne recovered consciousness he found the night watchman had notified the police. An alarm was sent out over the teletype system to five states. Mr. Pyne said the gun would be of little value to an ordinary criminal, but would be priceless to a foreign government, because it could be manufactured so much more cheaply than any other military weapon of its kind. The police suspect that the crime was the work of foreign agents, and fourteen suspicious persons were rounded up this morning. It is understood the FBI is actively interested."

The broadcaster went on to something else. Henry turned to Frieda. She saw suspicion in his little, fat-enfolded eyes.

"Why did they say nothing of you?"

249

"I can't imagine," Frieda said. "Perhaps you hit the old man so hard he doesn't remember I was there."

"No," Henry said. "He remembered hitting Louis. For some reason he did not tell the police about you."

"I think the police are not telling all they know."

Henry nodded. "That is what I think too," he said. Frieda thought he was satisfied with that explanation, but she wanted to change the subject as quickly as possible before he did any heavy thinking. This was the moment to let him know that the gun he was keeping hidden somewhere outside lacked one of its essential parts.

"Get the gun," she said. "I'd like to make sure it isn't rusted after last night."

"I dried everything and put grease on it last night before I went to sleep," Henry said. "The gun is not rusted. But I would like to put it together. I do not wish to give it to him in pieces. But first I will make breakfast."

He helped Louis out of bed and into a chair at the table and boiled eggs and made toast and got sausage and cheese and beer. When they had eaten, he cleared the table and went out to get the gun. Frieda noticed that it took him 10 minutes to get it.

He laid the parts out on the table as he took them from the bag. Frieda realized that she was leaning on her elbow with her chin in her hand, so her arms concealed the spot where she had hidden the piece of polished steel in her bra when she put on her clothes.

Henry pursed his lips as he looked at the parts. "I do not know what to do first."

"I think I remember," Frieda said. She put the longest coil spring in the buttstock, put the action rod in place, and fitted the bolt into the receiver.

"I need a cartridge. That is what the old man used."

Henry gave her a Luger pistol cartridge, but it was not long enough.

"Get me an ice pick or a screwdriver or something."

Henry got a screwdriver and she pushed the plunger down and put the barrel into the receiver. She looked at the few remaining

250

parts on the table. She felt the moment had come. She pushed the parts about as if she were looking for something.

"Give me the bag," she said sharply. She turned it upsidedown over the table. Nothing came out. She reached down into the bag, but there was nothing left in it.

"What is the matter?" Henry asked.

"The hammer," she said. She turned on him furiously. "You did not bring the hammer?"

"It is a bolt gun. Why would it have a hammer?"

"But it has," Frieda said, holding the gun upsidedown. "Look. Don't you see that there is nothing to connect the sear to the firing pin? That is where the hammer goes - on this pin. Otherwise when you pull the trigger nothing happens."

"Good God!" Henry said. "He will kill us!"

He walked back and forth across the room, his long arms swinging, his lips muttering.

"I will have to go back and get it," he said. "There is no other way."

"How would you get in again?" Frieda asked. "And how would you find it if you did?"

He stopped short. "You are a woman. You do not know what he is like when he is angry."

X

Joe Hill got home toward two o'clock that Saturday afternoon. J.M. Pyne had propped himself up in bed so he could read and smoke in comfort. The doctor had said he should stay in bed at least one day. Joe thought the old man looked as well as ever. He put the rifle he'd been carrying on top of the chest of drawers, where there was no danger that it would fall and knock the telescope sight out of adjustment.

"How are you?" he asked.

"There's nothing the matter with me except I'm hungry," the old man said. "It's nonsense for me to stay in bed. What did you find?"

Joe sat down and knew how tired he was. He'd got home at

251

three o'clock in the morning after his date with Betty and found a doctor and a policeman with J.M. Pyne. It had been close to daylight when the policeman left. Joe had talked to the old man and got a boat and gone down the river. He'd been on the river ever since.

"I've got to shave," he said. "I'm supposed to meet the Gaylords and that fellow Bostwick at the Highland Hotel for lunch."

"What did you find?" the old man repeated.

"It looked to me as if a couple of men had hauled a flat-bottom boat around that dam a mile below the plant. Of course, it might have been somebody else."

The old man sat up. "Did you see any sign that Frieda was with them?"

"I saw the footprints of a girl who was wearing high heels."

"So she did go with them."

Joe thought the old man said it sadly, as if he'd been hoping there was some other explanation for Frieda's disappearance.

"You still don't believe she was helping them steal the gun?"

"I don't understand why they'd want her to go with them," J.M. Pyne said.

"There's only one answer. She was one of them. That's why she came here to get you to make her a Pyne rifle. That's why she wanted to jam your old hat down over her face when she was shooting and she knew the news photographers were taking pictures of her. That's why she wouldn't pose for them when she got up off the ground. And that's why she hornswoggled you into getting the gun out of the safe when they were waiting behind the partition to take it."

"I've thought of all those things. I still think she's honest."

"I know how you feel. But you've always been a man to go by the facts."

"We don't know the facts," J.M. Pyne said. "We're just guessing at them. But I know the girl. She spent three days with me in my shop."

Joe went into the bathroom and shaved. He didn't want to believe it any more than the old man did. But he couldn't see

252

any other answer. He found a clean shirt and went back into the old man's room.

"I've got to hurry," he said. "I'm an hour late now. I'll stop at Brick's and tell them to send you some food."

"If they took the trouble to drag a boat around that dam, they didn't have a car waiting for them. There would have been no sense in going that far down the river unless they were holed up in the woods."

"That's what I thought. But I've been twenty miles down the river since I saw you this morning. I went ten miles below the Gaylord place to where the river widens out into a kind of lake and there's a resort with a lot of summer cottages. I rented a boat with an outboard motor and came back, watching the western shore. Then I went downriver again, watching the eastern shore. I couldn't find a trace on either bank. And they couldn't have gone ashore without leaving tracks, because the banks were mud after that rain last night."

"Just the same," the old man said, "they must have gone ashore."

"They may have," Joe said. He couldn't figure it any other way either. "I'll try to get back here in an hour or so."

He started down the stairs and the old man called to him.

"Yes," Joe said, sticking his head in the door.

"You like Frieda," J.M. Pyne said.

"I got off on the wrong foot with her," Joe said. "And now I have to admit she's probably a crook. But I can't help liking her better than any other girl I ever knew in my life."

J.M. Pyne nodded. "It isn't every girl that understands a man's wanting to shoot."

Joe ordered sandwiches and coffee at Brick's for the old man, and then drove to the Gaylord plant to get the two receivers for the Pyne rifle that he had milled out of the solid stock. He saw Frieda Guerdner's car standing in the factory yard. It wouldn't be long before somebody else would notice it and ask what had become of her. The watchman who had been on at the time of the robbery would be sure to report it. He had apparently been too excited to think about the girl when J.M. Pyne had staggered out at half past two in the morning to say he'd been slugged and robbed. But he would remember when he'd had a chance to think.

The old man had his nerve, to keep so important a piece of information from the police, especially when they were bound to find out that he had. But it wouldn't do any good to argue with him about it. He was sure that Frieda was innocent and he wasn't going to have her in trouble with the police.

He had been born in a Vermont village about the time the Civil War was over. He had never acquired the city man's fear of the police or his respect for them. He was an unreconstructed New Englander who had never granted that the police had any job more important than chasing boys on Halloween or putting the town drunk in the lockup until he was sober enough to go home. He must have read and heard about modern police organization and communication; he knew about the teletype. But his knowledge hadn't changed the belief he had grown up with in his village boyhood that in serious matters a man had better be his own policeman.

He had told Joe how he had felt when, making his first visit to New York and talking to a policeman, he had learned the fellow had never fired, let alone learned to shoot, the revolver he carried. The old man would admit that policemen in most places had target practice nowadays, but his prejudice remained.

Joe found the Gaylords in the grill of the Highland Hotel, after their lunch, with a man who looked like a young college professor, and he could see, as he approached their table, that none of them was happy. Reuben Gaylord had gone back into his pose of complete indifference, Connie Gaylord was anxious, and the college professor had been running his hands through his black hair until it looked as if it had never been combed.

"This," Reuben said to Joe, "is George Bostwick - and is he sore! He thinks we had the gun stolen on purpose to make it harder for him."

Joe Hill laughed and shook hands with Bostwick. He decided that he was going to like Bostwick.

"Where," Connie Gaylord asked, "have you been?"

Joe laid the shining steel receivers on the table next to Bostwick and sat down beside him. "I've been motor-boating," he said. "What's the news?"

"What do you mean - motor-boating?" Connie asked.

"The police were so sure the burglars got away in a car that the old man and I decided it would be a good idea to have a look at the river. So I did."

"And after many hardships you caught up with them with your trusty Gaylord woodchuck rifle and took the Pyne gun away from them," Reuben said.

"As a matter of fact," Joe said, "I did take that .25 caliber woodchuck rifle of the old man's - the one for the Krag case necked down. What do the police say?"

"They say what the police always say," Reuben replied. "And this time I think they're right. I think if it wasn't an inside job the burglars must have had information from somebody inside. They must have known that the gun was in the part of the Water Shop that Pyne had been using and that the night watchman didn't go through there and that they could go from the other end of the building, where no one would hear them breaking in, to Pyne's part by opening a few doors. The thunderstorm was a break for them. It meant there weren't any couples canoeing on the river to see them putting up a ladder. And on top of everything else, Pyne was working on the gun, so it wasn't in the safe when they barged in on him."

Joe nodded. He wasn't going to mention Frieda until the old man did, but he could see that it wasn't going to be too pleasant for either of them when the Gaylords and the police found out about her.

"The police have been working on our list of employees all morning and they intend to check on every employee we've got before they get through," Reuben went on.

"Oh," Connie Gaylord said, "let's forget about the burglary. Couldn't we talk about tooling up to make the gun, now that Joe has got here?"

"We've been talking about it for hours, darling," Reuben said. "I have been driven to the conclusion that George is right."

George Bostwick turned to Joe.

"Perhaps you could convince Mrs. Gaylord that I can't make an engineering study for the mass production of something that is not more than a memory. If I can't see a sample of the product that is to be made, I need drawings of it. So far, all I've seen is a bad reproduction of a photograph which makes the Pyne gun look like any other semi-automatic rifle."

Joe pushed one of the receivers toward him. "That's the most expensive part of most military rifles. It holds the works of the Pyne gun."

"I've been looking at it," Bostwick said. "You make it?"

Joe did not want to think about the rifle. He wanted to think about Frieda. But he knew he had to talk rifle or give up his hope of having the Pyne gun made in the Gaylord plant, and if Gaylord didn't make it, he doubted it would ever be made in the United States, though it might now be on its way to being made in Europe.

"That part will be a forging," Joe said to Bostwick. "We won't have to do much to the outside of it except clean it up. But boring it out and making the other cuts takes time."

"It should be done on a special machine designed for the purpose," Bostwick said. "I know a man who will build one for you in 60 days from the time he gets the blueprints and the specifications. What's the bolt like?"

Joe took a pencil and sketched the bolt in cross section on the menu. "I think we can machine most of it by fitting our lathes with the right tools and fixtures, and the lugs can be broached on machines we have."

"I'd have to study it," Bostwick said. "But it's really no use to start on any of this until we have at least one model gun."

Somebody kicked Joe under the table, and he could only imagine that it was Connie Gaylord. He looked across at her, and she made a gesture which he guessed meant, "For goodness sake, do something."

"We can't go all the way until then," Joe admitted, "but we've got to put up a front. Did Reuben tell you that he has a South American purchasing commission coming up here on Monday?"

Bostwick nodded.

"What do you think I'm going to do with them when I get them here, Joe?" Reuben asked.

"Sell them on the idea that we're remodeling the West Shop to build the gun, and if they want the first 10,000 rifles we make, they'd better get us a letter of intention right away quick, so we can clear their order with the State Department."

256

"How long," Connie Gaylord asked, "would it take J.M. Pyne to make a new gun? Ten days?"

They all looked at her and shook their heads at her hopeful ignorance.

"Ten months would be more like it," George Bostwick said.

"I think that J.M. Pyne and I could make two new guns in five or six weeks," Joe said. "We've got these receivers. We can use standard .30 caliber barrels. All we have to do is to fit the collars and ease the standard chamber a bit. The old man has a reamer for that. We can use Springfield trigger guards and triggers. We'll buy the coil springs. Really all we have to do is make a couple of bolts, a couple of hammers, a couple of action rods, a couple of magazines, and work out the exact relation of the parts again."

"Yes," Bostwick said, "just work out the mechanism the way the old man did when he invented the gun 10 or 15 years ago. That's all."

"And all I have to do," Reuben said, "is to sell these birds on a rifle that we haven't got, and hold them in line for five or six weeks while you and the old man make a model of what they're buying, so they'll know what it looks like."

"Of course we've got to throw a bluff," Joe said, "but it isn't as if they could buy anywhere else. They've been sent up here to get military rifles. And there aren't any military rifles for sale. Of course they'll wait five or six weeks."

"It's a lovely idea, Joe," Reuben said, "but it won't work."

"You're forgetting that there's a world war on, and one that looks as if it's going to be bigger than the last one," Joe said. "I know an outfit that sold a foreign government a two-million-dollar order when they didn't have a factory and didn't have the least idea where they were going to find one. They got enough cash down in advance to pay the cost of tooling up, and to buy all the steel they needed, and to meet the payroll for the first year."

"You mean," Bostwick said, "that all they had was a model or two of the thing they were going to make?"

"Exactly," Joe said. "That's all they had. No money, no tools, no factory, no nothing."

"But they had the model," Bostwick said. "Don't you see the difference?"

"Certainly I see the difference," Joe said. "But we have a factory. We've got many of the tools. We can raise some money. We're all set, compared with them."

"You almost convince me," Bostwick said. "You wouldn't if it hadn't been one of my dreams ever since I was in engineering school to engineer a rifle factory in the modern manner. The rifle factories I've seen were mostly planned in 1880 and everything they've added since is in the way of what they had before. What would you have us do today?"

"Go over to the West Shop with Reuben right now and begin figuring what you can use of the machine tools that are in there now. Get a crew in there first thing Monday morning and start moving things around. If you can't start what you want, start something. And when those South Americans arrive, Reuben will tell them what a great man you are, and take them in to let them see you work. They aren't engineers. They're army officers. They won't know what you are doing. All you need to do is to give them some action."

Connie Gaylord jumped up, her voice full of excitement, "Oh, Reuben, why don't you? Go now with George and show him the West Shop. Put on a show. Get that order."

George Bostwick grinned at Reuben. "Come on," he said. "Let's go."

Reuben Gaylord shrugged his shoulders. But he got up. "What about you, Joe?" he asked. "Will you be over when you've finished your lunch?"

"Joe needs sleep," Connie said. "He hasn't been in bed since night before last."

"I forgot," Reuben said. "How about bringing the old man out to the farm for Sunday breakfast - say 10 or 11 o'clock?"

"I will," Joe said. "I know he'd like it."

Reuben went off with George Bostwick, and Joe turned to the lunch he hadn't eaten.

"Oh," Connie Gaylord said, and all the excitement had gone out of her. "Why did the gun have to be stolen just when it looked as if we were going to get somewhere?"

"We've still got a chance," Joe said. "I meant what I said. Those

258

South Americans will wait. They'll have to. Put yourself in their place."

Connie Gaylord wasn't especially pretty. She had a rather small and impish face, but she was attractive and appealing. Joe told himself that any attractive woman who was so completely devoted to her husband would be appealing. But it was more than that. Connie Gaylord had something on the ball.

"We haven't got five or six weeks," she said. "Reuben didn't want to say so in front of George Bostwick, but we've probably got about five or six days."

"Don't be silly," Joe said. "You don't know how these things are. I hear it has taken 17 months for one factory to tool up to make 65,000 Garand rifles and it's one of our best factories."

"I wouldn't know about that, but I do know about Gaylord Arms. Winthrop Harris is trying to get a contract to make I don't know how many million rounds of ammunition. If he gets it before Reuben gets an order for the Pyne gun, it will be just too bad."

"Why?"

Connie Gaylord made a pathetic little gesture. "It's simple. Reuben owns 43% of the stock. Harris controls about 35%. Old Amos Brown owns about 16%. He always has been friendly to Reuben. He never blamed Reuben because the Company couldn't pay a dividend after he was made president. He saw that the times were against it. But now they aren't. Now old Amos would like to get a return on his stock. If Winthrop Harris walks into Amos Brown's office some day next week with an order for a hundred million rounds of ammunition and the figures to show a profit on it, Amos is going to listen. Reuben will be out, don't you see? He'll still own his stock. He might make a pot of money. But he'd be through, don't you see?"

Joe felt suddenly let down. "I see now," he said. "But no one ever told me that was the way it was."

"Well," Connie Gaylord said, "that's the way it is."

"You haven't eaten half your lunch," she said. "You've hardly eaten anything."

"I'm not hungry," Joe said. "I've got things on my mind."

He walked with Connie Gaylord to her car.

"Joe, there's something none of us has said. What if the gun is

259

made over there when we can't make it here? What if J.M. Pyne gave his best to invent a gun that will be used against us?"

"It's what we're all thinking about," Joe said. "We all know that's why the gun was stolen - because it's something that they want over there. And if I'd had any sense we'd have the drawings Bostwick needs. I could have made a whole set in half the time it took me to get out those receivers."

"You had no way of knowing what was going to happen. Go home and get a good sleep. You need it. And we'll see you and the old man at breakfast tomorrow." She looked up at him. "Why don't you bring the girl too?"

"What girl?"

"You know - the one you like so much - the beautiful redhead who was with you the day you shot the gun."

"What makes you say I like her so much?"

"You couldn't keep your eyes off her. Will you bring her?"

"I will if I can," Joe said.

XI

Joe started for home and thought better of it. He drove across town to the corner where Betty had told him to turn the night before. He drove slowly down the street, looking for the house. It had been raining so hard that she had insisted he must not get out of the car. She'd made a dash for the front porch. He remembered the house by the big maple tree in front of it, and stopped and went up and rang the doorbell.

A white-haired old lady answered his ring.

"Is Betty at home?" Joe asked. "Betty Foster."

"Why, no," the old lady said, "she isn't. She had to go to New York as soon as she got home from work this noon. Her mother's very sick. They telegraphed her at the office this morning to come home."

Joe thanked her and drove toward home. It might be true. The old lady certainly thought it was true. Perhaps it was just a coincidence that Betty had picked the evening before the robbery to say, as he met her in the hall, "Well?" in that smoothly flirtatious

260

way of hers, and because he wanted to show he was a wise guy and quick on the uptake, he'd said, "How about tonight?"

Perhaps she hadn't made a point of keeping him out late, and it had only seemed so because in the beginning he had hopes of getting back to the shop before Frieda left. There had been a time when he'd thought he wanted a date with Betty, but that was before he'd got his first glimpse of Frieda.

He ran up the stairs and into J.M. Pyne's room.

"It's only half past three," he said. "I've got at least five hours of daylight."

The old man had a drawing board on his knees and was working on a sheet of cross-section paper.

"I thought you'd want to go hunting again," he said. "I've been making a map of the most likely place. It's the old Legendre estate on the west side of the river, between here and Gaylords'. Renee Legendre bought up several thousand acres of poor hill farms and put a 7-foot wire fence around it and made it a game preserve in the '90's. He even imported European wild boar, but they got out and killed some good dogs and he had to give that up. He used to ask me over every fall to kill a buck. And after the hay was cut in the early summer I hunted woodchucks there. Legendre is dead now and the big house burned down, and I haven't heard what the heirs have done with the place. I haven't been there for more than 20 years."

Joe leaned over the old man's shoulder to look at the map.

"I saw plenty of no-hunting signs by the Legendre estate on the west bank of the river," he said. "They began about 5 miles below the shop."

"This isn't to scale, of course," J.M. Pyne said, "though I have kept it as near an inch to the mile as I could, and I've got the brooks and the ponds somewhere near right. If those fellows are in there, they'll camp near water. The trouble is there are so many places where they can find water. There are the three ponds, you see, and four brooks. And there are several good springs." He pointed to a cross. "I've marked the biggest one here. You've got a lot of ground to cover; the place runs three or four miles along the river and it must average two miles wide."

He took the thumbtacks out of the board and folded the map and handed it to Joe.

261

"Take my compass, so when you get lost you can figure out where you are."

"I won't get lost in a place that size."

"I've been lost there," J.M. Pyne said. "If you don't know where you are when it begins to get dark, you'd better figure on sleeping in the open. You'd better take some sandwiches."

Joe put on the dungaree jacket he had worn on his trip down the river that morning and felt in the pockets to make sure he had half a dozen cartridges and matches and a flash. "If you don't hear from me by daylight, you'll know I'm lost and you can tell the police to go find me."

"If I don't hear from you by daylight, I'll be out there hunting for you myself."

Joe picked up the woodchuck rifle. "You sight that gun in this morning?" the old man asked.

"Yes. It's shooting about an inch high at a hundred yards and dead on at about 150."

The old man nodded. "If you have to shoot at very close range, such as 10 feet, remember that telescope is an inch and five eighths above the bore, and hold low."

Joe smiled to himself at this last piece of advice as he went down the stairs. It was so like the old man to be concerned that Joe shouldn't shoot a man an inch and five eighths higher than he intended. It wouldn't make much difference to the man who got hit with that soft-nosed, copper jacketed bullet going close to 3,000 feet a second, but it would be most unsatisfactory to J.M. Pyne.

XII

Joe parked his car in a barway and walked across a field to a fence of woven wire higher than his head, with three strands of barbed wire hung outward on brackets at the top to make it hard to climb. A metal sign riveted to the fence said that the place was patrolled and that trespassers would be prosecuted. He walked along the fence for half a mile without finding any way to get over it. Then he saw a boy about 14 walking toward the fence from inside. He was carrying a woodchuck by the tail and he had a light rifle tucked under his other arm. The boy stopped where there was a 6 or 8 inch maple tree just inside the fence, and laid the woodchuck and his gun at the bottom of the fence. He climbed the tree, crawled out on a limb past the barbed wire, hung from his hands, and dropped to the ground on the outside of the fence.

Joe was within a few yards when the boy succeeded in getting his gun under the fence.

"Nice going," Joe said. The boy turned and saw him and got ready to run.

"Don't mind me," Joe said.

The boy looked at Joe, and then at the rifle Joe had cradled across his body.

"That's a bigger than average woodchuck you've got," Joe said.

The boy stared at the rifle and came nearer. "Mister," he said, without taking his eyes off the rifle, "is that a telescope sight on that gun you've got?"

"Yes," Joe said. "You want to look at it?"

The boy put down his gun and Joe handed him the Pyne woodchuck rifle.

"Gosh, it's heavy," the boy said, as he put it to his shoulder.

"It was made for hitting woodchucks at long range," Joe said. He held the muzzle up with one hand so the boy would get a look through the telescope sight.

"How far can you kill a woodchuck with that?" the boy asked, as he gave the gun back to Joe.

"Two hundred yards," Joe said. "Maybe 300 if I do my part."

The boy turned and pointed toward the hill inside the fence. "There's the biggest woodchuck I ever saw on the other side of that ridge. I got a shot at him, but I missed him. If you go over there and sit down under that apple tree, he might come out again. His hole is halfway down to the pond from the apple tree."

"Which pond is that?"

"I don't know what they call it." He pointed south and west. "The other ponds are farther that way."

"What about the men who patrol this land?"

"There's only two of them, and the only reason they work at it is so they can soak a man like you 5 or 10 bucks for not being arrested. They're both grafters."

"That's a break. Where do I find a tree on this side of the fence?"

The boy pointed south. "There's a handy one about a quarter of a mile down."

"Thanks," Joe said. "I haven't seen you and you haven't see me."

The boy grinned and Joe grinned back.

He found the handy tree where the boy said it was and got over the fence and started up the sloping meadow with the sun at his back. Toward the top of the slope he saw an old house site with two large white birch trees growing out of what had been the cellar. He went on to the apple tree the boy had pointed out, and as he topped the ridge he saw the pond that J.M. Pyne had called North Pond on his map. He sat down under the tree to have a long look. The pond lay in a pocket of the hills, like a mirror in the sun. The brush was creeping into the neglected meadows. It grew thick along the lines of the old stone fences.

He saw no sign of life. He was in the act of getting to his feet again, when, halfway down the slope a woodchuck sat up to look around. He guessed it was 150 yards. He lined the gun up, his elbows on his knees. He could see the chuck's bright, alert eye through the telescope. After half a minute the chuck dropped down again to feed, apparently satisfied that all was well. *For once,* Joe thought, *you guessed right.*

He took a look at the map the old man had made. He had it in his head so well by now that he felt he really didn't need it. He folded it up and put it in his wallet and walked on toward the woods that lay between him and Middle Pond. He was surprised at how long his shadow was as he angled across the slope. He looked at his watch. It was after 5 o'clock. He guessed he would be sleeping on the ground. He remembered then that he hadn't got the sandwiches the old man had suggested he take. He hadn't eaten much of his lunch either. It didn't matter. He wanted sleep much more than he wanted food.

He found himself presently in mixed woods that were quite unlike anything he was accustomed to - a few hemlocks, an occa-

264

sional pine, and oak and maple and beech and several kinds of birch, with an undergrowth of laurel. He kept as straight a course as he could while dodging the thicker stands of laurel.

He came out of the woods after more than an hour, on a slope that had once been meadowland, but that was now grown up to juniper and gray birch, with two twisted old apple trees, half their branches dead. He walked on across the field and into the woods again. The rifle was getting heavy. That was the trouble with a rifle - either it was too light for fine shooting or it was too heavy to carry comfortably. This one weighed more than 13 pounds with the telescope and the leather sling.

The country got rougher as he went on, with more outcroppings of ledge rock. He went down a slope so steep it was hard to keep his footing, and found himself in a marsh with many fallen trees, and so wet that he sank deeper with each step. He worked back up the slope until he found better going and came out on another small meadow. Downhill he saw what was left of an old stone wall, and lying across it the gray bole, two feet thick, of a dead chestnut tree.

The place was somehow familiar, as if he had seen it before. It was, he thought, a trick of memory. And then suddenly the scene righted itself, as a familiar city corner will right itself to a man who has got turned around in the subway, so that once again uptown is where uptown ought to be.

He had been there before. He had been there half an hour before. There were the junipers and the gray birches and the two twisted old apple trees, half their branches dead. He had been walking in a circle - as if he had no map, no compass, and no eyes for where the sun was.

He looked for the sun now. It was to his right instead of behind him.

He couldn't believe he had so far forgotten what he was doing. He got out the compass and found that the setting sun was in its proper place for the time of year - well north of west. He unfolded the old man's map. But he could not be sure which way he ought to go, because he did not know how far he had come since he had left North Pond, or in what direction.

He decided to climb to the top of the ridge and have a look around. After half a mile he walked out of the woods into a high meadow. The ridge was still higher. When he got to the top he saw a pond ahead much larger than North Pond. He sat down to rest. The opposite shore was heavily wooded, but in an opening toward the far end of the pond he saw the roof of a small building. He guessed it was a mile away. And then the last direct light of the sun behind him picked up a flame he couldn't believe was really there.

He lined the rifle up, his elbows on his knees, so he could look through the telescope. It was true.

She was standing in front of what looked like a rough summer camp. He could not see her face too well from this distance, but he could not be mistaken about her red hair. He would have known it anywhere, and the poise of her body too.

She turned and opened a screen door and went into the house, and he saw that she limped.

He got out the map again, comparing it with the long pond in front of him. It wasn't Middle Pond. It was South Pond.

He could only guess which was the easiest way. He chose to go left, which took him farther, for the time being, from the camp where he had seen Frieda. He walked fast, knowing it was a long way around and the light would soon be gone.

He went into the woods and bore downhill toward the shore of the pond. He did not dare go too far from the shore, for fear he would get lost again. He hurried on, climbing over fallen logs, but sure he was going in the right direction, because he got an occasional glimpse of the water.

It was getting dark fast now. He still had two miles to go, maybe more. The ground was so wet and soft he couldn't walk without getting in half way to his knees. He made a detour to find hard ground, and got into a laurel thicket. The tough, crooked little branches caught at his clothes, got between the barrel of his rifle and the telescope sight, knocked off his hat. He had to carry the gun butt foremost in one hand while he pushed the laurel away from his face with the other.

He slipped and fell, climbing over a fallen log. But he managed to save the gun as he fell, so the telescope sight was not put out of whack. He got out his flashlight. It gave only a feeble gleam. It had been all right early that morning when he had gone down the river, but it was almost useless now. He switched it off and put it back in his pocket and went on in the increasing dark.

At last he saw a faint light ahead. He walked toward the light.

He fell over a fallen log and got up and sat down on the log to listen.

He could hear voices, but not well enough to distinguish them. And then he recognized the odor of a steak cooking, and knew that he was hungry after all. He guessed that he wasn't more than 50 yards away, probably less. He lit a match and looked at his watch. It was nearly 9 o'clock. Presently the delicious odor was gone.

It was so dark he could no longer walk without bumping into trees. He crawled forward, holding the rifle clear of the ground with one hand, making slow progress, but feeling that he had plenty of time now. When he thought he was near the clearing around the cabin, he stood up. The light seemed to come from cracks between shutters. His eyes had become more accustomed to the dark now. He opened the rifle and took the cartridge out and held the faintly glowing flashlight at the muzzle and looked in the breech to make sure he hadn't got a twig in the barrel. The barrel was clear. He put the cartridge back in the chamber and closed the gun.

He thought there was an opening in the brush to his left, and walked toward it. He stumbled over something and fell heavily into a pile of tin cans. He lay there listening. The noise he had made seemed to him as loud as cowbells jangling. But of course it wasn't. He decided no one in the shack had noticed it.

He could hear voices occasionally, and, though he could not hear what they were saying he knew they were not excited voices.

He crawled around the pile of tin cans and toward the edge of the clearing around the shack. He lay there a long time, listening. Finally he turned the flashlight on to look at his watch. It gave just enough light so he could read the time. It was 25 minutes of ten. The moon would be up soon. He had to act before there was any more light.

He stood up and walked as quickly as he could, without making any noise, to the wall of the shack. He walked along the wall and reached a crack between the two shutters from which light came. He saw a small bedroom with a plain iron bed on either side. The door was open into another room, but he could see nothing except part of a stone fireplace with a large wire broiler leaning against it. He walked cautiously around the place, keeping close to the wall and putting his foot down for each step slowly, until he was sure he wasn't going to crack a stick or make some other noise. He had gone halfway around the building when he came to another crack between the board shutters. He put his eye against the crack.

Frieda was sitting at a table under an oil lamp that hung from the ceiling, playing checkers with a blond young man. She wasn't 10 feet away. He could see the long eyelashes lying on her cheek as she studied her move. Then she opened her eyes wide as she looked up at the young man, and for a moment he had the ridiculous feeling that she was looking into his eyes, and he was looking into hers. But of course she couldn't see him out there in the dark.

She lowered her eyes again, and though he could not see much of the checkerboard, he knew that she was studying her move. He stared at that gorgeous red head, and then she looked up from the board, smiling, one eyebrow cocked a little, as if she had just put something over and was waiting for her opponent to get it.

"Gracious lady," the blond young man said, "for the first time in all the games we've played, you have beaten me."

Joe turned away. Why did a girl who was everything he'd wanted have to be a crook? He could no longer doubt that she was, and the quicker he had the thing over with the better. He was sure now that there was no one except these two in the place. There must have been two men. The other one had probably gone to deliver the gun. But at least he could get Frieda and this young man. He had seen a lantern on a shelf. That would do for light. He would force them to walk ahead of him. He'd drive them ahead of him until he got out to a main road and found help. They would know the way. If they didn't, he'd make them go the hard way he had come. It would be a pleasure to make it tough for them.

He hugged the wall of the house as he walked toward the front door. He reached the corner and peered around it, and something fell on his head and the world went black.

XIII

Joe Hill heard voices before he opened his eyes. He heard the word "kill" repeated several times. He opened his eyes against the pain and found he was looking up at the underside of a roof. He started to raise himself up, and found he couldn't. His feet were fastened together. For some reason, that made it harder. And then an ugly face interposed itself between his eyes and the roof. It was not the face of the young man who had been playing checkers with Frieda. "He is coming to," the face said. "Now we will ask him."

He picked Joe up as if his 180 pounds were nothing and dropped him in a chair. Joe saw that the man was built like a heavyweight wrestler. He felt sick and dizzy. He clenched his fists, as if that would prevent the room from whirling.

"Where are the others?" the ugly man demanded.

"What others?" Joe asked.

Frieda was sitting across the table from him. But he could read nothing in her face. She was neither sorry nor glad to see him in the power of this man. Her eyes met his. But they said nothing. She must know what he thought of her. But she didn't care.

The ugly man drew a Luger pistol and pointed it at Joe. "If anybody else comes here, I will shoot you first. So tell the truth. Where are the others?"

"I came alone," Joe said.

Frieda put her elbow on the table and rested her chin in her hand, quietly thoughtful, as if she were interested, but not at all excited.

"How did you find this place?" the ugly man demanded.

"By pure luck," Joe said.

"By your bad luck. But how? What were you doing?" He made a gesture toward the corner of the room, and Joe saw his rifle standing there. "What is that big gun for?"

"It's a woodchuck rifle, Henry," Frieda said, "and it belongs to the old man. He showed it to me. If this man had been looking for us, he wouldn't have brought a single-shot rifle, nor one so heavy. And he would have had a pistol."

"That is true," Henry said, looking down at the table. "He had no pistol - nothing but that clumsy single-shot gun and so few cartridges."

He swept the things on the table into his big hands and put them in his pockets. Joe realized then that they were things that had come out of his pockets; he saw the micrometer caliper in a soft leather case that he always carried, as Henry took it. He tried to spread his feet apart fighting the dizziness, and could not. He looked down at his feet. His ankles were neatly lashed together with light braided line, wrapped around many times.

"How did you find this place?" Henry demanded again.

"I was on the hill over across the pond," Joe said, "when the sun was setting. It shone on the girl's red hair."

"Madam," Henry said, "I told you it was not good to show yourself outdoors when they might be looking for a redhaired lady."

Joe noticed how respectful he was in his tone and manner, as if he hardly dared to remind her that she had done something he had asked her not to. And she was not at all concerned about what he said. She did not even look at him.

"No one knows anything about her," Joe said, "because the old man didn't tell anybody that she was with him when you knocked him out."

"Why not?" Henry asked.

"Because she made him like her. He still thinks she's a friend of his who had nothing to do with taking the gun."

Henry's thick lips spread in a grin and his little eyes gleamed. He turned to Frieda.

"There is only one thing to do," he said. "I will take him off in the woods and do it with his own gun, so it will look as if he shot himself. Then we wait until he comes. He will take you with him."

She still looked thoughtful, her brows knitted, her chin in her hand. "I have been thinking," she said. "This is one of the two men in the world who knows the gun well enough to make a new hammer for it quickly."

Henry turned eagerly to Joe. "Could you do that?" he asked.

"Henry failed to bring the hammer of the semi-automatic rifle," Frieda explained to Joe. "He got everything else, but he didn't get that. If you could make a new hammer for the gun, it would be nice for us - so nice that it is possible that we might find some way to let you go on living."

"Could you do it?" Henry asked again.

Joe saw that the man was ever so anxious for him to say he could. That hammer meant a great deal to him.

"I would have to have tools," Joe said.

"What tools?"

"A hacksaw."

"I have a hacksaw."

"A drill of the right size."

"I have a whole lot of drills."

"Files."

"I have files."

"I'd need a vise, also."

"I have a vise," Henry said. The man seemed to swell with hope.

"The hard thing would be to find a piece of stock," Joe said. "But perhaps you have something around the place that I could cut a piece of steel from."

"How big?" Henry asked.

"Give me a pencil and paper," Joe said.

Henry got a pencil and paper.

"Wasn't there a half-dollar in the money you took out of my pockets?" Joe asked.

"Why?" Henry asked.

"I need it to make the drawing."

Henry reluctantly produced the half-dollar. Joe laid the coin on the paper and ran the pencil around it to make a circle, remembering the time when the old man had laid the hammer of the gun on a half-dollar and said, "There is a piece of steel that cost me 200 hours of work before I got it so it did what I wanted it to do. And though it's thicker than a half dollar, it isn't any bigger around and there isn't much more metal in it."

Working inside the circle, Joe placed the hole for the pin on which the hammer swung, and drew the longish flat which made the unique contact with the sear, and then the nose where it struck.

"That's about it," Joe said.

Henry picked up the half-dollar and looked at the sketch and went to the fireplace. He came back with an iron bar perhaps an inch and a half wide and a quarter-inch thick.

"Here," he said, "is one of the irons we use to hold up the broiler."

Joe guessed it was a piece of ordinary cold-rolled steel. The odd thing about the hammer was that it had no delicate or precise sear notch. The old man had made it of a proper alloy steel, and had hardened it so it would take the battering it got without changing its shape and so the hole for the pin would not wear rapidly. A hammer of soft steel should last for a number of shots without causing any trouble. But he did not see any reason for telling Henry this.

"Give me a file," he said.

"First you must saw a piece off," Henry said.

Joe knew then that the man was no mechanic in metal, however skillful he was in lashing a man's ankles together.

"Get me a file - a saw file if you have it - so I can find out what kind of stuff this bar is."

Henry went outside to get the file. Joe was alone with Frieda, unless the young man she had been playing checkers with when he had looked through the crack in the shutters was concealed in another room. He wanted to say something to her that would sting, and he didn't care whether he was overheard.

"You must like yourself for fooling me and the old man the way you did," he said.

She shrugged her shoulders in a gesture of distaste. "Only stupid men are as easily fooled as you are, and in our philosophy stupid people do not matter."

Henry came in the door as she finished what seemed to Joe the coldest, hardest statement he had ever heard a woman make.

Joe took the file Henry brought, a small three-cornered one in fair shape, and tried the steel bar from the fireplace. It was soft, too soft to be any good. But it would be easy to cut with hacksaw and files.

He looked up. Frieda's hands were trembling so hard that she could not hold them still.

272

"Is it all right?" Henry asked anxiously.

"It is not the kind of steel I would like," Joe said, "but perhaps I can make it do."

"Truly?" Henry said. "You can really make it?"

Joe saw that the man was so crazy to get the hammer made that he wasn't thinking about anything else. He wasn't considering Joe's position. Frieda had said that they might find some way of letting him live if he made the hammer. But of course they wouldn't. They couldn't. When they got the hammer he would be just as dangerous to them as he was before. They would still need to kill him to save themselves. But he would stall along, working on the hammer, in the hope that before the time was up he'd get a break.

"I can try," Joe said. "Where is the gun?"

"Why do you want the gun?" Henry asked.

"So I can see how thick the hammer should be and measure the size of the pin it works on."

Henry went to the door and whistled. Joe heard an answering whistle from out there in the dark. Presently he saw the young man who had been playing checkers with Frieda when he had looked through the crack between the shutters. He was using a pair of homemade crutches that were much too short for him. The lower part of one leg, from the ankle half way to the knee, was in bandages, and Joe guessed that he was the man J.M. Pyne had said he had hit across the shin with a rifle barrel.

"He is going to make us a new hammer, Louis," Henry said. "Take the pistol and watch him while I get the gun."

Louis sat down across the table from Joe, and Henry gave him the Luger pistol.

"Do not move," Louis said, pointing the pistol at Joe as Henry went out with a flashlight, "or I will shoot you."

Joe was interested to know that they had only one pistol between them. He was beginning to be himself again. His head ached, but the dizziness was gone. He felt the place that hurt. He had a lump over his left ear, but there was no blood. He guessed that he had been knocked out in exactly the same way that J.M. Pyne had been knocked out the night before, with a blackjack, and by the same man.

273

Henry brought in the gun and laid it on the table. Joe picked it up and looked it over.

"Who put it together?"

"I did," Frieda said.

Joe took the gun apart, wondering how he was going to measure the space in which the hammer moved. Of course Frieda had put the gun together. She had got Mr. Pyne to show her how before she helped these men steal the gun.

"I want that micrometer you took out of my pocket," he said to Henry. "It's in a leather case."

Henry took the case out of his pocket and laid the micrometer on the table. Joe measured the diameter of the pin. It was a hundred and eighty four thousandths. That was well under 3/16ths, but a 3/16ths hole would do.

"Get me your drill," he said.

Henry brought in a small hand drill and a little wooden box of twist drills. Joe picked out the three-sixteenths drill. He found it was a bit under standard size when he put the mike on it. But this was not going to be a Pyne job. All he had to do was make it look good to a man who was not a mechanic.

"Now give me my knife."

"That you cannot have," Henry said.

Joe grinned at him. "Then you don't get a hammer."

"Why do you want the knife?" Frieda asked.

"I want my knife and a small piece of hard wood. I'll cut the wood to fit the space in the gun and measure it."

"Give him the knife, Henry," Frieda said. "He can't do any harm with it while Louis holds the pistol."

Henry gave him the knife and got the end of an oak board from outside. Joe split off a piece and shaved it down until it would go into the space for the hammer. He measured the thickness with the micrometer. Then he measured the thickness of the iron bar.

"This is a piece of luck," he told them. "The bar is only a little too thick. It will not need much filing to get it down to size."

"Ah!" Henry said. "What next?"

274

Joe handed his pocket knife back to Henry.

"I want food. I haven't eaten since lunch. And I'm tired. I need sleep."

"Food you can have," Henry said, "but there is no time for you to sleep. The hammer must be done by 10 tomorrow morning."

Joe looked up at the oil lamp overhead. "I'll have to do most of the work by daylight. That lamp doesn't give a good enough light. Suppose you get me something to eat now and let me go to sleep. You can wake me up at daylight. I will have four or five hours of daylight before 10 o'clock. I can't do a nice job in that time. But perhaps I can make something that will work."

"While we are getting the food, you can cut off the piece of steel you want. I will get the hacksaw."

"I'll need a vise."

"The vise is part of the bench. I do not know if I could bring it in here."

"Haven't you got a small iron vise?" Joe asked. "The kind that clamps on a table?"

"That I have," Henry said happily.

Frieda started a fire in the fireplace and poured some charcoal from a paper bag on it. Joe noticed that one ankle was strapped up with adhesive tape and that she could not put much weight on that foot.

"Please," Louis said to her, "take back your crutches."

Joe saw that Louis did not look at her when he spoke. He kept his eyes on Joe, his right hand resting on the table as he held the pistol pointed at the middle of Joe's body.

"I'll take one crutch," Frieda said.

She took the crutch that Louis had leaned against the table and went into the kitchen. Joe watched her through the doorway as she lit the oilstove. She had no stockings on, and he saw that the good ankle was badly bruised.

Henry came in with a small iron vise and a hacksaw and a couple of blades.

"Put the vise on the edge of the table," Joe said. Henry did as he asked, turning up the clamp screw with a powerful hand.

275

"Now you will have to take the lashings off. I can't stand up and use the hacksaw unless you do."

"Sit still," Henry said. "I will fix it so you can take a short step."

He knelt down in front of Joe and took the cord off and put it back again, allowing a foot of quadrupled cord between Joe's ankles.

Joe stood up. The dizziness came back, so he had to hold on to the table with both hands, but after a minute or two he was all right.

He was trying to measure from the end of the bar with his circle the size of a half-dollar when Henry gave him a carpenter's folding rule. Joe had to smile at the crudity of his tools. But he was too much a disciple of J.M. Pyne not to be interested in finding out what he could do in the circumstances. One of the old man's pet stories was of the day when he and three of his friends arrived at a rifle match to learn that the conditions called for open sights. J.M. Pyne had made open sights for them out of stiff paper and fastened them on with rubber bands, and he and his friends had taken three of the first five places in the match.

Joe put the bar in the vise and adjusted the hacksaw and started in. The table jiggled. He got Henry to sit on it. His weight steadied the table enough so it was possible to work.

Frieda came in with a piece of steak. The charcoal was glowing now and she put the steak in the broiler and tried to balance it on the one iron bar that remained.

"One minute," Henry said, "and we will have this bar. He is using only a little piece of it."

The hacksaw went through. Joe broke the piece off. Henry took the bar over to the fireplace and set up the broiler over the charcoal fire. Joe studied his piece of stock. He had no way to locate the hole he was going to drill. He would be lucky to get it within an eighth of an inch of where it should be, with the tools he had at hand. It would be tough to get it exactly right in a tool-room. There was nothing to do but take a chance.

"Get me a prick punch," he said to Henry, "and a hammer."

When Henry came back with the punch and the hammer, Joe laid the piece of steel bar on the stone hearth, because it was the only really solid thing in the room; he guessed where the hole should be and struck the punch.

He put the piece back in the vise and started to drill the hole. He realized how tired he was before the drill went through, but the sputtering of the steak in the fireplace urged him on. He sat down when he had drilled the hole.

"That's all for tonight," he said.

Frieda brought him steak and creamed potatoes and bread and butter and mixed salad.

"Now I will take the pistol, Louis," Henry said.

He put the pistol in his back pocket and walked back and forth, his protruding lips moving as if he were talking to himself, while Joe ate his dinner.

Frieda sat down and put her elbow on the table and rested her chin in her hand. Joe thought there was something odd about this gesture. She did the same thing every time she sat down at the table. He wondered if her hand still trembled as violently as it had before, and she wanted to steady it in this fashion. And why, underneath her calm pose, was she so frightened? She treated Henry as if he were an inferior person. She gave him orders and he obeyed them. He seemed eager to please her. And Louis' eyes followed her as if he were in love with her, when he did not have the responsibility of holding a pistol on Joe.

"Madam," Henry said to her, "where shall we put him? Where will he sleep?"

She made a motion with her head toward an open door. "In there, of course. There are two beds."

"But that is your room."

"There is no other place," she said. "I am not afraid of him."

"I will tie him to the bed," Henry said.

"Naturally," Frieda said. She went into the kitchen, got coffee, and gave it to Joe.

"Tonight," Henry said, "someone must watch. It is now 11 o'clock. Louis can sit here with the pistol while I sleep. After three hours he will wake me up. Then he can sleep and I will sit here."

"You can keep awake by playing your beloved waltzes on the phonograph," Frieda said.

Joe could not be sure whether she was being kind to him or kidding him. But it was plain Henry thought she was being kind.

"It would not wake you?" he asked.

"I am so tired," she said, "that nothing will wake me."

Henry got a hank of braided line from the kitchen, and a candlestick. He tapped Joe on the shoulder. "You have eaten," he said. "Come now."

Joe hobbled into the bedroom, unable to take a step more than a foot long. Henry told him to lie down. He doubled his braided line and went to work. He made several turns around one of Joe's wrists and led the line to a bedpost, carrying it under the spring, and back to Joe's other wrist, and from there to the opposite bedpost. Then he lashed Joe's feet to the bottom of the bed. He did it as if he had done the job many times before and knew exactly how it should be done.

"Now," he said, "you can sleep. But you will not get away. Only men who have learned how and have practiced much can do it."

He took the candle and went out, shutting the door behind him. The room was dark, except for a thin bar of moonlight. Joe guessed that it came through the crack left between the two shutters on the window. He experimented with the lashings, and learned that Henry had done a clever job. He could move his hands, but not enough so he had any chance to reach the cord with his teeth. He heard Henry at the shutters outside, and knew by the sound that he was fastening them with a hammer and nails. The bar of moonlight disappeared and the room was black dark.

Lying there in the dark, seeing no way out, knowing that Henry would shoot him when he finished the hammer, Joe remembered that J.M. Pyne had said he would come to find him if he didn't get home by daylight.

The old man had been kidding Joe about getting lost when he had said it. But he'd come just the same. He'd start out hunting when he failed to hear from Joe. He would come alone too. And if he found this place he'd walk into a trap, just as Joe had.

The thought of the old man meeting sudden death on his account completed Joe's despair. But even this new and bitter fear couldn't keep his exhausted body awake.

XIV

Joe dreamed that a girl was close beside him, stroking his face and calling, "Joe! Joe! Wake up!" and that from somewhere came the sound of violins.

He awoke, and the dream was true, except that the girl wasn't calling out his name. She was whispering it in his ear. He stirred and would have spoken, but she put her hand over his mouth.

"Sh-h-h," she whispered, her lips against his ear. "Whisper. And listen to the phonograph, so you can stop when it stops."

Joe listened. The phonograph in the next room was playing a waltz. He guessed it was the one called "Tales from the Vienna Woods", and it was almost over. He realized, coming wider awake, that Frieda was sitting on the floor beside his bed. He could not imagine why.

The violins finished the waltz. He heard a chair creak as Henry got out of it in the other room. He wound up the motor of the machine and started a new waltz record. Joe didn't recognize it, but it had the lovely lilt of the previous one.

"I've got a knife," she whispered. "I can cut the cords he tied you with. But I'm afraid it wouldn't do any good. He nailed up the shutters, so you couldn't get out of the window without making a lot of noise."

The girl talked as if she had been planning how to save his life, even at great risk to herself. He couldn't understand why she should pretend such a thing. He wanted to trust her. He wanted her, too, in spite of the dirty trick she had played on the old man, getting him to make a rifle for her, so she could steal his gun. He understood for the first time in his life how women who were spies could get information out of men. If you loved them you trusted them, even if you knew better.

"Joe," she whispered, "have you still got the blue pill?"

He still had the blue pill in his watch pocket. He had stuck his thumbs casually inside his belt before Henry had tied him up, and had felt it. Henry hadn't searched him well enough to find it when he was knocked out.

"What good would it be? I haven't got much chance of making a hammer that will fire it."

The record on the phonograph stopped. She did not speak while

Henry was changing the record in the other room.

"I've got the Pyne hammer," she whispered when the music had begun again.

She put her hand on his arm and found his hand. She gave him a small, irregular piece of metal. He knew it by the feel. It was the hammer from the Pyne semi-automatic rifle. There could be no other piece of steel in the world of that shape.

For the first time he had hope. Maybe the girl wasn't what she seemed. Why would she give him the hammer if she wasn't trying to help him? But he remembered how she'd been with Henry and Louis. There must be some catch. "Where did you get this?" he asked.

"I took it out of the bag they carried the gun away in, and when we got here I hid it."

"Why?"

"So the gun wouldn't be any good to them, of course."

"I mean why do you give it to me now?"

"I thought if you had the real hammer and the blue pill, maybe we'd have a chance."

"Who is 'we'?" Joe asked.

"You and me," she whispered. And then she must have realized what was in his mind. "You don't think I'm one of them, do you?"

"They didn't tie you up."

"Of course. They think I'm one of them."

"How can they, if you aren't?"

"Because I have red hair. Their boss seems to like redheads. They were told that a redheaded girl in the Gaylord plant was giving him information and helping any way she could. She's probably the girl from the information desk you had a date with last night."

"Her hair isn't red," he said, wondering how she knew he'd gone out with Betty Foster.

"Of course it is."

"Not like yours." He supposed you could call Betty Foster's hair red. He had never thought of it as red, exactly.

"Anyway, when Henry and Louis found me in Pyne's shop, they thought I was the boss's girlfriend. So they offered to take me with them. I was so scared I didn't know what to do, but I thought, as long as they figured I was helping them, I'd surely have a chance to save the Pyne gun."

The phonograph stopped, so he could not tell her how happy she had made him. He knew that she was telling the truth. She wasn't what he had been afraid she was. He couldn't see her face now in the dark, but he could picture her as she was in Pyne's shop facing Henry and knowing what a thug he was, and deciding to go with him, on the chance of beating him. He started to put his arm around her, and couldn't. The cords that bound him checked him sharply. He couldn't even reach her hand to tell her that he could do things, with a girl like her to help.

"You're wonderful," he said, when the music began again. "We'll work out something with the blue pill."

She caught her breath so sharply he knew how much that single cartridge meant to her. "Oh," she said, "you've got it."

"Yes," he said. "Now tell me all you know. Have you any idea who the boss is or what he's like?"

"They always call him 'he'. They never use his name. But I'm sure he's Winkler - the man Pyne told us about at dinner that first evening - the one with the big Doberman who was at the Gaylords'. Because this man breeds Doberman pinschers, and he has some arrangement for using the country around here for training his dogs. Henry was so frightened this afternoon when I showed him that the hammer of the gun was missing that he had to talk. He told me quite a lot about his boss. He never comes to this camp. Louis has never seen him. He comes within a quarter of a mile or so, working a dog, with a whistle. When Henry hears the whistle, he runs to meet the boss. But tomorrow morning Henry is going to take me with him. He thinks the boss will be pleased with him for rescuing me and taking me back to him. And if he's the kind of man Henry says he is, he'll shoot me."

Joe realized Winkler would have to kill her. He couldn't do anything else and save himself. And no one could stop him, unless Joe Hill could.

"What did Henry say about the man?"

"From what Henry said, I think he's a murderous madman - a sadist who loves to torture and kill."

"He must have something on Henry and Louis," Joe said.

"I don't know whether Henry is a loyal slave or if he's so afraid of the man that he does what he's told. I'd guess it's both."

"And Louis?"

"Louis was a nice simple boy once. He's been made into a criminal who's learning Henry's trade. They haven't given him a pistol of his own yet, and he's afraid that his letting Pyne cripple him will be a black mark against him. I think both he and Henry are hoping I'll put in a good word for them with the boss."

The phonograph stopped again. It was silent so long that Joe was afraid Henry wasn't going to run the machine any longer. But at last it came - Vienna Woods again.

"In the morning," Joe said, "I'll go to work making the hammer for Henry. I'll have to work the stock down so it looks like the sketch I drew. Even then I can't switch to the real hammer while he's sitting on the table to steady it for me, the way he was tonight, or hanging over my shoulder. We've got to figure some way to get him out of the room for a minute. Even then, Louis will be there."

"I'll distract Louis," Frieda said.

"Another thing - I don't want to use the blue pill until I'm forced to. I've got to save it for Winkler, in case we run into him. I can't possibly bluff Henry in the house. He'll be too confident he can get me with his Luger at six feet. But he's no pistol shot."

"How do you know he isn't?"

"Didn't you see the way he held his gun tonight when he pointed it at me? He's never learned what to do with his thumb. He doesn't know what can be done with a pistol at 50 yards. If I can get him far enough away, he'll know he has no chance against a man with a rifle."

They whispered to each other for half an hour, pausing only when the phonograph stopped, planning exactly how they would get Henry where they wanted him, and then Frieda struck a match and saw that it was half past four.

282

"I think we've got it," she said. "And it isn't safe to talk any longer. Henry will be coming in to wake you up."

He hated to give up the intimacy of their whispering; their cheeks touching again and again as he whispered in her ear and she whispered in his.

"Good night, Joe," she said.

"If I could get my arms free - " he said, straining at the cords.

"You can't," she said.

And then his predicament struck them both as funny and they started to laugh together. She stopped it. She put her hand over his mouth and put her face down in the pillow. It was half a minute before they recovered their control.

The phonograph stopped and they both held their breath, for fear Henry would open the door. But he put on another waltz.

"Someday I want to laugh a lot with you," Joe said. Frieda stood up. Then she leaned down and took his face in both her hands and kissed him on the mouth and stole across the room to her own bed.

XV

He was still awake when Henry opened the door. He closed his eyes, pretending to be asleep. Henry took him by the shoulder and shook him hard.

"It is time," he said. "It is nearly 5 o'clock."

"All right," Joe said.

Henry cast off the lashings, leaving only the one that prevented Joe from taking a step more than a foot long, and helped him to his feet. Joe stole a look at Frieda. In the light from the open door he saw her, a lovely shape in the wrinkled green cotton dress, her hands clasped under her chin, her face pale against her red hair, dark circles under her eyes, apparently asleep.

Joe hobbled into the other room after Henry and sat down at the table. The piece of stock he had drilled the night before was in the vise. A dozen files lay on the table.

Joe picked up a file. Henry set a cup of coffee down in front of him. Joe tried files until he found two that cut well, and drank his coffee.

283

"Hurry," Henry said. He pointed to the alarm clock that hung on the chimney breast. The clock said two minutes of five. "You have till 9:45 - not one minute longer."

Joe went to work. He could hear Henry in the kitchen, getting breakfast.

He was so tired from lack of sleep that filing was labor. But he knew he had to go ahead exactly as if he expected to finish the job, until the moment came when he could put the Pyne hammer in place and load the blue pill into the gun.

He filed steadily until Henry brought in soft-boiled eggs and sausage and bread and cheese and beer and more coffee.

Henry sat down opposite Joe and they ate. Henry was plainly hopeful. He slapped Joe on the back when he was taking the dishes away.

"I know you can do it," he said. "You are a good workman."

Joe filed away at the surfaces of the piece, taking pains to file them true, and checking frequently with the micrometer caliper. It took him more than an hour to thin the piece down to size. Then he began to file the edges to shape. Henry sat on the table, holding it down and watching him, with his little eyes as interested as a child's.

Frieda came out at 8 o'clock. Joe didn't dare look at her, for fear his face would give him away.

"The sound of filing doesn't help one sleep," she said.

"I'm so sorry," Henry said, "but you know it has to be done. It means much to you - maybe as much as to me and Louis."

"It wasn't I who left the hammer behind," she said.

Louis called out from the other bedroom. Henry helped him out to a chair at the table.

Joe got the new hammer into the gun at 9 o'clock while Henry watched anxiously.

"How is it? Will it work?"

"Not yet," Joe said.

Joe found that by a fluke he had got the hole in the hammer within a couple of hundredths of the right place. He had plenty of stock above the hole for the hammer nose and enough below the hole for the long sliding contact with the sear. He filed steadily on.

"It is now a quarter past nine," Henry said. "At most you have only 30 minutes more."

Joe nodded and went on filing while Henry bent over his shoulder.

"It is half past nine!" Henry cried. "You have only 15 minutes more! Can you finish?"

"Not if you keep on bothering me." Joe said.

Joe stole a glance at Frieda. She was watching him closely, but so was Louis. She must have understood his look, because she asked Louis if he didn't want to play a game of checkers.

"You know how I love to play checkers with you," he said, and his voice told how happy he was to have her ask him.

Frieda got out the board and sat down close to Joe, so that Louis was across the table from him.

Henry pointed at the clock. "Look," he said. "It is ten minutes of 10, and he is never late. Sometimes he is early."

Joe tried the hammer in the gun. It was so nearly right by now that he thought it would probably fire a cartridge. He wasn't taking any chances on it. But he felt a little proud of his job.

"How is it?" Henry asked.

"A few minutes more," Joe said.

Joe took the new hammer out of the gun and fastened it in the vise.

"Hurry!" Henry said.

Joe sat down in front of the vise and picked up a file and reached with his foot for Frieda's foot.

Frieda threw up her head. "Henry," she cried, "there's the whistle! Don't you hear it?"

Henry rushed to the door and out into the yard to listen, just as Frieda had said he did when he heard the whistle.

Joe slipped the real hammer into the gun, and took the blue pill out of his pocket. He saw that Frieda was opening her purse.

She leaned down with the vegetable knife she'd taken from the kitchen the night before, and cut the cord that fastened his ankles together.

Louis half rose to his feet and yelled, "Look out, Henry! Look out!"

Joe ran to the door. Henry was fifty feet away at the edge of the brush and turning toward the house in answer to Louis' yell.

"Put your hands up," Joe said, as he raised the gun.

Henry almost laughed. "Your gun isn't loaded." he said.

From somewhere behind Henry in the woods came two blasts of a whistle. Henry yanked at the Luger in his back pocket, and Joe knew he'd have to shoot. But as the sights swung on, he couldn't bring himself to kill the man. He fired low at his right shoulder.

Henry staggered and dropped his pistol as the ferocious muzzle blast of the blue pill echoed from the hills. With surprising speed, Henry picked up his pistol with his other hand and dived into the brush. Joe could see the brush waving as Henry ran staggering toward the sound of the whistle.

Joe turned. Frieda was right behind him. Louis had almost reached her when the gun butt struck him in the chest and knocked him down.

Joe took Frieda's arm and together they ran down the path, turned into a woods road, crossed a roaring brook on the rough bridge covered with rotting planks that she had told him about, and down another old woods road.

"Can you keep it up?" Joe asked.

"I can run a mile," she said.

They ran on. He had told her the night before that South Pond couldn't be more than two miles from the Gaylord's footbridge. Joe was afraid that Winkler's dog could trail them. But Winkler wouldn't guess any more than Henry had that Joe had no more ammunition for the Pyne gun. He'd be pretty careful about coming up on them.

"Take it easier," Joe said. "Jog."

They slowed down to a dogtrot. He saw that she hardly limped at all. They came to the end of the old woods road after half a mile and saw a meadow ahead.

"I've got to rest!" Frieda gasped.

Joe stood with one hand under her elbow, taking her weight off the bad ankle, while they panted for breath.

"We'll go across the field and get on the other side of that stone wall," he said.

The wall wasn't high enough to conceal them, but the brush growing on either side of it would help.

"Can you run some more?"

She nodded. They jogged across the meadow and got over the wall, and stopped to look back. There was no one in sight. They walked along the wall.

"We're way out in front," Frieda said.

"Yes," Joe said.

If the dog was trailing them, he certainly hadn't got out of the woods as yet, and Winkler couldn't come as fast as the dog.

"We'll have to change our course at the next wall," Joe said, "and go more south."

"There's another wall," Frieda said.

They climbed the next wall and walked along it, feeling better every minute.

"We can't be much more than a mile from the Gaylord's now," Frieda said.

"Just about a mile, I'd guess," Joe said.

He looked up at the sun. He guessed their right course was almost into the sun. There were several big boulders in the field, some of them as big as a small car. It looked as if they had been too big to blast and drag away on a stoneboat, even for a New England farmer of a hundred years ago. Then Joe looked back over his shoulder and saw the dog. He had his nose to the ground, but now he lifted his head and saw them and came racing toward them - a big short-haired dog with the black coat and tan markings of a Doberman pinscher.

"It's Winkler's dog," Frieda said.

"Yes," Joe said.

The dog caught up with them. Joe poised the Pyne gun, butt foremost. If the dog tried to jump at Frieda's throat or at his, the butt should stop him. But the dog did not jump at them. He ran around behind them, rushing in to snap viciously at them, but keeping out of Joe's reach. Joe saw that he was wonderfully quick - much quicker than a man.

The dog's rushes, always ending just before he reached them, forced them to stand still. Joe tried walking straight forward, as if the dog wasn't there. The dog leaped at Frieda, his jaws open. Joe pulled her toward him and the dog turned in mid-air. The dog was trained to do just what he was doing. Joe remembered what Connie Gaylord had said about Winkler - that his hobby was training his dogs to catch and hold criminals.

"We've got to keep on going, whatever he does," Joe said.

The dog ran around them, rushing at them from behind and then from one side, making one of his magnificent feinting leaps every minute or two - leaps that let Joe know the dog could get a throat hold when he tried. It was a long time before Joe realized that the dog was forcing them farther out into the field. He was driving them in a particular direction.

Joe stopped short, his arm under Frieda's elbow, and looked around.

Winkler stepped out from behind the big rock ahead with a gun half raised to his shoulder. "Put your hands up," he said.

Joe stood there, staring at the man. He couldn't quite believe what he saw. Winkler leveled his gun.

"We'll have to do what he says," Frieda whispered.

Joe dropped the Pyne gun in the grass and held up his hands. He saw that the gun Winkler had was some kind of light submachine gun with a magazine that held many cartridges. You really didn't have to aim with a gun like that, at 30 feet. It was a weapon built to spray bullets as a hose sprays water.

Joe dropped his hands and put one arm around Frieda. But he was utterly helpless to protect her.

Winkler must have known the country so well that, guessing they would make for the Gaylords', he could take a short cut. The dog had done the rest. The dog had been trained to drive people toward his master, into ambush. All the time he had been making those false rushes and those feinting leaps he had been forcing them to go to the place where Winkler was hidden.

Winkler pointed to his right. "Walk over there," he said.

Joe and Frieda did what he told them to.

"Stand still," Winkler said. He moved behind them.

"Turn around," he said.

When they turned around, he was standing by the Pyne gun.

"You will understand why I must kill you both," he said.

Joe saw that he was the kind of man no one believes in until it is too late. You read about his kind in the papers every day - men you thought of as existing only in prisons or insane asylums - until you saw the headlines over stories of violent death. They weren't civilized, but they had a kind of reason, a logic of their own. They took what they wanted, not honestly, but by lies, not under the law, but by force. They could win that way, not because they were clever, or because they had more force, but because they used force when better men did not expect it.

"You wouldn't shoot a woman," Joe said.

Winkler smiled faintly. He was a tall, broad-shouldered man, rather elegantly dressed for a day in the field, training a dog. His hat had a long feather stuck in the band. His tweed jacket was a nice shade of beige, and he wore it with a beige shirt, a beige tie and beige slacks of a lighter shade. The dog stood at heel, part of the costume.

It was plain from his dress that he fancied himself, though how a man who fancied himself could use a submachine gun for his private use when he had a choice was beyond Joe's comprehension. It implied a special weakness, a lack of confidence under the showy and arrogant exterior. The gun in Winkler's hands was final evidence that he was a killer, and nothing but a killer - a man who sprayed bullets at close range, instead of placing them precisely.

"I shall make it easier for her by shooting her first," Winkler said.

Joe knew how little good it was to feel superior to Winkler. He had to appeal to the man, to touch his sporting instinct, if he had a trace of it.

"I'd like to say good-by to her," Joe said.

Winkler smiled that faint smile again. "Make it snappy," he said.

Joe took Frieda in his arms. "I love you," he said. She put her arm around his neck to hold him closer. "I love you," she said.

There was no more to say. She turned up her face for their last kiss and clung to him, warm and sweet and trembling. For a long moment neither of them breathed.

Joe heard the mild crack of a .22 rifle and, almost in the same instant, the smack of the little bullet against a stone close at hand. Winkler was looking toward the sound, his gun poised. Joe turned. J.M. Pyne was down yonder in the meadow, 200 yards away, on the other side of a stone wall. Joe saw him duck behind the wall. But he couldn't understand how the old man could have shot so wildly. The bullet must have struck a stone a yard away from Winkler's feet.

Winkler fired a burst of shots, faster than Joe could count them. He heard the bullets smacking against the stone wall behind which the old man had hidden. Some of them sent little spurts of dirt beyond the wall.

Winkler stopped firing, the gun still at his shoulder.

The old man's hat appeared in a little open space where there was no brush above the wall. Winkler fired instantly - a stream of shots. The hat disappeared.

"Oh, no - " Frieda cried, "he got him!"

Winkler stood, his gun at his shoulder, the barrel pointed at the place where Pyne's hat had been, but dropped a little, so he could look above the sights.

From the middle of a bush two yards along the stone wall from where the hat had been came the crack of the .22 again, and close at hand the thud a bullet makes when it hits flesh. Joe jumped for Winkler as his gun sagged in his hands. He grabbed the small of the stock with his left hand and drove at Winkler's jaw with his right and gave it everything he had. The man went down and Joe had the submachine gun.

The dog ran up to his master and got down beside him, whining and licking his face.

"Is the old man coming, Frieda?" Joe asked, not daring to take his eyes off Winker.

"He's coming," she said. "I didn't know he could walk so fast.

290

And he's got the rifle he made for me."

Joe saw that Winkler wasn't out. His right hand was moving ever so slowly toward his hip. Joe stepped hard on the hand and called to Frieda. When she had taken Winkler's pistol from its holster, the man grasped his left elbow with his right hand, and Joe knew that was where the bullet had struck - in the elbow joint, which, when he was holding his gun ready to shoot, must have been in front of his heart. Hitting heavy bone, the little bullet hadn't had the power to go on through.

J.M. Pyne was winded when he got there. He paused and got his breath. "I didn't kill him, did I?"

"No," Joe said. "His elbow stopped the bullet."

The old man nodded and walked over beyond Winkler and picked up a stone about four inches in diameter. It had a gray splash of lead on it. He tossed the stone away.

"I hoped I'd get the elbow instead of killing him," he said. "Dead men don't talk. We want this man to talk."

"Joe," Frieda said, "where's Henry? Do you suppose he's some-where behind a boulder?

"We'll have to watch," Joe said. "But I don't think he came far. I hit him pretty hard."

"Was it you who fired that shot?" - the old man pointed toward the camp - "down yonder 10 or 15 minutes ago?"

"Yes," Joe said.

"I hoped it was," J.M. Pyne said, "but I didn't remember that the woodchuck rifle had such a crack as all that."

"It wasn't the woodchuck rifle," Joe said. "It was one of your blue pills in your semi-automatic rifle."

"What? You got the gun?"

"There it is in the grass."

The old man took charge then, as a matter of course. "I guess you're elected to go over to the Gaylords and get help, Joe," he said. "Frieda and I'll stay here. She can take her rifle, and I'll take that submachine gun, and you can have the pistol Frieda's got."

The old man handed Frieda her rifle.

"It's sighted dead on for the distance I shot," he said. "I guessed it at 200 yards and I paced it coming up, and it was 197."

"You'll watch for Henry," Joe said. "I don't think he stayed on his feet long after he made that first dash to warn Winkler. But you can't take a chance."

"We'll watch," J.M. Pyne said. "You take the semi-automatic rifle with you, too."

Joe saw a party on the Gaylord terrace as he crossed the foot-bridge, and remembered he had promised Connie Gaylord to bring the old man and Frieda to breakfast.

At the time he'd had no idea where Frieda was or if he'd ever see her again. But he'd said he'd bring her if he could.

They all stood up and came toward him as he got nearer - Reuben and Connie and George Bostwick.

"Here," Joe said to Bostwick, "is the rifle you wanted a look at. It's just been test fired with a proof cartridge."

It took five minutes for them to telephone the police and tell them where to look for Henry and Louis, and where to find Winkler, and to hunt up a box of .30-06 ammunition. Then they all started out across the bridge. Joe walked ahead with the Pyne semi-automatic rifle, knowing that the magazine was full and there was an eleventh shot in the barrel. He didn't expect to use it, but it was a nice feeling to have so many cartridges in the gun.

Joe sat beside Frieda at breakfast on the terrace, an hour later. Joe had her hand in his, and across the table the old man beamed on them. You could see that he was proud of himself, and Joe felt he had a right to be. He wanted to say something, and he couldn't think of any way of expressing his affection for J.M. Pyne except by kidding him a little.

"You're the only man in the wide world who would go on a man hunt with a .22 target rifle," Joe said. "I think you had your nerve!"

"I couldn't help myself," J.M. Pyne said. "There wasn't any other rifle in the shop I could use. I'd have had to stop and cast bullets for my 200-yard target gun, and I didn't have time."

"I can understand that," Joe said dryly. "But I can't understand how you missed Winkler by 5 or 6 feet with that first shot of yours."

"Missed?!" the old man said. "That shot was dead on. Didn't you see the bullet splash on that stone I picked up? I hit it practically plumb center."

"What did you shoot at the stone for?" Joe demanded.

"I didn't know if I'd guessed the distance right. I just had to have a sighting shot to be sure."

Joe turned to Frieda. "What can you do about a man like that?"

Frieda smiled back at him. "Nothing," she said, "but love him, I guess."

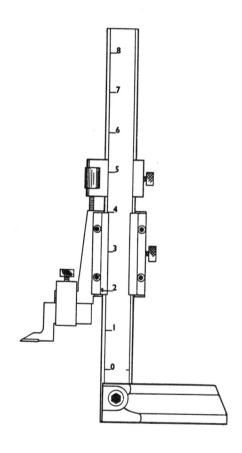

THE GUY WHO HAD EVERYTHING

Jimmy Clark saw that it was no soap. The bevel gears under the apron had taken all they were ever going to. And the last drill he had made wasn't cutting any better than the others. He would have to tell Margie he was licked. And Margie would be sunk. She wouldn't say so, but she would be.

He stopped the machine and looked at the work. He was a garage mechanic. He had done occasional jobs on a lathe and on a mill. But he wasn't a machinist. He had spent the last four or five weeks trying to learn what it takes a good man four or five years to learn. He had learned something from the catalogs and the handbooks that he studied every night. He had learned, for instance, that a machinist called the piece he was machining "the work".

The work he had in the old lathe was a thick round bar of tempered alloy steel five feet long. When it was finished it would be the shaft of a torpedo, with a three-hundred-horsepower engine on one end of it and two opposed propellers on the other, a torpedo that cost fourteen thousand dollars when bought in lots of five hundred - fourteen thousand dollars worth of destruction able, if it hit just right, to do fourteen million dollars worth of damage to an enemy battleship. Only it wouldn't have much chance of hitting just right unless its intricate interior was fitted with watchlike precision.

Jimmy was glad he wasn't responsible for that part. The Bowman Machine Company had only one operation to perform. It had taken a subcontract from Braid & Barnes to drill a hole two inches in diameter through bars of tough stock five feet long. That was all.

George Bowman, who had run an automobile agency until the Government stopped sales of cars, and then used every cent he had to buy a machine shop, so he could give his old employees work and feel he was doing something worth while, hadn't known why so many companies had ducked that contract for deep-hole drilling. He had been sure it would be easy for Jimmy to drill the hundred shafts in the trial order. Then they'd get an order for five hundred more, or a thousand.

"After all," George had said, "you're the best mechanic we ever had. Here's where Bowman Machine turns the corner."

With that he had hopped into his car and gone off to hunt more money, and to hire more automobile salesmen that he'd expect Jimmy to turn into deep-hole drillers overnight.

Jimmy walked slowly down the aisle between the machines, stopping now and again to see how the work was going. Five of the men had worked in a machine shop before, or said they had; three of them were automobile salesmen from George Bowman's agency, one was a taxi driver; one was an ice man. The best of the lot was a plumber named Joe Gotch. Jimmy was foreman, learning at night out of a catalog what he told a man the next morning. The funny part of it was that it worked. The simple jobs were going all right.

Jimmy felt like a tired old man. He wasn't thirty and he was tough - the wiry kind. He had worked more than ninety hours in the last week, and studied at night instead of sleeping. But he had to smile when he opened the office door.

Margie Bowman was standing at her high bookkeeper's desk. She was wearing an old brown sweater and a baggy old brown skirt, and she had a big smudge of machine shop dirt beside her turned up nose. She was lovely.

He had known Margie six months now. They were friends. He knew they'd never be anything else -- Margie rated something better than a guy who could never get all the black oily dirt out from under his fingernails.

"I'm stuck," he said.

"When you admit you're stuck, Jimmy, that's sum'pin."

"I should have admitted it sooner. So far, I haven't got a hole half an inch deep. I should have told George before he left that I just didn't know enough."

"It wouldn't have done any good," Margie said. "You know how George is."

They both knew that George was a nice guy, but inclined to believe in miracles. George was out combing the state for more men to drill more torpedo shafts when they hadn't been able to drill one.

"I think I'd better call up T.W. Walker at Braid & Barnes, long distance, and ask him to send us a man who understands deep-hole drilling."

"What if he says we can just load those pieces on a truck and send them back to Hartford?" Margie asked.

"They shopped that job around a lot before we took it. They don't really want to take it away from us."

Margie thought a minute, and then she looked at him and grinned. She had an impish grin. Jimmy loved it.

"I'll call up," she said. "If he asks me embarrassing questions, I can say I don't know. You can't."

She sat down at George Bowman's desk and picked up the telephone. Jimmy spread a newspaper over the seat of an old wooden tavern chair, so he wouldn't get oil from his clothes on it.

He couldn't hear what T.W. Walker was saying at his end, but he could appreciate the job Margie did on him, hearing what she said, and watching her face change expression from second to second.

"We get the man," she said, as she hung up. "He'll be here late this afternoon. We pay him two dollars an hour - half time for travelling - time and a half for overtime, and five cents a mile. How far is Colesville from Hartford?"

"Maybe two hundred and fifty miles. Have you got enough money to pay him?"

"It depends on how long he stays."

"You don't have to pay me this week," Jimmy said, "I've got some money."

Margie looked at him. He'd been taking half his pay in stock in the company.

"You can't keep on this way," she said. "It isn't fair. What do you think stock in Bowman Machine will be worth if we lose this deep hole drilling job?"

Jimmy smiled at her. "We haven't lost it yet."

"One thing I forgot to tell you - this man Walker is sending has the authority to take this job away from us. If he doesn't like the looks of this place, he will."

"We'll have to get him so interested in the drills he'll forget to ask about the drill rig," Jimmy said.

He went out to the shop and took the work out of the drill rig and laid it to one side; then he got the drill and the head of the drill tube out and put them on the bench with all the other drills he'd made. He couldn't figure out why his drills wouldn't cut. He'd used King Double A alloy steel. He had never seen a deep-hole drill. But he had copied a deep-hole drill he'd found pictures of in a catalogue.

Jimmy heard a car in the yard outside at five o'clock that afternoon and looked out of the window. It was the kind of 1940 convertible coupe that Jimmy had wanted ever since he'd seen the first one. His own 1934 roadster had a pick-up body where the rumble seat had been; its upholstery was shot and you could see that it had been painted three different colors during its long past. If it ran like a sewing machine, it was only because he had fitted new main bearings, and new pistons, and new timing gears, and ground the valves.

The handsome blond young man who got out of the coupe was wearing the kind of clothes that Jimmy would have worn if he'd had the money. Well, maybe the pearl-gray felt hat with the bright little feather in the band was too flashy. But the double-breasted dark blue suit with the pin stripe was the nuts.

While Jimmy stared, the fellow opened up the rear deck of his car and dragged out a real machinist's toolbox - the kind that opens up to show a double bank of shallow drawers lined with purple felt. Jimmy recognized the make and model. It was No. 8 in the catalogue - the "Toolmaker's Pride" - price $21.60.

Jimmy grabbed up a drill and put it in the vise of a smaller miller with a high-speed head on it. The head had a flat abrasive wheel he'd been using to sharpen the drills with. He had no tool for getting the drill at the right angle in the vise except a cheap protractor. And it was hard to tighten the vise without letting the drill shift position. He hadn't got the drill quite right when he saw Margie coming down the aisle with the blond young man.

297

He wished he looked like this guy - like a man a few years out of college with a job that paid better than a hundred a week.

He could see that Margie was impressed. She had got that smudge off her cheek and used her lipstick and fixed her hair. And she wasn't her usually confident self. She was sort of fluttery.

"Jimmy," she said, "I want you to meet Mr. Morgan."

Jimmy wiped his hand on a piece of waste so he could shake hands.

"Forget the mister," Morgan said. "I'm Bill."

"Okay, Bill," Jimmy said, thinking the guy said it in a nice way.

"What's your trouble?" Bill asked.

"Drills," Jimmy said. "It seems I don't know how to make a deep-hole drill."

"There aren't many mechanics who do," Bill Morgan said. He hoisted his toolbox up on the bench. "Let's see your drills."

Margie smiled at Bill Morgan. "This is going to be deep stuff, so I won't stay. But if there is anything I can do, you'll find me in the office."

Bill Morgan stared after her as she walked down the shop. Jimmy could guess what was on Bill's mind. Nobody could meet Margie without thinking, "Nice girl!"

Bill turned back to the bench when Margie was out of sight. He didn't say anything. He opened one of the drawers in his toolbox and took out a universal bevel protractor with a vernier. Jimmy had never seen one before, but he recognized it instantly. It was No. 439 in the Starrett catalogue, price $24.75. You could measure to 5 minutes of a degree with the vernier.

Jimmy watched while Bill Morgan went to work with the beautiful shining tool, measuring the angles of the drill lips.

"Show me the tool you made these drills on."

Jimmy showed him a bench lathe fitted with a tool-post grinder. Bill checked over the lathe and the grinder.

"This the best you've got?" he asked.

Jimmy nodded.

298

Bill Morgan asked questions for ten minutes and Jimmy learned that his drills were wrong in several different ways. When Bill started to ask him about the drill rig, Jimmy showed him the way he had been sharpening the drills. Bill looked at the high-speed head and the drill in the vise of the miller, and shook his head.

"You've got to use a soft cup wheel," he said. "And you'll never get both lips the same without a fixture."

Jimmy couldn't help liking the man. He didn't rub it in. He just told you the facts. And no one listening to him could doubt he knew his stuff.

"The thing that's bothered me most," Jimmy said, "is that my drills won't cut."

Bill Morgan took a file out of his toolbox and tested one of the drills. Then he tried all the others.

"How did you harden these?"

"Sent them to a hardening shop in Newark."

"The guy let you down. He's got a kind of skin on these, but they aren't hard. Of course they won't cut."

Jim felt pretty foolish. He should have known enough to test the drills. He'd taken it for granted the hardener knew his business.

"It isn't your fault, Jim," Bill Morgan said. "You never did any deep-hole drilling."

"No," Jimmy said. "But I'd like to learn."

"Let's go talk to the boss," Bill Morgan said.

They walked down the aisle to the office. Margie was sitting at George Bowman's desk. Jimmy saw that she'd been doodling on a pad, and he knew that she'd been worrying while she waited for Bill Morgan's decision.

"Margie," Jimmy said, "this guy's a real all-round machinist. I guess he's what they call a toolmaker. If I knew what he knows, I'd never have had to yell for help."

"Oh," Margie said, "how wonderful!"

Jimmy thought the smile she gave Bill Morgan should have made his heart go faster.

"So," she added, "you're going to make new drills for us?"

299

"I'd like to," Bill Morgan said. "I'd like to stick around where you are, Margie. But I can't make proper drills on that bench lathe and tool-post grinder you've got out there."

The thing that registered on Jimmy was the way he said it: "I'd like to stick around where you are, Margie." He didn't hesitate. He just said it. And the way he said it -- well, it was all right. It must be all right, because he could see the color in Margie's cheeks and the brightness in her eyes.

Jimmy would have given anything to be able to say a thing like that. This man just tossed it off. He had a way with women.

"It means so much to us," Margie said. "We've just got to get this job going."

"I'd take most any excuse to stay here," Bill said. He didn't actually say that he wanted to stay because of Margie, but it was plain that was what he meant.

"But," he added, "T.W. Walker is no dope. He told me I was probably wasting my time coming down here. If I stay I've got to get results."

"Of course you have," Margie said. "Maybe we can dig up what you need."

"I need a lathe with a tool-post grinder that's in some kind of decent shape."

Margie looked at Jimmy. "Couldn't we find something second-hand?"

Jimmy knew she didn't have the money to pay for a secondhand lathe with a tool-post grinder, even if they could find one in a hurry. He remembered his friend Doc, a dentist who had a shop in his basement as a hobby. The lathe was one he'd got from a mailorder house. But it was new.

"What about that outfit Doc Ennis has?"

"Do you think he'd lend it to us?" Margie asked.

"He'd lend you anything you asked him for, Margie."

Margie turned to Bill. Jimmy could see that she was herself again.

"Let's go down there and look at it," she said.

Jimmy watched them go. This guy had got farther with Margie

in an hour or two than he had got in six months. It was a gift. Jimmy heard the starter of that beautiful convertible coupe outside - Bill Morgan had something more than words to offer.

Jimmy had eaten his supper at the dog wagon and gone home to the room he rented from the grocer and his wife when Margie called him up.

"The Doc was fine," she said. "He's lending us his stuff."

"Did Bill think it would do?"

"He made some cracks after we'd left the Doc's. He says the Doc's lathe is more of a kid's toy than a toolmaker's lathe. But I kidded him along. He said he guessed he could make it do. What do you think? About Bill, I mean."

"That guy has everything," Jimmy said. "Why?"

"Oh, nothing. He tried to make a date with me to go dancing in Clintonville."

"If that guy said anything out of line I'll knock his block off," Jimmy said.

Margie laughed. "Don't be silly. He was a perfect gentleman, of course. I just thought maybe he was a fast worker."

Jimmy went to bed, but not to read and not to sleep.

He asked Joe Gotch to help him with Doc Ennis' lathe the next morning. They had it all set up on the bench when Bill Morgan came in at half past eight. He said he'd had to drive all the way to Clintonville to find a decent meal and a decent place to sleep.

He took off his pin-striped, double-breasted suit and put on his overalls and went to work.

Jimmy watched him and learned things. Bill Morgan made half a dozen new drills by quitting time, and he showed Jimmy that they didn't vary much more than half a thousandth in diameter.

When they'd washed up, Bill opened the office door.

"Listen, sweetheart," he said to Margie, "I've got to drive to Newark tomorrow and stand over the hardener and see he does them right. How'd you like to go along?"

"I'd love to," Margie said. "But I can't. I've got to stay here."

Bill got back with the drills about four o'clock the next afternoon. He showed Jimmy a soft cup-shaped abrasive wheel he'd bought.

"That's the kind you need," he said. "The one you've got there is too hard. It just burns the drill. Tomorrow I'll make a fixture to hold the drills while they're being sharpened."

Jimmy shook his head over the simplicity of the fixture Bill made the next day. He laid out the angles with that vernier protractor of his on a piece of flat cold-rolled steel, and put three dowel pins in it. When you laid the flat drill against the pins only one angle could be exposed to the sharpening wheel. And having sharpened one lip, you turned the drill over in the fixture, and the angle of the other lip had to be the same.

Bill Morgan sharpened a drill in it while Jimmy watched.

"See the stream of sparks," Bill said. "That means she's cutting."

"How about letting me try it?" Jimmy asked.

"Sure," Bill said. He was so nice about it that Jimmy couldn't hate him. Jimmy sharpened all the rest of the drills while Bill kept an eye on him and corrected his mistakes. They worked until after six, when everybody else in the shop had gone home.

Jimmy called up that night to tell Margie how well everything was going. Her sister-in-law answered the telephone. She said Margie had gone to Clintonville with Bill Morgan.

"It's taken longer than I thought to get this job going," Bill Morgan said the next morning. "Walker told me he expected to hear from me within three days. This is my fourth day and I haven't called him, so he'll be calling me. If I can't tell him I'm drilling, he'll be sore."

He got the work into the headstock of the lathe with Jimmy's help. He put the drill in the head of the drill tube and made it fast. He checked everything carefully. Then he started the machine and moved the drill gently up against the revolving work.

Jimmy watched anxiously. Bill dipped his cupped hand in the trough that caught the coolant as it came away from the drill. He let the liquid run through his fingers until only the chips remained.

"There," he said. "That's the way chips look when a drill is right."

But even as he spoke the bevel gears under the apron went. Jimmy stopped the machine.

"Why didn't you tell me this rig had no feed?" Bill yelled.

Jimmy couldn't tell him the answer to that one. He'd been afraid for three days that Bill would discover it.

"What kind of a feed should it have?" Jimmy asked.

"Hydraulic."

"What's that?"

Bill shook his head impatiently, as if he were annoyed at Jimmy's ignorance. "You have a tank and an air compressor. You fill the tank almost full of oil. Let's say your compressor keeps a pressure of 20 pounds to the square inch on the surface of the oil and that surface is 100 square inches. That's 2000 pounds total. You take off that pressure through a pipe that's one square inch. Forgetting the friction losses, you've got one ton on that square inch to push a tool with."

"We'll have to build one," Jimmy said.

Bill just looked at him.

"I know where we can get a second hand compressor. It's easy enough to get a tank and fittings and valves and stuff."

"The tough part is the piston and cylinder. Where are you going to get that?"

"Couldn't we make it?"

"No," Bill said. "And even if we could, do you think T.W. Walker is going to let me stay here and fool around with this kind of a machine?"

He started for the office and Jimmy followed him. They had to hang on to Bill Morgan. If Bill went, the deep-hole-drilling job went with him.

"I'm sorry, Margie," Bill Morgan said, "but we're through."

"Through!"

"Yes, through, finished, all washed up."

"I thought you'd made new drills that were right."

"I did." He went on to explain to Margie that the lathe wasn't a deep-hole-drilling machine, and never would be unless it was fitted with a hydraulic feed. In order to force a 2-inch drill through five feet of tough steel you had to have force, either a heavy screw feed or a hydraulic feed. There was no way to fit the lathe with a heavy screw feed. He should have noticed it the first day. He'd never be able to explain to T.W. Walker why he hadn't.

"I get it," Margie said. "Let's go find a secondhand hydraulic feed."

Jimmy knew she didn't have the money to buy one, even if she found it.

"If you did find it," Bill said, "it would be part of some big machine. They wouldn't sell it separately."

Margie looked out of the window. It was one of those summer days that come sometimes in spring. Then she looked up at Bill. "It would be fun to go looking - on a day like this."

"But T.W. Walker - " Bill began.

"I'll answer the phone, when he calls," Jimmy said. "I'll fix it."

Margie jumped up. "I'll have to go home and change my clothes. But it won't take more than fifteen minutes."

Jimmy stood at Margie's desk after they'd gone, making rough sketches and trying to think where he had ever seen a hydraulic cylinder, instead of thinking about Margie riding beside Bill Morgan. The top would be down and the wind would be blowing Margie's hair.

The telephone startled him. It was plain from T.W. Walker's tone that he was annoyed. He wanted Bill Morgan, and he wanted him quick.

"He isn't here right now," Jimmy said. "He had to go to Newark to get some stuff."

"Oh, he did, did he? When he comes back, you tell him I'm coming through Colesville on my way to Wilkes-Barre tomorrow, and I'm going to stop long enough to inspect this job myself."

Jimmy walked out into the shop when Mr. Walker had hung up. It was half past nine. He had twenty-four hours - maybe a little more - to build a feed for that drilling job. But he remembered now where he'd seen a hydraulic cylinder and piston. He went

304

over to the machine where Joe Gotch was working.

"You used to be a plumber," he said. "I need you."

They got into Jimmy's old roadster with the pick-up body and went first to the savings bank. Jimmy took out all the money he had - a hundred and fourteen dollars.

The two of them were kneeling in a pool of oil on the machine-shop floor at two o'clock the next morning, making up pipe with Stillson wrenches, when Margie came in.

She was wearing her new suit and her new hat - a brown felt hat with a wide brim that turned down on one side and up on the other. Jimmy thought she looked like Park Avenue. And he knew something had happened. He could only guess that Bill Morgan had been making time.

"I saw a light, so I came up here," she said. "What on earth are you doing?"

"We don't know yet," Jimmy said. "Where's Bill?"

"He's gone on to Clintonville. I just left him about five minutes ago. Aren't you two going to quit now and get some sleep?"

"No," Jimmy said.

He could guess that Bill Morgan had taken her some place where they could dance. You couldn't hunt for secondhand machinery after six o'clock in the evening.

"I guess I'm only in the way," Margie said. "I'll go home."

T.W. Walker arrived early the next afternoon. He came down the aisle with Margie - a big man who looked mean.

"Well, Morgan," he said to Bill, "what have you got to say? Why didn't you report to me?"

"It took longer than I thought it would, Mr. Walker," Bill said. "This rig didn't have any feed. We had to build the one you see. But the job's going fine now. The first piece took five hours to drill. I don't think this one is going to take quite that long."

Mr. Walker stood watching the machine for five minutes without saying anything. Then he walked around it, studying it.

"Morgan," he said, "come on back to the office." He looked at

Jimmy. "You too."

Jimmy put Joe Gotch on the machine and told him what to watch for, and went on to the office.

Mr. Walker sat down. The rest of them stood up.

"Morgan," he said to Bill, "you're a good deal more ingenious than I ever thought you were. Where did you get that hydraulic cylinder you're using out there?"

"Off an old coal truck," Bill said. "It's the cylinder they used to dump it with."

Jimmy stared at Bill, but Bill avoided his eyes.

"That was pretty smart. I'll remember that." He jerked his thumb at Jimmy. "Can this helper of yours keep the job going without you?"

"Sure he can," Bill said. "I've shown him how to make the drills and how to sharpen them. He sharpened the drill that's in there now."

Mr. Walker took a notebook out of his pocket and found the place and turned to Margie.

"We gave you an order for a hundred pieces?"

"Yes," Margie said.

"You had no business to take the job when you didn't have a deep-hole-drilling machine. But that scheme Morgan has worked out for you seems all right. I'm going to let you go on and fill the order if you can."

"Mr. Walker," Jimmy said, "I hope you noticed that we have several lathes like the one we're using. If you were to give us an order for five hundred pieces we could afford to rig a couple of those lathes with hydraulic feeds like the one we have."

Mr. Walker got up to go. "We'll talk five hundred when you've got out one hundred." He found his hat. "Morgan," he said to Bill, "how soon can you start for Hartford?"

"As soon as I wash up and change my clothes."

"Get going."

Jimmy could see that Bill was glad to get out of that room, away from his eyes and from Margie's. He wasn't happy about taking the credit for that hydraulic feed. Mr. Walker said good-by and went out to his car. Margie made a little gesture toward the door through which Bill had gone.

"That's the guy you said had everything - that louse."

"At least he told Mr. Walker I knew how to get the job going."

"You bet he did. If he hadn't, I'd have told Walker who got that hydraulic cylinder off a coal truck and who built that rig out there."

"I thought you liked him," Jimmy said.

Margie looked at him. Her eyes were very blue, and he felt he could see deep into them.

"Maybe I did. Maybe I wanted a good time too. He's the only man I've met around here that ever offered to take me out. But now I know he was a phony."

Margie was wearing her old brown sweater and her baggy old brown skirt. They made her seem nearer to him than she had seemed the night before when she had come into the shop all dressed up. Jimmy took a step toward her. She was very near.

"Margie," he said. "Margie, would you mind going places with me in that old roadster of mine?"

She looked as if she were going to cry. He had to take her in his arms. And when he did she turned her face up and he saw that she was smiling at him. He didn't know the right thing to say, but he knew the right thing to do.

HOW'S THAT?

Jim Ross was young enough to need to make a hero of some-body. He had still to learn that there are no heroes, but only men who, for the moment, seem to be. Jim liked the Captain and believed in him. He continued to believe in him in spite of the gibes of old How's That?

That is what they used to call Colonel Burke - "How's That?" The Colonel, retired now, was a loud, ruddy man, not unkind, but with the long habit of having his own way. They called him "How's That?" because he had a trick of finishing nearly every comment he made with the question, "How's that?" He said it in more than one way, but most often with a hard rasp in his voice, as if the phrase were a challenge. There was always a rasp in his voice when he said it to the Captain.

Jim Ross had a bad spill that winter, playing his first season with the hockey team. He broke his left shoulder, and the upper arm as well, not long before the second-term exams. He spent two months in hospital, and when he got out, with his shoulder in bandages and his arm in a sling, it was too late to go back for the last term. So he lived with his mother on East 71st Street and tried to do some of the reading he thought he ought to do, and was restless. All his friends were away at school.

Colonel Burke lived down the street. He had been a friend of Jim's father. He came in to ask how Jim was getting on and stayed to talk about Jim's father, who had died when Jim was a small boy. His father had been a famous pistol shot and a mem-ber of the American teams that had won international matches from the French before the war. Jim knew the drawerful of medals and the cupboardful of cups his father had won.

Now, as the Colonel talked, Jim Ross got a glimpse of an Ameri-can tradition that his father had helped to carry on. The pistol had, centuries ago, made commerce possible in a Europe infested with bandits. But it had remained for Americans to discover that a man who knew how could hit things at a distance with a revolver.

The Colonel told a story of how Jim's father had astonished Gaston Renette's in Paris where the French duelists went to practice, by the way he could shoot a .44 American revolver. One of them had asked him if he could put a bullet through the opening in a powder can, and Jim's father had said he didn't know, but it was a sporting proposition. They had taken the cap off a pound powder can and laid it down at twenty yards with the hole toward the firing point. The men who had been practicing for duels, shooting at one another with wax bullets, had taken off their masks to watch. Jim's father had put a .44 bullet through the hole without touching the edge of it. The Frenchman who had asked him to do it congratulated him effusively and disappeared. He returned an hour later with eighteen or twenty French duelists. He had gathered them from all Paris to see the American master do it again. Jim's father had protested that he had been lucky the first time. But he was the only American present. He could not refuse to try. And again he had put a bullet through the hole without touching the edges.

"Your father," Colonel Burke said, "was that kind of a man."

Jim smiled, picturing the scene and taking pride in his father. "I've got your father's guns," Colonel Burke said. "They're yours as soon as you learn to use them and get a police permit to possess them. How's that?"

"I'd like to have them," Jim Ross said.

Colonel Burke took Jim Ross down to the Murray Hill Club the following Tuesday evening. The Colonel had a leather kit bag that looked heavy. He talked about the club in the taxi. The Murray Hill was, he said, in its own special way, one of the most exclusive clubs in New York. Jim's father had been a member. Not that it mattered to the Murray Hill who your father was. If you weren't seriously interested in pistol shooting, it was hard to get in. And you mustn't annoy the other members by handling guns in an ignorant manner, or you would get thrown out.

Dr. Moorhead Tolliver, who was one of the two surgeons called in when a king of finance was dying the other day, and Doctor Tolliver's chauffeur, Joe Biddle, were both members. But the king of finance was not a member, and no doubt never wanted to be and could not have been for long, if he had wanted to be. He had died by shooting himself accidentally with a revolver while cleaning it. The Murray Hill would never have stood for a man who handled a revolver in so extraordinary a fashion.

"The Murray Hill has no clubhouse," Colonel Burke continued when they got out of the cab. "Never has had. We've shot in a lot of places in the last forty years. Lately Hicks & Hewitt, the sporting goods people, have opened a range. We've rented it for our exclusive use on Tuesday nights. How's that?"

The Colonel led the way downstairs to a large basement room. At one side Jim saw a row of firing booths. In a back corner he saw, sitting behind a table, a man in a shabby blue serge suit. Jim noticed him particularly because, though a man in his 30's, he wore a beard that almost covered his face. He heard two of the club members address him as "Captain".

The Colonel introduced Jim to his friends.

"Bill," he'd say, or "Joe," or "George," or "Mike," as the case was, "this is young Jim Ross. He's our Jim Ross's boy. How's that?"

They asked Jim if he could shoot the way his father shot, and he assured them he couldn't. It was embarrassing. He wanted a chance to stand back and look on, and then to talk to somebody who would explain the place to him. Why, for instance, did everyone speak in a hushed tone amid the crack of pistols? He was glad when the Colonel picked up the kit bag and took him over to the man in the corner. Jim saw, when the man stood up, that he was tall and lean and powerful. His beard gave him a slightly arty look. But that was by the way. He caught a glimpse also of a revolver, heavy and thick, in a holster, a little to the left, at the waistline, as the man caught the flap of his double-breasted jacket and buttoned it. The Colonel saw it also.

"So, you're still carrying that thing," Colonel Burke said. "I told you it was nonsense to carry a gun like that in New York City. It's silly."

"I'm sorry you don't like my gun, sir," the man said.

Jim felt that the Colonel was picking on the man. He liked the man's quiet, polite but wholly unyielding reply. They called him "Captain", but he was plainly some sort of attendant.

"I don't like it," Colonel Burke said. "You'll be getting into a jam

310

one of these days that will give those silly asses in Albany one more excuse for passing another stupid law that serves no purpose except to assure every crook in the city that nobody but a crook has a gun or knows how to use it. How's that?"

"I hope not, sir," the Captain said.

"Here, Woodhull," the Colonel said. He put the kit bag on the table. "Look after Mr. Ross."

Jim noticed that the Colonel did not address the man as "Captain". The Colonel was being intentionally rude, which was not like him. The Colonel turned to Jim.

"There are your father's target guns," he said. "Have a look at them. If you want to shoot, Woodhull will give you ammunition. I haven't seen Joe Milligan for a long time. I want to talk old times with him."

Jim opened the bag and took out several guns wrapped in green felt covers and tied with black tape. One was a slender .22 target pistol, and one was a heavy .44, and a third was a .38 with the longest barrel Jim had ever seen.

The Captain pointed to it. "That's a Pyne," he said. He picked up the revolver and turned the barrel to the light and showed Jim the name. Jim read, "J.M. Pyne" in small Roman capitals cut in the steel.

"He didn't make the whole gun," the Captain explained, "just the barrel."

"But why so long?" Jim asked.

"The rules allow ten inches between front and rear sights. Pyne liked to take the limit."

"It's at the opposite extreme from the gun you carry," Jim said. He was hoping that the Captain would let him see the gun to which the Colonel had objected. But the Captain did not take the hint.

"My gun was designed for a different purpose," the Captain said. "But if you don't mind a suggestion, I'd try the .22 pistol. It doesn't make as much noise, and the recoil is less."

"I'm not afraid of noise," Jim said.

311

"No," the Captain said, "of course. But some of the men are shooting a match. They won't like the sound of a .44 while they're trying to make a score."

"So that's why everybody is so quiet," Jim said.

The Captain picked up the target pistol and aimed it at the wall. "You're holding on the black - or trying to - and pressing the trigger hard enough so just another fraction of an ounce will fire the gun when everything is just right. If you overhear what somebody behind you says, the gun is likely to go off. You can't hear what people are saying, you can't even let yourself think about anything else, and shoot."

"It's a game, then, like billiards or golf. There's nothing practical about it."

"It's a game," the Captain said. "At its best it's a fine art. And maybe it has its practical side."

He got a box of ammunition and some targets and took Jim over to an empty firing booth. He laid the pistol on the shelf, elbow high, in the booth and showed Jim how to hang a target and how to run it out to twenty yards by means of an electric carrier. The target was about ten by twelve inches, with a round black bull in the middle, two and a half or three inches in diameter. Inside the bull were the eight, nine and ten rings. The ten ring was about the size of a quarter.

The Captain showed Jim how to hold the pistol, his hand as high as possible on the grip, his thumb extended along the left side of the action toward the target, and warned him that the important thing was to pull the trigger with a slowly increasing pressure.

Jim loaded the pistol. He could use his left hand a little in spite of its being in a sling - enough to hold the pistol while he put a cartridge in the breech with his right hand. He raised the pistol and aimed it at the target. The front sight came on the target and swung clear across it and back and up and down in irregular zig-zags, impossible to anticipate. The gun went off on one of the wild swings. He missed the target.

He tried again and again. He found he could hit the paper seven or eight times in ten. He took the pistol back to the Captain when he had fired fifty shots. He was sweating with the effort he had made. He was at once exasperated and fascinated by the difficulty of shooting a pistol. He told the Captain how it was.

312

The Captain suggested that he come in and get some coaching. The range was open to the public except when it was reserved by the Murray Hill group.

"You're here every day?" Jim asked.

"From ten to six," the Captain said. "If you come early, there won't be any other men here."

Jim told the Colonel on the way home that he was going to take a lesson in pistol shooting. He said the Captain seemed to know about pistol shooting.

"Captain!" Colonel Burke said, "Captain! Why do you call him Captain?"

"I heard some of the members call him Captain," Jim said.

"If he's a Captain, I'm the Rajah of What-do-you-call-it," the Colonel said. "How's that?"

"You don't like him," Jim said.

"He's a fake. What does he know about shooting? Whoever heard of him? Woodhull! Did you ever hear of anybody named Woodhull doing any shooting? I'm tired of seeing that belly gun of his. Does he think he's Wild Bill Hickock? I say it's a kid's trick to carry a gun like that. He's pretending he's a killer. That man wouldn't kill a fly. How's that?"

The Colonel went on at length, savagely. Jim said nothing. He thought the Colonel was prejudiced. He thought the Colonel was merely sounding off. But he couldn't argue with the Colonel. He was a boy of seventeen. The Colonel would think him impudent.

Jim went down to the range the next morning. He got there at three minutes after ten and found the Captain alone. The Captain coached him, with great patience, for an hour. Jim would have liked to stay on and talk. He would have liked to ask the Captain why he carried a belly gun. He felt that the Captain was all right. But it did seem silly for a man to carry a gun like that in New York City.

A bank guard came in, much perturbed. The bank was getting tough. The bank was insisting that its guards learn how to shoot.

The guard said he had to make a better score or he would lose his job. The Captain went patiently to work to teach the guard how to shoot. Jim went home. He wondered, thinking about the Captain, why was he working at such a job. It couldn't be a great job. The Captain must have come down in the world. His blue serge suit was shiny with wear.

Jim went down to the range every morning after that. The Colonel had to go to Washington, but he urged Jim not to miss the weekly meeting of the Murray Hill. Jim went down Tuesday night. He was gratified to find that under the Captain's coaching, he could keep all his shots on the target. He had made a marked improvement in a week. Afterward he accepted an invitation to go down the street with eight or ten of the members who were going to get a beer and a sandwich. He heard Mike Falls ask the Captain to go along. But the Captain said he had to go home.

They all walked down the street to a saloon and restaurant in Third Avenue. There was a bar along one side of the room and a series of benches on the opposite wall. The waiter put three tables together to make one long table. Most of the Murray Hill men had bags or briefcases in which they carried one or two or three target guns to the range. They piled the bags in the corner of a bench and somebody sat next to them, so there was no danger that any of the saloon's other patrons would pick up a bag and walk off with it. Jim Ross sat by and listened.

They talked about guns and shooting for a couple of hours. It was half past two when Jim got home. But he went down to the range early the next morning, as usual.

"You asked me if there was anything practical about slow-fire target shooting with a pistol," the Captain said. "I've been thinking about that. Mostly you shoot a pistol for the same reason that you play golf - because you get a kick out of trying to do it better, and succeeding. If you aren't in competition with other men, you're at least in competition with yourself."

"I understand that," Jim said. "It's got me. But most people think of shooting a revolver as a way of killing somebody before he kills you."

"That takes speed," the Captain said.

"Exactly," Jim said. "You don't do that by taking half a minute to aim and fire one shot."

"You have to learn to do it slowly first," the Captain said. "You have to learn to hit. It's no good being fast, if you don't hit."

He took the gun he carried out of his holster. He took the cartridges out of the cylinder and handed it to Jim. It was an ugly gun. It was so plainly made for "business".

The Captain pointed out the way in which his gun had been modified. The whole front of the guard had been cut away, so your finger would have no interference in finding the trigger. The front sight had been rounded, so it would not catch in the holster as you drew the gun. The thumbpiece of the hammer had been cut off for the same reason.

"It's quite different from the guns you see in movies - Western movies," Jim said.

"The purpose is the same," the Captain said. "The technique is different, because here and now the gun has to be worn concealed."

Jim asked him to show him how the quick draw was done. The Captain did not seem to move fast. But Jim heard the snap of the falling hammer before he could see just what the Captain did. The Captain did it again in slow motion. Jim saw that the Captain's hand grasped the butt of the revolver and drew it without moving more than a few inches. He fired as the muzzle came clear of the holster, his hand close to his belt.

"You can't see the sights," Jim said.

"No," the Captain admitted. "And no man can do fine shooting without sights. But if you practice long enough, you can be sure of hitting a man at fifteen or twenty feet."

Jim liked the Captain. But he wished the Captain did not carry a gun like that. He felt it was beneath the Captain's dignity.

"Do you carry that gun all the time?" Jim asked.

"Yes," the Captain said, "I do."

"Why?"

"You're thinking of what the Colonel said."

"Yes," Jim said.

"The Colonel is right. I can't see carrying a gun day in and day

315

out on the remote chance that you will need it."

"But you do it," Jim protested.

The Captain looked at him gravely. "In my case," he said, "the chance is not remote."

"That's different," Jim said. He was greatly relieved. He was still curious. But he knew the Captain was telling the simple truth. He wondered how the Colonel could think the Captain was a faker. It was so plain, when you talked to him, that he was real.

"I'd hate to have to have to shoot a man," Jim said.

"Most of us hate to do it so much that we're slow to do it when we should be quick - unless we've made up our minds to it beforehand."

"You've made up your mind?"

"Yes," the Captain said. "I've made up my mind. But if there's time, I'll try to stop them rather than to kill them."

Jim noticed that he used the plural. It occurred to him that the Captain had men in mind whom he would have to shoot.

"I suppose," Jim said, "it's different in war."

"Yes, it's different. Mostly you don't see the men you are shooting at, and even when you do, it's more impersonal."

Jim got his father's target pistol out of the locker. He couldn't take it home because he had no permit. He was, at 17, too young to be granted a pistol permit. Shooting a .22 target pistol seemed a mild thing to do, compared with carrying a .44 belly gun that you expected to have to use.

"Did you ever do any slow-fire pistol shooting before you learned the quick draw?" Jim asked.

"I shot .22 target pistols for years," the Captain said.

"Did you ever win any matches?" Jim asked.

Jim heard two men coming down the stairs from the street level as he spoke. The Captain picked up the cartridges he had laid on the table and loaded his belly gun and put it in its holster and buttoned the lowest button of his jacket. He didn't hurry, but he was done before the two men opened the door. They were not dangerous, as Jim hoped. They were two employees of an armored car company that specialized in carrying money from one bank to another.

Jim Ross went down to the range as usual the next morning. The Captain was in a firing booth.

"I'll be with you in a minute," the Captain called out.

He fired two shots and brought his target back and looked at it and crumpled it up and dropped it in the wastebasket beside him. When he came out of the booth, Jim saw that he had a particularly handsome pistol. He took it over to the cleaning bench. There was a flat, rectangular case of fine leather on the bench. Jim waited patiently while the Captain cleaned the pistol and oiled the bore. He expected that the Captain would hand him the pistol, so he could get a good look at it. But the Captain put the pistol in the case, which, Jim saw, was fitted for it.

"Aren't you going to let me see it?" Jim asked.

The Captain lifted the lid of the case. But he did not take the pistol out. Jim saw, on the side of the frame, a gold star, inlaid. There was a legend engraved around the star. He read: NATIONAL PISTOL CHAMPIONSHIP.

The Captain dropped the lid of the case before Jim could see the date.

"A friend of mine gave it to me," he said.

"It's a beautiful gun," Jim said, wondering why the Captain did not want him to see all of it.

"Yes," the Captain said. "A bit on the gaudy side, but nicely done."

Jim fired fifty shots that morning. He didn't do so well as he had been doing. He was thinking too much. He wondered if the Captain would talk more freely to a grown man. He told himself he had to remember that he was a boy of seventeen. The Captain was in his thirties. He must be older than that. He had once said that he graduated from West Point before the United States declared war.

Old How's That? came back from Washington that week. The

Colonel came back and called up Jim and asked him to come over. Jim sat in a big leather chair opposite the Colonel and told him what he had been doing.

"You've seen a lot of this Woodhull," the Colonel said.

"Yes," Jim said. "And Colonel, I think he's quite a man."

"You do, do you?" the Colonel said.

"I do." Jim said stoutly. He was surprised at his own tone. It was almost defiant. He had great respect for the Colonel as a man and as an old friend of his father's. He did not wish to seem defiant.

"Why?" the Colonel asked.

"Well," Jim said. "I like the way he looks at things. I don't know why he's running the range for Hicks & Hewitt. It seems like a comedown for a Captain in the Regular Army. But..."

"Captain!" the Colonel roared. "Didn't I tell you he wasn't a Captain?"

"He told me he was a West Point man," Jim said.

"Did he?" The Colonel asked the question so casually that for the moment Jim thought he was accepting the fact.

"Yes," Jim said. "He did. And I think he's quite all right."

"What does he carry that belly gun for?" the Colonel asked.

"Because he expects to have to use it," Jim said.

"I see," the Colonel said. "And suppose he did. What then?"

"He's very good on the quick draw," Jim said.

"Is that so?" the Colonel asked.

"I've seen him do it," Jim said. He says when you've practiced it enough, you can be sure of hitting a man across the room."

"No doubt," the Colonel said. "No doubt you can, if you aren't scared green."

Jim had to tell the Colonel something that would hit him between the eyes.

"He won a national pistol championship once," Jim said.

The Colonel didn't seem impressed.

"Jim," he said. "I'm sorry. You aren't the first boy who's been taken in by a smooth talker like this Woodhull. I know how hard it is to learn that a man you've admired is a fake. But it's something you have to learn. This guy might have fooled me, too, if I hadn't checked up on him."

The Colonel took a thick folder from his desk drawer.

"I have a letter here from the commandant at West Point," the Colonel said. "He writes that he has had the files gone over and he finds no record of the man. He never entered West Point - much less graduated." The Colonel leafed through other letters in the dossier. "You can read them if you like," he continued. "They all say the same thing. Nobody has any record of such an officer."

Jim sat silent. He didn't know the answer to the problem. But there must be an answer.

"Now," the Colonel said, "let's look up the pistol-shooting records." He took down a bound volume. He found the right place. "I didn't know Woodhull was claiming any pistol championships."

"He didn't claim it," Jim said. "I saw it on a pistol he had."

"This is an official list of national pistol championships," the Colonel said. "There isn't any Woodhull in the list of men who have shot high scores in national championships."

"He didn't say he won it," Jim said. "He never mentioned it. I saw it on a pistol he had."

"He let you see it, didn't he?" the Colonel asked.

Jim said nothing. He was almost sunk.

"I'm sorry, Jim," the Colonel said. "But you see how it is. I can't wink at this thing. The man has gone too far. He's masquerading as a Captain when he isn't. He's let on he's won national pistol championships when he hasn't. And he's carrying a .44 belly gun. He's likely to pull some boner and get the Murray Hill in a jam just when we've convinced the powers that be that it isn't such a bad thing that there are men who care enough to learn how to use a gun, and that it wouldn't be unfortunate if more than one policeman in a hundred knew as much about a revolver and what it's for as every man in the Murray Hill knows. How's that?"

Jim stood up. He remembered the way the Captain looked and talked and acted. There must be some mistake.

"You see how it is, Jim," the Colonel said. "I've got to call this guy."

Jim got out of the Colonel's apartment somehow. He went home. But he couldn't go to sleep.

Jim Ross hurried downtown the next morning. It was Tuesday. The Murray Hill was meeting that evening. He had to do something. He got down to the range before it was open. He had to wait ten minutes for the Captain.

"You're early," the Captain said.

"I wanted to talk to you," Jim said.

The Captain unlocked the door and they went downstairs.

"I guess," Jim said - "I guess I've been talking out of turn. I told Colonel Burke you won a national pistol championship."

"I'm sorry you told him that, Jim," the Captain said.

"There's more than that," Jim said. He knew he had to warn the Captain. He would have to tell the Colonel he had warned him. If the Colonel felt he had betrayed a confidence - well, perhaps he had. But he had an obligation to the Captain. He felt that the Captain was a friend. But still he hesitated.

"Maybe," the Captain said - "maybe you'd better not tell me the rest."

"But - " Jim said. "But -."

"You've said enough," the Captain said. "I can guess the rest. I can see that I've been a fool. I should never have let Hicks & Hewitt call me Captain. I should have stopped that in the beginning."

"But -" Jim began again.

"That's all right," the Captain said.

Jim could see how worried he was. But he wasn't so worried that he forgot to be kind.

Jim tried to shoot that morning. But he couldn't hit anything. He was thinking too much. He'd put the pistol up and try to hold it on the bull while he gradually increased the pressure on the trigger, and the thought would go through his mind that maybe there was an answer - maybe the Captain wasn't a fake, and the gun would go off, and sometimes the bullet wouldn't even hit the paper.

He went home. It was hard waiting until it was time to go down to the Murray Hill. He left the house an hour early, so he would not have to ride down in the Colonel's taxicab. But at the range he only waited for the Colonel to come in. He had to tell the Colonel. He hated to, but he had to. It wasn't so bad when the Colonel came in and he could tell him.

"Colonel," Jim said, "I told the Captain that I told you he won the pistol championship."

The Colonel looked at Jim. "I didn't ask you not to, did I?"

"No," Jim said, "but --"

Jim waited miserably for the evening to be over. The Captain came over and spoke to him in a low voice.

"Jim," he said, "I wish you'd do me a favor. If nobody else asks me to go with the crowd to that saloon in Third Avenue tonight, I wish you'd do it."

"Of course I will," Jim said.

Jim didn't have to ask the Captain. Several other men asked him. Jim walked beside the Captain. He had a protective feeling for the Captain. He was a boy of seventeen and the Captain was old enough to be his father. But he wanted to protect the Captain.

The waiter put three tables together as usual. The Murray Hill men piled the bags and cases in which they carried their target guns in the corner of the long bench, as usual. Jim took a seat beside them. The Captain sat at the end of the long table next to Jim. The Colonel was at the other end of the long table. Jim noticed that the Captain looked about as if he expected to see

321

somebody. He seemed to be studying every man at the bar and at the other tables.

Somebody ordered beer and sandwiches. The talk was more subdued than usual. Jim wondered how many of them knew that something was likely to happen. He knew by the set of the Colonel's jaw that something was going to happen.

The waiter brought the beer. Somebody near the Colonel leaned forward and called down the table to the Captain.

"Captain," he said, "you were an officer in the war. What did you carry - a .45 automatic or the 1917 revolver?"

"I carried the .45 automatic," the Captain said. "I believe all the officers of the Regular Army did. The revolver was used later, because the Government couldn't get automatics fast enough."

The Colonel leaned forward, and his face was hard, and when he spoke, his voice had a nasty rasp in it.

"Listen, Woodhull," he said. "You weren't an officer in the war. I'm tired of hearing that you were. How's that?"

The Captain said nothing. It was pretty awful.

"You aren't a Captain in any branch of the service. You never were. How's that?"

Still the Captain did not speak. The Murray Hill men were looking down at their beer glasses, making wet circles on the table top.

"You never won a national pistol championship either," the Colonel said. "How's that?"

The Colonel leaned farther forward to say one more thing. "You're going to quit carrying that belly gun. How's that?" he rasped.

Jim thought, when the Captain got to his feet, that he was going to run away. He thought the Captain had had enough. And then he saw that the Captain had his mind on something else. He was looking at two men standing at the bar. They turned as he started toward them. They must have seen him in the mirror.

"You're under arrest," the Captain said.

And then a gun roared. Jim couldn't see who fired first. The

322

Captain was between him and the two men. He tried to remember afterward how many shots were fired. You couldn't count the shots from an automatic. They came too fast. But when it was over, the Captain was on his feet and both the other men were down.

The Captain stooped and picked up a .45 automatic and took out the magazine and made sure the chamber was empty and laid it on the table beside the Colonel.

"How's that?" he said.

He turned to the Murray Hill men. They were all standing up now. Two of them were madly opening bags and cases to get guns. All over the room, men were picking themselves up out of the sawdust on the floor.

"Somebody get a doctor," the Captain said. "I've got to call Governor's Island. The police can't have these two. They're Army prisoners."

"Woodhull," Colonel Burke said. "Woodhull."

"Woodhull is my middle name," the Captain said. "Hicks & Hewitt knew who I was. And they would call me Captain. I've been trying to get those two gunmen and deserters for weeks. They killed the best top sergeant I ever had. We knew they were hanging around this neighborhood. I thought I could get them into the range. They were always betting they could beat each other shooting, when they were in the Army. I thought they couldn't resist a pistol range, and they wouldn't know me with a beard. But they never came in. And until yesterday only one of them ever came in here."

They all heard the wail of a police siren down the street.

"I've got to telephone," the Captain said. "The police can't have these men."

The Colonel held out his hand and apologized. They shook hands.

Jim Ross took a long deep breath. He was happy. He was so happy he was afraid there were tears in his eyes.

323

I SHALL NOT BE AFRAID

Sigrid put on slacks and a sweater and walked half a mile up the mountain that afternoon, as she had so many times before. She sat on a rock and looked down at the fjord. The summer fog was rolling in. And presently she saw her father's yacht running under power for her mooring. The Germans were not good sailors; not good enough to patrol the fjord in the fog. She wished she could show them how you handled the *Trillebrok* in a fog. If you knew the fjord you knew where you were by the sound of the motor as it was echoed back to you by the cliffs and the valleys. But the real fun was sailing her outside, in the open sea.

The *Trillebrok* was no racing yacht, but a cruiser after the fashion of a Norwegian pilot boat, cutter-rigged, double-ended and full in her sections, as a boat of fourteen meters needs to be to stand offshore in a winter gale; and with all her ballast inside.

Sigrid watched the Germans pick up the mooring and then the fog hid them. The fog slowly hid everything. The big house on the slope below her disappeared, and then the thicket of birch trees half-way between her and the house, and then the big rock twenty yards away. She loved being alone in the fog, where no one could see her. Her secret seemed so safe.

But she wanted to get back to the house before Lieutenant Schultz came up from the fjord. He would not object to her taking a walk, of course. She was free to go about as she pleased, and if she did not it was only because she wanted him to think she never saw anyone in the village. Ever since the Lieutenant had quartered himself in her house, she had been careful to do nothing that might make him suspicious. She was always polite to him and she made old Anna be polite to him too.

He was not a bad man, only dull. She knew he was aware that she was young and pretty, but he treated her as if she were his social superior, though he was one of the conquerors and she was one of the conquered. He had never even mentioned her habit of wearing a knife on her belt with her sports clothes. The knife was small, like a Norwegian peasant's knife, except that hers had a silver ferrule and a silver medallion on the butt of its birch root handle, and it hung lightly behind her right hip.

Sigrid got up to go and knew, without knowing how she knew, that she was not alone. She stood still, ready to run, listening. She saw the shape of a man in the fog and knew that he was coming toward her. She did not run, because she was too proud.

"You are Sigrid," he said, and she knew that he was neither a peasant nor a fisherman.

She could see him plainly now - a tall young man without a hat. The fog glistened on his blond head.

"Yes," she said.

"I am Nils," he said.

"I do not know you," she said, guessing from his speech that he must have come from Oslo and wondering how he could have got permission to travel so far unless he was one of those Norwegians who had gone with Quisling.

"I come from the right people," he said. "You can trust me."

And, looking at him, she felt she could trust him. But she was not trusting anyone. "Trust you with what?" she asked.

"I have been sent here to take the *Trillebrok* away. Can you get word to Lars and Ole to come at once?"

"I do not know any Lars or any Ole," she said. She did, of course. The two fishermen had helped her father when he had brought the trucks from Oslo. The Germans would shoot her father, as well as Lars and Ole, if they found out what they had done.

He smiled for the first time and she liked him better than ever when he smiled. But this was a thing not only of life and death. It was the only big responsibility she had ever had.

"I am trusting you," he said again.

"You know who I am?"

"They gave me photographs of you to study and remember and they told me where to wait for you. But I do not believe in you

325

because of what anyone said about you. I can see with my own eyes what kind of girl you are."

"That is foolish of you," Sigrid said.

He shook his head. "We all know the real thing when we see it. I see it in you and you see it in me. Now will you take my word to Lars and Ole?"

He was not angry. He was matter-of-fact. He was so quietly intent on his business that she could not understand her longing to say that she would do anything he asked. She lifted her head high, stiffening herself against a feeling so absurd.

"No," she said.

"So," he said, "you feel it too."

"Feel what?" she asked, though she knew what he must mean.

"That it would be pleasant to forget the hard things we have to do and remember that you are a woman and I am a man, especially when we shan't see each other again. But there isn't time. I must get the *Trillebrok* out tonight in this fog. Have the Germans questioned you?"

"About what?"

"Then they haven't. That means they don't know your father had anything to do with it."

"Where is my father?"

"In London."

She did not try to conceal her relief.

"Your father will want to know how safe you are."

"Oh, perfectly safe," she said.

"You are sure?"

"Yes," she said. "I am so nice to the Lieutenant that he tells me his troubles. He is so jealous of the Gestapo man he cannot keep it to himself. I know how to manage him."

"I am not as glad as I should be. If you weren't safe I should take you with me. As it is, I have no excuse."

For a moment she had the wild hope of going to a land where you could breathe gain. But trying to get her aboard the *Trille-*

brok would double the chance of being caught.

"That would be silly," she said.

"No, not silly. But wrong. I cannot have it that way. And now you will get my message to Lars and Ole?"

She hesitated, feeling he was a true Norwegian, but remembering how careful she must be.

"They have hidden the food and the gasoline three kilometers up the fjord," Nils said. He pointed in the right direction. "Now will you take my message to Lars and Ole?"

"Yes," she said.

"Good-by then, Sigrid."

"Good-by, Nils."

She went down the mountain as fast as she could, the fog so thick that she could see the path for only three or four yards in front of her feet. She paused near the house to get her breath. There was no reason to be breathless. What she had to do was quite easy. It had been long planned. She was not frightened. But she was aware that her thought of going to a free country was not wholly honest. Her real thought had been of going with him. And she was surprised at herself for having such a thought about a man she had known for only ten minutes.

She went to the kitchen door. Old Anna was cooking 'fatligmansbakkes' in a kettle. She looked up, a little anxious. "You are late," she said.

"Am I?" Sigrid said. "Is the Lieutenant back?"

"No," Anna said. "Won't you have coffee?"

Sigrid sat down at the kitchen table and she was oppressed by the silence of the big house. It had been full of laughter and young people every summer, before the Germans came.

And now, Sigrid told herself, *I am like an old maid who falls for the first man she sees.* But she knew better.

"What happened?" Anna asked, as she put the coffee and a plate of cakes on the table.

"Nothing," Sigrid said, pouring coffee.

"There is color in your cheeks," Anna said. "And you are smiling

327

again, the way you used to when life was good."

"Really?" Sigrid said, looking up at her and feeling that she was blushing.

Anna was the small, dark Norwegian type, old now, and wrinkled, but her eyes still had the spark of revolt in them. She stood waiting for Sigrid to tell her what had happened, and Sigrid knew she could not pretend nothing had happened - not to Anna. She was glad to hear a knock on the door.

"Ah," Anna said, "that is little Gerta."

She opened the door and a girl of eight or nine came in, in a patched dress and worn-out shoes. She had ash-blond hair in two pigtails braided tight to her small, square head, and the pink-and-white face of an angel.

Anna went to get the cookies. It was the bright spot in her day when Gerta stopped on her way to get the family cow in the high pasture.

"Sit here by me, Gerta," Sigrid said. "I have something to tell you."

She put her arm around the little girl, but as she lowered her voice to give the message for Lars and Ole she heard Lieutenant Schultz coming. He knocked on the door, as he always did, and waited for Anna to open it.

"Ah," he said, "the little Gerta!"

Sigrid knew that he would have liked to pick up the little girl and hug her. He had a daughter of the same age, back in Germany, whose photograph he carried in his pocket, and liked to show.

"May I have coffee?" the Lieutenant asked.

The Lieutenant had coffee every afternoon, alone in the dining room at an oak table built to seat eighteen or twenty people.

"I will bring it at once," Anna said.

The Lieutenant bowed to Sigrid. "Would it be too much to ask, *Fraulein*, that I have my coffee here in the kitchen?"

Sigrid was surprised that he should ask such a thing. But this was no moment to refuse. "Not at all," she said. "Please sit down." She turned to Anna. "Bring a cup for Lieutenant Schultz."

Sigrid saw Anna's face take on the stolid look which meant she was angry. But she obeyed.

"I wish I could tell you how I feel," Lieutenant Schultz said. "I know you dislike me. But I do not dislike you. I am homesick. And this kitchen with little Gerta, who might be my own dear daughter sitting here; and you, *Fraulein*, who might be my wife's younger sister, and Anna - we have a word for all of this in German. *Gemutlich*. It means everything that is homelike and friendly and warm."

"I know the word," Sigrid said.

She thought to herself that the word described one of the two things that the Lieutenant was sworn to destroy in Norway. The other was the freedom without which people who have once had it cannot truly live. But she did not want to quarrel with the Lieutenant. It would do no good. And, besides, he was full of German *Heimweh** He was shorter and plumper and rounder than a Norwegian, and his pale blue eyes looked as if he were about to cry at the thought of his own kitchen, back in Germany, so *gemutlich*.

Gerta licked a crumb from her lips and stood up. *"Tak for maten,"** she said, like a well-brought-up child who has eaten in the house of friends. "I must be going."

Sigrid had intended to tell Gerta just what she must do and she could not do that in front of the Lieutenant. But, if Gerta remembered, it would not be necessary.

Sigrid picked up two cookies. "Here, Gerta, take these - one for little Lars and one for little Ole."

"Ah," the Lieutenant said, smiling at Gerta, "you have brothers."

Gerta looked up at the Lieutenant. "Yes," she said.

"And why don't they get the cow instead of sending you, a girl?"

Sigrid held her breath for a fraction of a second, for fear the child had forgotten what she had been told.

"They are too little," Gerta said, with a touch of that scorn with which an older child regards a younger.

Sigrid loved the bland expression of the child's face as she told this lie, so like that of her elders when they were questioned by

* (homesickness)
** (thank you for the food)

329

the Germans. There was, she felt proudly, nothing so stupid-looking as a Norwegian when he feels himself in danger, and his mind is busy.

The Lieutenant bowed again to Sigrid when Gerta had gone. "I am sorry if I have intruded," he said.

Sigrid stood listening to his footsteps as he crossed the dining room and went on. Then she shut the door.

"So nothing happened out there in the fog?" Anna said.

Sigrid trusted Anna completely, but it was a rule that you told no one anything that was not necessary. Anna knew what the cookies for little Lars and little Ole meant. But she did not know the secret of the *Trillebrok*.

"Yes, of course something happened," Sigrid said.

"He must have been handsome."

"He is," Sigrid said.

Anna grumbled under her breath, but she knew better than to ask any more questions.

Sigrid sat down again at the table. The fog was so thick that she could not see out of the windows, though the light came through. It would be that way all night, for the sun never really set in this season and there was no true darkness, only the fog. She could not help thinking about what was going to happen out there. Lars and Ole would not be long in joining Nils. The three of them would scull a boat out to the *Trillebrok*. There would be only one German aboard her. In two or three minutes the *Trillebrok* would be running up the fjord to the place where Lars and Ole had hidden the food and the gasoline they had stolen from the Germans. In an hour she would be clear of the fjord. Lars and Ole would have her sails up while Nils laid her course, for the Faeroes, or for Iceland, as his Viking ancestors had done for a thousand years. He'd have a fine German chart to do it with.

Looking into the fog, and knowing how the wind was blowing out there, Sigrid could see the *Trillebrok* with her lee rail awash and the big seas sliding by, and a tall young man in oilskins with little drops of water glistening on his bare blond head as he leaned against the oak beam of the tiller. The wind would soon be making a song in her rigging.

"Your dream must be pleasant," Anna said.

330

Sigrid came out of it instantly. She could hear the Lieutenant coming toward the kitchen. Anna opened the door on his knock.

"*Fraulein*, may I see you for a moment?" he said.

Sigrid saw that he was excited. "Yes, of course."

She followed him through the dining room and down the wide hall with the elk horns over the stone fireplace and into the library, which he had taken for his office.

"Sit down, please," he said, and shut the door.

Sigrid took the chair at which he pointed. The Lieutenant sat down behind his desk. "*Fraulein*," he said, "I meant it when I said that I liked you. I thought also that you were a person of good sense. Now I find that I am mistaken. But I still wish to save you. If you tell me everything quickly I believe that I can."

"But I have nothing to tell," Sigrid said, and knew that her face was taking on that stupid look of a Norwegian in danger.

"If you behave that way, I can do nothing. You will certainly go to the concentration camp. You may be shot."

"But how can I tell you what I do not know?"

The Lieutenant shook his head. He was no longer full of *Heimweh*. He was angry. "It is no use," he shouted. "You were seen with him."

Sigrid guessed that someone in the neighborhood who had gone with Quisling had seen her and Nils. It couldn't have been anybody else. She asked herself desperately if their voices could possibly have been loud enough so anyone far enough away to be hidden by the fog might have understood what they were saying. But she must not show she was afraid.

She took a case out of the pocket of her slacks and lighted a cigarette. It was, she decided, no use to play with the Lieutenant. He knew she wasn't stupid. But she could see he was startled that she should light a cigarette -- as if this were a social occasion.

"There has been some mistake," she said. "I took a walk up the mountain this afternoon as I often do. I like to watch the *Trillebrok* coming in to her mooring. I have had so many good times sailing the *Trillebrok* with my father and my brothers. I am often homesick for those days, just as you felt homesick when you came to the kitchen to have coffee. But --"

"Fraulein," the Lieutenant interrupted, "it does not go. There has been no mistake. At noon I received orders to find this man at once, and bring him in. He is a dangerous enemy. I sent all my men out. And what happens when I come back here? I have not been here an hour when I have word that you met him within a kilometer of this house!"

Sigrid tried to smile a skeptical smile.

"If you will not tell the truth like a sensible person, there are ways of getting the truth out of you, and I am going to use them right now. Do you think I am going to let the Gestapo get him first and laugh at me?"

Sigrid saw that the thought of torturing her was not wholly unpleasant to him. He was a sentimental man, more sentimental than seemed proper to a Norwegian, but he had also the capacity for brutality. She wondered how a man could be both sentimental and brutal, but she knew this man could.

He leaned across his desk, thrusting his chin out at her. "Do I need to tell you what I will do to you?"

Sigrid waited. The fact that she said nothing seemed to enrage him. He stood up, one plump German lieutenant, who had the power of the entire German Army behind him.

"I will call in my orderly and tell him to take off your clothes and beat you with his belt until you tell me where that man is," he said. "If necessary I will help him."

Sigrid knew that he was not bluffing. The Germans had stripped women and beaten them to make them talk. She wondered how long she could hold out after it began. She took a deep breath and clenched her hands. She would fight. If the Lieutenant thought he could do it alone, he was mistaken. His orderly, a big, strong, rough peasant, was something else. But she could hold out long enough - until she was sure the *Trillebrok* was under sail in the open sea.

"You have one minute to decide," Lieutenant Schultz said.

"I have decided," Sigrid said. "I will tell you nothing."

The Lieutenant looked at her. Sigrid knew he wanted to beat her with a leather strap. And then the moment's stillness was broken by the sound of voices outside.

Lieutenant Schultz jerked the door open. Sigrid could not see through the open door into the hall from where she sat.

"What does this mean?" he demanded.

Sigrid recognized the voice of the orderly, and heard the last part of what he said.

"This man says he comes from Oslo to see you, but he has nothing to show who he is."

Lieutenant Schultz took his automatic pistol out of its holster. "Search him."

Sigrid heard nothing for two minutes while the Lieutenant stood in the doorway with his pistol half raised, and then the orderly reported that the man had nothing - no weapon, no money, and no papers.

"Bring him in here," the Lieutenant ordered.

Nils stepped into the room.

Sigrid sat rigid, fighting to show no sign that she had ever seen him before. Something had gone wrong with the plan. But why had he made it worse? They hadn't caught him. He was here of his own accord.

"Who are you?" Lieutenant Schultz asked.

"I prefer to tell you when your man is out of hearing," Nils said.

The Lieutenant hesitated. Then he spoke to the orderly. He didn't turn his head. Sigrid wondered why she hadn't noticed before that when he spoke to a private he only changed his voice instead of moving his glance.

"Take the girl into the dining room. See that she doesn't get away."

"No," Nils said. "I shall need the girl, I think."

The Lieutenant kept on looking at him. He was plainly puzzled. But it was just as plain that he felt he had to act. Still without turning his head, he told the orderly to go out and shut the door. Then he laid his pistol on the desk and sat down behind it. Sitting down seemed to make him surer of himself.

"Now," he said, "I will hear who you are."

Nils laughed. "I am the man you are looking for," he said.

Schultz stared at him.

Nils laughed again. "When I have finished talking to the girl you shall turn me over to the Gestapo."

"I have orders to arrest you," Schultz said. But he spoke with the manner of a man who had to cling tightly to one simple fact because events were moving too fast for him.

"I also have orders, Lieutenant," Nils said.

"Show them to me."

Nils smiled patiently. "My orders are in my head. I am to find out what was done with a part of the Norwegian gold reserve which disappeared at the time of the occupation. About five tons of it. In pigs. Thirty million kroner. It is known to be hereabouts. I should know exactly where it is if you had left the girl for me to deal with. That was all arranged this afternoon. But when I come here to get her to show me where it is, I find you about to make it impossible for her to lead anybody anywhere! You left me no course except to interfere. If I had not done so, I am afraid the Gestapo would not have been too well pleased, Lieutenant - with either of us."

Lieutenant Schultz swallowed. "Thirty millions! And she knows where it is?"

"Look at her," Nils said.

There wasn't time for Sigrid to get the stupid look back into her face.

"Ah," the Lieutenant said.

"She knows," Nils said. "That will be all we need to tell the Gestapo."

Sigrid saw the Lieutenant's eyes narrow and his mouth tighten. She could almost see him thinking. The Gestapo wasn't going to find that gold. Lieutenant Schultz was going to find it. No. Not Lieutenant. Captain Schultz. Or even, perhaps, Major Schultz.

"Possibly it will not be necessary for us to trouble the Gestapo. The *Fraulein* is intelligent." His eyes considered her. "The Gestapo, *Fraulein*, will not use belts. Not even to begin with."

Nils turned to Sigrid. "That is so," he said. "You will tell them, before they are through with you. It will be better if you tell us now. Much better."

334

Sigrid looked into his eyes, amazed that they could look back into hers without shame. She was not the only one who had trusted those eyes. There would be others who would trust them, true Norwegians who would die because they would believe that this man was true.

She put her face down into her hands. She had believed in him. She had made it easy for him to trick her into telling him - but she hadn't told him! Even when, because he knew so much, she had taken it for granted that he knew where the gold was, she hadn't said anything that could have told him where it was. He didn't know. And there was a way to prevent him from ever knowing. A simple way. It was only necessary for her to die. But she must die quickly, before they could beat her into something that was no longer a woman, that would tell them.

She remembered the knife in her belt, hidden from them, behind her. She had never thought of it as a thing to kill with. Her father had given it to her because one needs a knife on a boat, as a tool. But it could kill. It was small, but it was sharp. She needed only the chance to get it out of its sheath. There wouldn't be time for them to stop her.

She made herself ready, breathing deeply, letting her muscles relax so that when she tightened them they would be quick and sure. And then, suddenly, she saw that it was too soon, that there was more for her to do than merely to die. She lifted her head. "Very well. I will show you where it is hidden. But it will be necessary to use a boat. There is no way by land."

"The boat? In this fog?" The Lieutenant's face went hard with suspicion. Then it cleared, and he laughed. "But of course! I was forgetting. A fog means nothing to you, *Fraulein*. It will be no more difficult for you than walking through your own room in the dark."

"It will not be quite so easy," Sigrid said. She must not seem too anxious. "It is very thick, this fog."

"But you will find your way," Nils said. His voice was quiet. He did not need to say what would happen to her if she didn't find her way.

"Yes," she said. "I will find it."

She knew that she could find her way. To that rock where the water went straight down for fifty fathoms. If she could hit the rock, even at half speed, she wouldn't have any trouble about

335

dying. And neither would they. No one could live long in that water, only a few degrees warmer than ice. She was eager, suddenly, to start; so eager that she stood up almost too quickly. But neither of them seemed to notice.

The Lieutenant opened the door and called to the orderly. He stood back, motioning for them to go out ahead of him. Nils went out first and the big private followed him. Sigrid was next, with the Lieutenant close behind her. They walked down the path to the shore and found a boat. The soldier rowed while Sigrid, sitting beside the Lieutenant in the stern, directed him. It was nearly half a kilometer out to the *Trillebrok* and Sigrid was fearful she might miss the yacht, but presently, when the Lieutenant hailed the man on board, there was an answer, startlingly close, and in a moment they were alongside, and the Lieutenant put his pistol into its holster to help her aboard.

She slid down into the deep cockpit. The Lieutenant ordered the man who had been left aboard to start the motor and told his orderly to go forward and cast off.

"You, *Fraulein*," he said to Sigrid, "will be so kind as to take the tiller."

Sigrid stood beside the tiller, waist high. The feel of the wood as she put her hand on it steadied her. Lieutenant Schultz leaned over, looking down the hatch at the man who was cranking the motor. Sigrid felt something touch her back lightly. She stiffened involuntarily. And then she knew what was happening. Nils was pulling the knife out of its sheath.

Sigrid turned quickly, but before she could snatch at the knife she remembered that she didn't need it any more. She could kill this man without it. She was glad she was going to kill him.

The motor roared. At the sound, as if that was what he had been waiting for, Nils slashed hard down along the Lieutenant's hip, cutting the strap that held the holster. The pistol fell on the deck. Nils caught the Lieutenant's wrist in both his hands and, turning and bending his back at the same time, threw him clear of the cockpit coaming into the water.

He picked up the Lieutenant's pistol and ordered the man at the motor up on deck and overboard. The man at the bow could not see the cockpit in the fog. It was only as he got halfway aft along the narrow deck between the rail and the cabin house that he saw Nils with the pistol. He jumped overboard.

Nils threw in the clutch. "Give her the gas," he said.

Presently he cast off the line to the boat they were towing and then he stopped and picked up her knife.

He would have handed it to her, but she shook her head. She couldn't have put the knife back in its sheath. She hadn't the strength. He must have seen how she was trembling. He put his arm around her.

"It is not good to kill," he said. "They have not taught us yet to do it gladly."

"It isn't that," she said. "It is - all the rest."

His arm was firm around her. "I know," he said. "You thought I was one of them. I hated to let you think so, but there was no other way. The little Gerta came to tell me that Lars and Ole had not come home from their fishing. I came to the house to find you, and when I stood under the window and heard what the Lieutenant was saying to you, I could not stay outside."

"Why couldn't you?" Sigrid said. She knew why, but she wanted to hear him say it.

"I needed you," he said, "to steer the boat for me."

"Oh," Sigrid said.

"But I did not think about the boat till afterwards," Nils said. "All I thought of outside the window was just that I needed you."

"Oh," Sigrid said again.

They were silent for a long time. Sigrid looked at the compass, listened to the echo of the motor, and changed the course a little.

"You are not afraid anymore?" Nils said.

"No," Sigrid said.

"We sail for Iceland. It is a long way."

She turned her head toward him. "I shall not be afraid," she said.

It was a long time before either of them remembered to be glad about the gold, five tons of it, in pigs that had been painted with red lead, like the iron pigs on top of them, which were the ballast of the *Trillebrok*, burying her rail in the long gray seas of the open ocean.